AVAILA

The programs described in Chapter available on disk for your IBM PC (ar for Chapter 7 have been written in PASCAL and those for Chapter 8 have been written in C. You will need the appropriate compilers to run the programs.

Order the Program Disk today priced £12.50 (+ VAT)/$24.75 from your computer store, bookseller, or by using the order form below.

Pidd: **Computer Modelling for Discrete Simulation**—*Program Disk*
Please send me .... copies of Pidd: Computer Modelling for Discrete Simulation—Program Disk at **£12.50 (+ VAT)/$24.75** each
0 471 92428 8

POSTAGE AND HANDLING FREE FOR CASH WITH ORDER OR PAYMENT BY CREDIT CARD
☐ Remittance enclosed .... Allow approx. 14 days for delivery.
☐ Please charge this order to my credit card (All orders subject to credit approval)
Delete as necessary:—AMERICAN EXPRESS, DINERS CLUB, BARCLAYCARD/VISA, ACCESS
CARD NUMBER ☐☐☐☐☐☐☐☐☐☐☐☐☐☐☐
                              Expiration date ....
☐ Please send me an invoice for prepayment. A small postage and handling charge will be made.
Software purchased for professional purposes is generally recognized as tax deductable.
☐ Please keep me informed of new books in my subject area which is
....
NAME/ADDRESS ....
....
....
OFFICIAL ORDER No .... SIGNATURE ....

Site Licences which allow multiple copies to be made of the programs are also available. For further information please contact:

Helen Ramsey
John Wiley & Sons Limited
Baffins Lane
Chichester
West Sussex
PO19 1UD
England

Affix
stamp
here

Customer Service Department
John Wiley & Sons Limited
Distribution Centre
Shripney Road
Bognor Regis
Sussex
PO22 9SA
England

COMPUTER MODELLING FOR DISCRETE SIMULATION

COMPUTER MODELLING FOR DISCRETE SIMULATION

Edited by
Michael Pidd

The Management School
Lancaster University

JOHN WILEY & SONS
Chichester · New York · Brisbane · Toronto · Singapore

Copyright © 1989 by John Wiley & Sons Ltd.

All rights reserved.

No part of this book may be reproduced by any means,
or transmitted into a machine language
without the written permission of the publisher.

Library of Congress Cataloging in Publication Data:

Computer modelling for discrete simulation/edited by Michael Pidd.
   p.   cm.
   Bibliography: p.
   Includes indexes.
   ISBN 0 471 92282 X
   1. Computer simulation. 2. Discrete-time systems. I. Pidd,
Michael.
QA76.9.C65C654   1989   89-5264
001.4' 34—dc19   CIP

British Library Cataloguing in Publication Data:

Computer modelling for discrete simulation.
   1. Simulations. Applications of computer systems
   I. Pidd, Michael
   001.4' 24

   ISBN 0 471 92282 X

Phototypeset by Dobbie Typesetting Limited, Plymouth, Devon
Printed at the Bath Press, Bath, Avon

To Sally, Karen and Helen,
a model family

Contents

List of Contributors		xiii
Preface		xv

1 DEVELOPMENTS IN DISCRETE SIMULATION 1
M. Pidd
- 1.1 **Computer Simulation: An Attractive Technique** 1
  - 1.1.1 When all else fails? 1
  - 1.1.2 Experimentation and simulation 2
- 1.2 **Modelling** 3
  - 1.2.1 Modelling: logic 3
  - 1.2.2 Modelling: stochastic behaviour 4
  - 1.2.3 Modelling: policy comparison 5
  - 1.2.4 Modelling: validation 6
  - 1.2.5 Modelling: two general principles 7
- 1.3 **Programming** 8
- 1.4 **Experimentation** 10
  - 1.4.1 Experimentation as gaming 10
  - 1.4.2 Classical experimentation 11
- 1.5 **Looking Back** 11
  - 1.5.1 Origins 12
  - 1.5.2 Taken for granted 14
  - 1.5.3 Power to the user 17
  - 1.5.4 Software consolidation 18
  - 1.5.5 Personal computer power 19
- 1.6 **References** 22

2 THE IMPLEMENTATION OF SIMULATION LANGUAGES 23
S. C. Mathewson
- 2.1 **Introduction** 23
  - 2.1.1 Interrelated products 23
  - 2.1.2 An overview of developments 23
- 2.2 **The Implementation of Simulation** 25
  - 2.2.1 Problem definition 26
  - 2.2.2 Model development 28

		2.2.3	Decision support	30
		2.2.4	Approaches to providing such facilities	32
	2.3	**The Robot Cell**		33
	2.4	**Simulation Language Features**		34
		2.4.1	Modelling a system's static state	36
		2.4.2	Provide extensive list processing capability	36
		2.4.3	Modelling the dynamic interactions of data objects	37
		2.4.4	Provide statistical sampling	45
		2.4.5	Collect data	45
		2.4.6	Data analysis and reporting facilities	45
		2.4.7	Monitoring the model and debugging the program	46
	2.5	**Simulation Language Implementations**		46
		2.5.1	Event-based	46
		2.5.2	Three-phase	47
		2.5.3	Process	49
	2.6	**Object-Oriented Simulation Languages**		52
		2.6.1	Object orientation	52
		2.6.2	Parallel processing	53
	2.7	**Conclusions**		54
	2.8	**References**		55
3	SIMULATION SUPPORT ENVIRONMENTS			57
	S. C. Mathewson			
	3.1	**An Overview**		57
	3.2	**Generalised Graphical Building Blocks with Transaction Flow**		58
		3.2.1	Simple building block systems	58
		3.2.2	Queuing networks	61
	3.3	**Application-Specific Systems**		66
		3.3.1	PCModel	66
		3.2.2	SIMFACTORY, MAST and SAME	68
		3.3.3	WITNESS	70
		3.3.4	XCELL	71
		3.3.5	ModelMaster	72
		3.3.6	Other systems	72
	3.4	**Simulation Pre-Processors**		73
		3.4.1	DRAFT	74
		3.4.2	CAPS	81
		3.4.3	The Dialog approach	81
	3.5	**Support Environments**		83
		3.5.1	TESS	83
		3.5.2	SDL	85

Contents

		3.5.3	RESQ	85
		3.5.4	RESQME	86
	3.6	**System-Theoretic Representation**		88
	3.7	**Current Research and Progress**		91
		3.7.1	Model specification	92
		3.7.2	Automatic program generation	92
		3.7.3	Program debugging	93
		3.7.4	Simulation experiments	94
		3.7.5	Project management and documentation	94
		3.7.6	Management access	95
	3.8	**Conclusions**		97
	3.9	**References**		98
4	GRAPHICS AND INTERACTION			101
	R. D. Hurrion			
	4.1	**Introduction**		101
	4.2	**The Graphics Approach**		102
		4.2.1	Graphics methods for simulation	103
		4.2.2	Management science graphics simulation history	104
	4.3	**Visual Interactive Simulation**		105
	4.4	**Graphics and Simulation Examples**		106
	4.5	**Display and Interaction Methods**		109
		4.5.1	Schematic display	109
		4.5.2	Logical display	110
		4.5.3	Passive versus interactive graphics	110
		4.5.4	Entity interaction	110
		4.5.5	Menu interaction	111
	4.6	**Phases of a Management Science Simulation Project**		112
	4.7	**Intelligent Visual Interactive Simulation**		113
		4.7.1	Monitoring	114
		4.7.2	Learning	115
		4.7.3	Simulation experiment advisor	115
	4.8	**Conclusion**		116
	4.9	**References**		117
5	ARTIFICIAL INTELLIGENCE AND SIMULATION MODELLING			121
	Ray J. Paul			
	5.1	**Scene Setting**		121
		5.1.1	AI and simulation	121
		5.1.2	At the research stage	122
		5.1.3	The computer-aided simulation modelling project	123

		5.1.4	Artificial intelligence	125
	5.2	**Natural Language Understanding**		126
		5.2.1	Basic concepts	126
		5.2.2	Syntactic and semantic analysis	127
		5.2.3	Classification of NLUSs	129
	5.3	**Expert Systems**		131
		5.3.1	Basic concepts	131
		5.3.2	Knowledge representation	132
		5.3.3	Production systems	135
	5.4	**Comparing the Modelling Approaches**		137
		5.4.1	A production system view of three-phase modelling	137
		5.4.2	AI languages in simulation	141
	5.5	**References**		144
6	**COMBINING AI AND SIMULATION**			149
	Ray J. Paul			
	6.1	**Natural Language Processing Concepts in CASM**		149
		6.1.1	Fundamentals of the CASM NLUS	149
		6.1.2	Syntactic and semantic analyses in the CASM NLUS	150
		6.1.3	Validation and successive refinement in the CASM NLUS	152
		6.1.4	Trapping ambiguous and meaningless responses in the CASM NLUS	152
	6.2	**Simulation Program Debugging using an Expert System in CASM**		154
		6.2.1	An outline of SIPDES	154
		6.2.2	System control in SIPDES	155
	6.3	**Other Examples of AI Tools in Simulation**		156
	6.4	**Automatic Program Generation**		157
		6.4.1	CASM.AUTOSIM	157
		6.4.2	Other interactive simulation support tools	159
	6.5	**Other Uses of AI in Simulation**		160
	6.6	**Simulation Support for AI Applications**		162
	6.7	**Conclusions**		164
	6.8	**References**		166
7	**SIMULATION IN PASCAL**			171
	M. Pidd			
	7.1	**Developing Simulation Programs**		171
		7.1.1	Option one: simulation languages	171
		7.1.2	Option two: using FORTRAN	172
		7.1.3	Option three: using data-driven generic models	172

Contents

	7.1.4	Option four: use some other language	173
7.2	**Discrete Simulation Libraries**		173
	7.2.1	Simulation system routines	174
	7.2.2	Useful general-purpose routines	175
	7.2.3	Application-specific routines	176
7.3	**Characteristics of Discrete Simulation Programs**		176
	7.3.1	Typical mode of development	176
	7.3.2	Logic not computation	177
7.4	**An Array-Based Executive in Pascal**		183
	7.4.1	Essential type definitions	183
	7.4.2	The A phase	185
	7.4.3	The B and C phases	186
	7.4.4	Other useful procedures	186
	7.4.5	An example	187
7.5	**A Simple Pointer-Based Executive**		193
	7.5.1	Type definitions	194
	7.5.2	The A, B and C phases	197
	7.5.3	Scheduling entities	199
	7.5.4	Adding and deleting entities	201
	7.5.5	Creating classes	204
	7.5.6	Finding entities	204
	7.5.7	Creating queues	205
	7.5.8	Finding queue members	206
	7.5.9	Adding entities to queues	208
	7.5.10	Removing entities from queues	208
	7.5.11	Other procedures	208
7.6	**An Example: An Encore for the Harassed Booking Clerk**		209
7.7	**Pascal for Discrete Simulation?**		213
7.8	**References**		215

8 SIMULATION USING C
J. G. Crookes   217

8.1	**Introduction—Simulation in General-Purpose Languages**	217
8.2.	**Why C for Simulation?**		218
	8.2.1	C Much better than Pascal	218
	8.2.2	Disadvantages of C	221
8.3	**How to Write Simulations in C**		222
	8.3.1	Overall design	222
	8.3.2	Executive design	224
	8.3.3	The heap module	230
	8.3.4	The queue module	233

	8.3.5	The grafmod module	236
	8.3.6	The machine-dependent module	239
	8.3.7	The hungry philosophers model	239
8.4	**References**		240

APPENDICES 241
Appendix 1 241
Appendix 2 248
Appendix 3 250
Appendix 4 252
Appendix 5 256
Appendix 6 258
Appendix 7 260

Author Index 265
Subject Index 269

List of Contributors

S. C. Mathewson
School of Management
Imperial College
London

R. J. Paul
London School of Economics
London

R. D. Hurrion
School of Industrial and Business Studies
University of Warwick
Coventry

M. Pidd
The Management School
Lancaster University
Lancaster

J. G. Crookes
The Management School
University of Lancaster
Lancaster

Preface

Computer simulation, especially the discrete methods employed in management science, has increased in popularity and practicality over the decade of the 1980s. As a subject it emerged during the early days of computing during the 1950s and its progress has been tied to that of computing ever since. This book puts that development in context and describes the important progress since the mid-1970s.

The original idea was that this book would be a follow-on to my text, *Computer Simulation in Management Science*, which is now in its second edition. Like *Computer Simulation in Management Science* it focuses on the *modelling* work involved in producing working simulations within a reasonable time-scale. This book, however, concentrates exclusively on the *computer modelling* and explores these developments in discrete simulation.

Rather than writing the entire book myself, I invited four others, all internationally known for their contribution to these developments, to collaborate. Stephen Mathewson is known for his pioneering work on simulation support environments, especially for DRAFT, a program generator which is growing into a fully fledged support environment. Thus Stephen has contributed Chapters 2 and 3, which outline the state of the art in support environments for discrete simulation. Ray Paul started and led the CASM project, which aims to provide computer-aided support for simulation modelling. With his co-workers he is especially known for his efforts to link developments in artificial intelligence to discrete simulation. Chapters 4 and 5 reflect his long experience, as a researcher, practitioner and communicator. Bob Hurrion developed and implemented the ideas for visual interactive simulation during the late 1970s and has written extensively on this theme. All along, his aim has been to produce tools which are usable in decision support and this comes through clearly in Chapter 6. John Crookes is almost the grand old man of computer simulation, having worked with Keith Tocher and having been responsible for a major research centre in simulation. John is particularly interested in the development of simulation systems which are easily portable from machine to machine, and which make effective use of available hardware. Thus, in Chapter 8, he presents a simulation system written in C.

As well as to my collaborators, I am grateful for the support and encouragement of Diane Taylor of John Wiley & Sons Ltd. This book has had a long gestation period and its birth is very welcome. I hope it proves useful to my colleagues around the world.

M. Pidd
Lancaster, 20 July, 1988

Computer Modelling for Discrete Simulation
Edited by M. Pidd
©1989 John Wiley & Sons Ltd

1
Developments in Discrete Simulation

M. Pidd

1.1 Computer Simulation: An Attractive Technique

Computer simulation has long been a popular tool in management science, dating back almost to the first digital computers which were commercially available. Early simulations were limited by the small size and poor reliability of the available computers. Nevertheless, many of the principles which were originally laid down are still applicable today. The difference is that the computer power now available in small boxes means that the dreams of the pioneers are now a reality. Not only is simulation theoretically attractive, it is now cost-effective and proven in thousands of applications. Indeed, its use is becoming so routine that some have argued that management scientists should move on to other things. The authors of this book still think otherwise.

1.1.1 When all else fails?

As a technique it is attractive for two reasons. Firstly, it is possible to simulate many very complicated management systems. 'When all else fails' is a suitable slogan for many such simulations. This should not be used to justify the inappropriate use of computer simulation for, sometimes, analytical methods can be much cheaper, much faster and more accurate than a simulation. However, it is surprising how often the last resort of simulation is necessary. Secondly, the technique itself is straightforward and does not rely on a great degree of mathematical abstraction but can allow the correspondence between a simulation model and some 'real' system to be clearly seen. Indeed this is probably the main reason why discrete simulation is so often useful in management science. That is, a particular simulation can be very closely tailored to fit the system being simulated, there being no need to squash the system into an ill-fitting set of mathematical assumptions.

1.1.2 Experimentation and simulation

Computer simulation is based on the idea of experimentation. Instead of experimenting on the real system, the trials are made on a dynamic model. If the model is a valid representation of the system, then the results of the simulation ought to be transferable to the system itself. Once it is clear that simulation is the approach to use, then the process of simulation can be thought of as three stages (Pidd, 1988):

modelling
programming
experimentation.

However, it is rare for the three stages to be entirely distinct; for example, when developing a system model, the analyst will certainly have an eye to its programming implications. When programming, the analyst would be wise to design the programs for easy and accurate experimentation. Particular experiments, though, may lead to revisions in the model and thus in the program. In addition, Mathewson argues in Chapter 2 that the stages are cyclic rather than a single-pass run-through. That is the three stages are repeated throughout a simulation project. Hence the stages are a useful way of thinking about simulation, but are no more than that. As will be clear later in this book, they do indicate where the major effort is needed in a simulation project. For present purposes they provide a list of headings which illustrate the main problems facing the simulation analyst.

1.2 Modelling

1.2.1 Modelling: logic

As employed in discrete simulation, a model has three main components. The first is an attempt to represent the rules which govern the behaviour of the system being simulated. These rules are usually modelled by a contingent logic. Thus, a simulation program often consists of conditional statements of the form

If ⟨condition⟩ *then* ⟨contingent actions⟩

For example, it may be necessary to test whether an item of equipment is in an acceptable state in order to decide what action to take next. If the state is acceptable, then a job and associated material might be allocated according to some plan. Thus statements of the following type must be found somewhere in the model.

If Item. State in [ok, ready] then
   Begin
   Engage (Item)
   . . . .
   . . . .
   End;

It is normal to break down these logical rules into individual blocks of code in the simulation program and the same blocks should sensibly be used when modelling. As described in detail in Pidd (1988), these blocks are termed activities, events or processes depending on the approach being used. In Chapter 2 Mathewson shows how the various simulation programming languages and systems each employ one or more of the approaches. The approaches have their own plus and minus points, which means that simulation analysts are unlikely ever to agree that one approach is wholly the best in all circumstances. Whichever approach is adopted, it needs to be understood properly and used consistently, otherwise any advantages will be lost and the resulting program will be very difficult to maintain.

   Any complete model must capture the essence of the logical interactions of the system being modelled. Therefore, whether the modelling approach is based on activities, events or processes, these rules and their consequences must be present somewhere in the model. Thus one important part of the modelling task is to identify the important rules of the system. Simple though this may sound, it often turns out to be far from straightforward. Often new rules come to light as a result of trying to compare the behaviour of the model with that of the system of interest. Thus analysts should be encouraged to write programs with a strong modular structure, the idea being that the modules can be separately compiled and debugged as they are added to the model. This is especially important if a large model is being planned; it should, however, be noted that small models have a habit of growing over time, and that a modular structure is always advisable.

The simulation model needs to be validated, and an essential part of this validation is the attempt to check that the rules embodied in the model are a valid representation of those in the system being simulated. Graphical representations of system logic are a great help here. Even simple devices such as activity cycle diagrams (described in Pidd, 1988) are useful for validating the logical rules. The availability of graphical and interactive systems, as described by Hurrion in Chapter 4, are also of great value. They can be used to show the dynamic effects of the logical rules embodied in the model, and may thus make certain aspects of validation much simpler than walking through code. Both activity cycle diagrams and interactive graphics can be used by the analyst to show the client of the study what are the essential features of the logic of the model. Indeed, they can allow the analyst and client to develop the model logic co-operatively and thus reduce the need for post-hoc validation.

1.2.2 Modelling: stochastic behaviour

A second feature of discrete simulation models is the representation of stochastic behaviour in some way or other. Most often this is done by taking samples from appropriate probability distributions. The determination of which distributions are most appropriate is a task which requires considerable skill. After all, no model is any better than the assumptions which it embodies; therefore using the wrong distributions may lead to very strange results.

The vendors of simulation software are increasingly stressing that their products are easy to use. So easy to use, some claim, that they may be always successfully used by non-specialists. As so often, these claims are somewhat two-edged. As Mathewson makes clear

Modelling

in Chapter 3, these packages certainly make it possible for non-programmers to write discrete simulation programs which will run properly in a computing sense. They do this by easing the modelling of system logic and by eliminating the need for detailed coding of programs. Unfortunately, a program which executes correctly on a computer may still be full of errors, in that the model which is embodied is full of wrong assumptions and rules. In particular, the vendors of such packages tend to make light of the need for careful statistical modelling to be carried out. It is almost implied that the statistical side is irrelevant — would that this were really true. Occasionally it may seem not to matter, within certain limits, what distribution are used in a particular model. In such cases this may well indicate that a simulation is unnecessary, and that a much cruder approach will do.

In some simulations it may be necessary, usually for validation purposes, to simulate an actual pattern — say of arrivals or of orders. In such cases these events will not be generated by sampling procedures but by taking a sequence of values from some pre-established timetable or externally generated list. The timetable or list may well be drawn from a computer file, this file coming possibly from some existing database. Using such a timetable will allow the client and the analyst to satisfy themselves that the model closely fits the behaviour of the system of interest. A cautionary note should, however, be sounded here. Using such timetables can be dangerously misleading other than for validation. Their repeated use implies that a particular sample is equivalent to the full population of such arrivals or orders. In fact, a particular sequence is only one pattern amongst a very large set of such patterns. Thus, useful though timetables are for validation, they should be used sparingly.

1.2.3 Modelling: policy comparison

The third component of discrete simulation models is the algorithms and policies which are being compared in the experiments. The policies embody the alternative actions which are open to those controlling the system. Sometimes the full range of available actions is known in advance; however, it is not at all unusual for possible options to appear during the experimental phase of a simulation project. That is, the full list of alternatives is very often unknown at the start of simulation modelling. This implies that the model should be designed so as to allow the easy substitution of one policy alternative for another. Again a modular approach is much to be commended.

One approach to this is, as far as possible, to separate the logical rules due to the policies from the invariant system rules. It thus then becomes easier to substitute one policy for another during experimentation. For example, supposing a simulation is being used to design a new continuous production plant. The individual sections of the plant may be well defined and their logic may be directly incorporated into the model. However, their precise configuration and sequence may be unknown, and may be one reason for undertaking the simulation study. Thus the configuration and sequence may be regarded as parameters of the model; the model itself being a description of the individual sections and their responses to particular conditions within the simulation. Thus the resulting program might use the configuration parameters as input data to the model, thus defining the links between the processes at run-time and avoiding the need to re-compile the program for each experiment.

1.2.4 Modelling: validation

It cannot be overstated that a model is an abstract representation of a system. But a model is also a simplification of the system. Were this latter point untrue, then the model would be just as complicated as the system being modelled. Because models are simplified abstractions then the question of validity is important, if not crucial. The task of the modeller is to produce a valid yet simplified abstraction of the system of interest. This is not easy and may, in some circumstances, be almost impossible. Nevertheless, this is certainly the task of the modeller and some more detailed advice is given in Pidd (1988).

A further difficulty, from a simulation perspective, comes from the common need to simulate systems which do not yet exist. Thus there is no way to be certain that the model is a fully valid representation of the system. It is often possible to test parts of the model against parts of existing systems. However, the aim of the simulation may be to see how these components behave when they interact. If the interaction were fully known, the simulation would probably be unnecessary. There may be no way to validate the modelling of these interactions.

Modelling

Validation can occur whilst the model is being built, as well as after the event. Often the main source of validation information is the client of the study. Thus any device which makes the model logic transparent to the client should greatly aid validation as model building proceeds. As mentioned earlier, activity cycle diagrams and interactive graphical displays are a great aid in this regard. As the modelling proceeds it is also the responsibility of the modeller to ensure that the statistical distributions employed are the best for the intended purpose. Books such as that by Hastings and Peacock (1974) can be a great help in this regard. It is also possible to imagine that expert systems could be devised to aid in the selection of appropriate distributions.

1.2.5 Modelling: two general principles

The preceding pages suggest two things about any approach to simulation modelling. First, it should be modular. That is, it should break down the system into relatively independent blocks whose interaction produces the system behaviour. If this modular approach is followed, then the modules at least can be independently tested, and specific interactions can be compared. There is still no certainty that the interactions are correct, but at least the source of the interaction behaviour can be pinpointed in the model. A further advantage of such modularity is that extra components can be tested and added to the model as required. This allows the modeller to first develop the overall, if simplified, structure of the model. Components can then be added in turn in order to reach the required degree of complication. This modular approach clearly fits well with the idea of easy substitution of policy alternatives during experimentation. Similarly, it allows timetables to be used during validation and their replacement by sampling processes during experimentation. Also, it allows a black-box approach to be taken to various components of the system being modelled. These parts may be modelled initially on a crude input–output basis and refined later as necessary. It should be possible only to edit the appropriate module.

The second desirable feature is that the modelling should concentrate on the rules which govern the behaviour of the model. The rules at least can be tested or argued over by the team working on the project. The more explicit these system rules, the easier it becomes to identify the reason for particular behaviour in the model. Putting these two requirements together suggests very strongly that a modular approach based on system rules and their predictable consequences should be the basis of simulation modelling. This is exactly what characterises the main approaches to simulation modelling. That is, the activity, event, process interaction and three-phase approaches (Pidd, 1988) are all attempts to build modular models.

1.3 Programming

When producing a small, or 'toy', simulation it matters little whether the program is written sensibly. If it works, then that may be enough. However, many practical simulations are large; that is, they have many entities, many state changes and there are many possible interactions between the entities and many possible experiments. Thus for practical simulations it is important to take very seriously the computing aspects of the project. Most of this book is devoted to the detail of these computing aspects. Nevertheless, there are some general points which are well worth noting here. The first is this: a modular model should lead to a modular program. Using a proper simulation programming language will force this modularity on the programmer. When writing in other more general-purpose languages, then the programmer may need explicitly to choose such an approach. Even when using simulation languages, care should be taken to ensure that the program blocks are short and relatively independent. Thus it should be possible to alter a single block and to be sure what the consequences are for the entire simulation program.

Thus simulation programs should be strongly structured. The rules devised by the advocates of structured programming and software engineering should thus be taken seriously by writers of simulation programs. Successful programs may well be maintained over several years by more than one programmer. A strong and sensible structure will greatly ease this task. A modular approach will also aid the simulation group in establishing the notion of a simulation software library. Rather than devising subroutines and procedures from scratch, task-oriented procedures can be devised and held in a library as re-usable code. For example, complex queue handling may be a feature of many models, and hence suitable routines may be made available from a library. They are then included as necessary in new programs, sometimes in their pristine, off-the-shelf state or, at other times, modified in specific ways.

Programming

Secondly, the program must be designed for ease of experimentation. The development of full simulation support environments (see Chapters 2 and 3, by Mathewson) is an important step in the right direction. The need for easy experimentation applies whether the software is to be delivered for use by a relatively unskilled client, or for use by the analyst personally. In general it implies that the simulation program itself should contain at least three sections.

1. *Parameter editor*: ideally, this should allow the user to specify an experiment or a new run without the need to re-compile the program each time. Thus, a convenient way of producing and editing a parameter file is needed. Nowadays this often means devising attractive and easy-to-use screens and menus. To devise these from scratch can be extremely time-consuming. Thus, if possible, this task may be best done using a common spreadsheet or database manager, or from a library of suitable screens. The file which is produced then becomes data for the simulator itself.

2. *Simulator*: this is the guts of the program. It contains the logic and rules of the system being simulated. That is, it simulates the operation of the system over time. In many cases it will be necessary to provide dynamic screen displays as the simulation runs. Hurrion gives details of this in Chapter 4. It should be noted here that various types of such output are possible; notably text, iconic graphics and graphs. In addition, the simulator should be programmed so as to make updating and editing as simple as possible.

3. *Report generator*: if the results matter, then they should be presented properly and in a way which avoids the need for further manual calculation. The reports must also make clear the precise nature of the experiment whose results are displayed. As with convenient data input, this part of a simulation program can be very time-consuming to write from scratch. If sophisticated time-series analyses are needed, then the results might as well be written to a file in some convenient format. This will allow the use of readily available statistical packages to analyse the results. Similarly, spreadsheets can allow convenient data analysis and manipulation and thus it may be sensible to produce the results in file formats which can be accessed by some favourite spreadsheet. If screen displays are used for reports, it should be possible to obtain a printed copy in all cases.

1.4 Experimentation

This is the reason for making the effort to develop and program simulation models, and it should not be regarded as an afterthought. Experimentation can be thought of as two linked types, gaming and classical experimentation. The two are not necessarily to be regarded as simple alternatives; one may lead into the other.

1.4.1 Experimentation as gaming

The first approach to simulation experimentation is to adopt a gaming approach. The ready availability of cheap graphics screens has led to many developments in this area, and a more complete description is given by Hurrion in Chapter 4. The idea is to display information about the simulation model state as the simulation proceeds. The display should be one which is readily understandable by the experimenter. To game with the program, the experimenter is provided with some way to interact with the computer. This might be via a keyboard, mouse, light pen or whatever. The devices are used to allow the experimenter to reset values of specified variables and to see the effects of these changes. For example, jobs in a machine shop may be re-routed in order to simulate emergency intervention at times of high demand. This can be a great aid in convincing clients that the model is valid, as it can be seen that appropriate behaviour follows from this interaction.

A second use of this interaction might be to reduce the need for many long classical experiments. That is, an interactive approach is used to isolate a small feasible set of policies for proper (i.e. classical) experimentation. In this way, gaming and classical experimentation may be regarded as complementary. Providing interaction facilities which are safe and easy to use is not straightforward. The user must be protected from making disastrous mistakes. At the same time the mode of interaction must be one which allows sensible and unambiguous options. To do this properly requires careful planning. It also usually implies a need for fast disk access and a large main memory on the computer. This is because it is usually a good idea to dump the current system state when interaction occurs. Such dumps are then available for later analyses. Thus interaction facilities should be carefully planned and not provided as an afterthought. See Chapter 4 by Hurrion for details.

1.4.2 Classical experimentation

The second type of experimentation, which is also important, is the properly designed experiment. These experiments are usually used to gain estimates of particular response variables or to compare experimental alternatives. A proper understanding of the nature of stochastic variation is important if major blunders are to be avoided in such experiments. In many cases conventional experimental design and analyses of variance methods may be used for such experiments.

However, this is certainly not always the case. Simulation results often include autocorrelated variables, and this means that many of the assumptions underlying conventional statistics no longer hold good. One problem with the use of simulation packages by non-specialists is that they may be blissfully ignorant of such considerations. A good simulation support environment might be able to identify such problems for the user.

As mentioned before, these two forms of experimentation can happily feed off one another. A gaming approach can be a very valuable way of reducing the number of alternatives which require formal comparison. At the same time the analyst ought to be aware that short-term dynamic effects in a particular simulation run may be misleading. Thus care may be needed in interpreting the results of any game.

1.5 Looking Back

A general description of the basic ideas of discrete simulation was given in the previous sections. The current section provides a brief historical review of the development of some of those ideas. Since the early 1950s, developments in discrete simulation are inextricably linked to progress in general computing. After all, without a computer no computer simulation is possible. Alongside these changes have been new applications of some statistical ideas, though probably relatively few wholly novel contributions. Although management scientists may have no professional interest in history, an understanding of how things came to be as they are may provide same insight into future possibilities. Hence this section.

1.5.1 Origins

Curnow and Curran (1983) report how difficult it is to be certain when and where the first digital computer was built. At least part of their problem stemmed from the difficulty of knowing how precisely to distinguish a stored program digital computer from other calculating devices. Different definitions lead to slightly different claims as to who was first. In their case a further complication comes from the classified nature of much early computing work, taking place as it did in the Second World War. Both of these issues arise when considering the early work on discrete simulation. Various threads can, however, be identified (Tocher, 1963).

One such thread was Monte Carlo analysis, a way of evaluating mathematical functions which are not amenable to direct analysis. It was developed before digital computers were available, often being the only feasible way to evaluate certain functions. The idea is that the computation of randomly selected points can be used to estimate a multi-dimensional integral. Some writers still use the term Monte Carlo simulation to describe what is here termed discrete event simulation, even such simulations may include no proper Monte Carlo evaluation. See von Neuman (1951) for an original paper describing the Monte Carlo approach.

Another thread was the theory of random sampling. If the behaviour of some object can be recognisably described by some probability distribution, then samples from that distribution may be used to simulate its behaviour. Further, if a particular system can be described by the combined effects of several distributions, then a combination of samples from these could be used to estimate the likely distribution of the system. Indeed, unless the combinations are very simple, then such a sampling experiment may be the only way to estimate the combined distribution. Many discrete event simulations can be regarded precisely as such complicated sampling experiments, though this is often played down by software vendors.

The final impetus seems to have come from the emergence of operational research, later termed management science. OR practitioners attempt to take a scientific view of their work. Such a stance often requires the use of formal models of systems of interest. Given that the systems being studied are often large and complex, appropriate models will rarely be simple. After all, there may be many interactions to be considered. Add this to the observation that the components of many systems display stochastic behaviour, and the attraction of a simulation approach becomes clear. A further attraction is that in many cases estimates of expected values are not enough. Often the analyst needs to know how the system might behave under extreme conditions.

Despite these three threads, simulation (and possibly OR/MS too) may not have taken off without a further obvious development; that is, the digital computer itself. Though the original computers, built during the late 1940s and early 1950s, were intended for numerical calculations, it soon became clear that simulation was possible on them too. However, it must be remembered that the early machines were very crude by today's standards.

The first-generation computers were physically very large and yet offered little processing power in today's terms. The working memory was small, programming might be done by physically setting switches, and the machines were not very reliable. But, compared with what was available before, they offered tremendous scope for some kinds of work. Main memory was limited because, in the more sophisticated machines, it had to be built slowly and laboriously by hand as a matrix of magnetic cores. Programming and data input, if not achieved by setting switches, might be by paper tape — a very frustrating method of imput. Reliability was low partly because logic had to be achieved by using thermionic valves. The early computers tended to overheat because many banks of valves were needed, and each value emitted some of its radiation as heat energy. Fault-finding in a hot, hard-wired device can be a very fraught and time-consuming business.

These first-generation machines were built individually for specific applications. Well-known examples, though not the first, were UNIVAC and the Ferranti Mk I for scientific computing, and LEO for business transaction processing. All these machines were expensive, complex to program and needed careful attention if they were to work at all. Not surprisingly, therefore, their use tended to be restricted to research staff or to routine tasks such as producing a payroll. In all cases, programming a computer was regarded as a deep and mysterious business by those unskilled in its practice.

Therefore, as far as simulation goes it should be no surprise to realise that only fairly small simulations were possible. Even these had to be very carefully written so as to fit in the small machines, and so as to complete their runs within a tolerable time limit. Before the development of problem-oriented languages such as FORTRAN, the programs had to be written in machine code or some marginally higher-level language. Given the early emphasis on computing and statistics, it should be no surprise that the first simulation text

(Tocher, 1963) was written by a man with a unique reputation in both fields.

Among the frustrations and excitement of this early work, some lessons did emerge which are still relevant today. The first was the realisation that no simulation program need ever be written wholly from scratch. It became clear that a modular approach could be taken. The activity within the system of interest could be broken down into relatively self-contained blocks. The interaction of these blocks could be used to simulate the logic of the system. The interaction itself could be controlled by a general-purpose executive, or control program, which would attend to the sequencing and scheduling of the blocks. Similarly, routines were quickly developed for sampling from standard and empirical probability distributions. This modular approach is still to be wholly commended today.

What also emerged was the need to make the best use of the finite computer resources available. Despite first impressions, the same is still true today. As machines offer more power and more storage, there is a temptation to assume that speed of execution (say) becomes unimportant. Not true. The faster the response experienced by analysts and users, then the greater is their expectation. Thus the need to write programs which are accurate, easy to amend and debug, and run fast still remains. Like faith, hope and love, the need for computationally efficient programs is likely to remain for ever.

1.5.2 Taken for granted

Once computers were established for transaction processing in organisations, they began to be taken for granted. Certainly they were still very expensive. Certainly they required many skilled people to work them properly. However, many organisations soon began to rely on them for what had been basic clerical tasks. The questions for many large organisations became 'which computer?' and 'what tasks?' not 'do we need a computer?'. To meet this market, computers were designed on a modular basis and it became almost possible to buy a machine off-the-shelf. The beginnings of a second-hand market also appeared. In both regards the IBM 360 series is perhaps the best example. The modular design allowed most configurations to be delivered without recourse to special production. This standardisation reduced both the cost of a computer and the risk inherent in its purchase. It also made possible the emergence of a professional group of programmers and analysts whose output need not be solely restricted to a single machine on a single site. Thus some portability of software became feasible.

The realisation that commercial computing was here to stay led to a demand for more powerful machines and for better input and output. Maybe as a spin-off from the US space missions, integrated circuits appeared in commercial computers during the 1960s. These replaced the valves and magnetic cores of the first generation of machines, thus increasing their reliability and allowing designers to pack more power into the machines. Backing store became faster and more reliable as magnetic disk-packs replaced extensive use of tapes and drums. Though punched cards remained the dominant mode of input through the 1960s, direct-key entry started to appear. Thus the hardware became more reliable, cheaper and more powerful.

This same period saw the dawning of the software revolution. Many of today's programming languages appeared and enjoyed widespread use. In order to encourage numerical processing, IBM sponsored the development of FORTRAN. For commercial use, COBOL was introduced as suitable for applications which involved much file-handling and input/output. Both of these are still in widespread use, though enhanced somewhat since the early days. ALGOL was mooted as a way of describing algorithms and in due course became a programming language. These and other languages allowed the programmer to concentrate on the task of problem-oriented computing, rather than having to worry about the details of machine architecture. The agreement on standards for these languages and their compilers allowed the limited porting of software from one machine to another.

The standardisation of hardware and software opened up possibilities for computer simulation which were quickly developed. Packaged routines in the form of subroutine or procedure libraries began to appear on the market. These were aimed at users who already knew a host language such as FORTRAN or ALGOL. The routines provided at least

an executive
sampling routines
queue handling facilities
report tabulations.

Examples were GASP, which provided FORTRAN routines, and the ALGOL library of SIMON. Whatever their drawbacks, these packages at least meant that an analyst no longer had to program the simulations from scratch.

As well as these libraries, 'proper' languages for discrete simulation started to appear. Examples were SIMSCRIPT (Markowitz et al., 1963), which employed a FORTRAN-like syntax, and CSL (Buxton and Laski, 1962). The latter was developed jointly by IBM and ESSO in the UK and went through a two-stage translation, the CSL source generated a FORTRAN program, which was itself compiled into object code and could be run. The intention was that such systems might be usable by analysts who knew no 'real' programming languages. The reality was that they eased the task of the already proficient programmer. At the very least they provided a syntax which made the programs relatively easy to read and to relate to the underlying model. For this reason program verification became slightly less difficult, and the programs themselves could be shorter.

More ambitiously, flow diagram languages (see Pidd, 1988, for details) appeared in the guise of GPSS (Greenberg, 1972) and HOCUS (Poole and Szymankiewicz, 1977). Both required the user to model the system of interest as a flow diagram which showed how the entities interacted to produce the system behaviour. GPSS was originally designed jointly by IBM and Bell Labs for the simulation of telecommunication networks, its syntax betrays these origins. HOCUS is based around the idea of activity cycle diagrams. In both cases the idea was that the user would submit a set of punched cards to the main program which were formalised descriptions of the flow diagrams. This description then became data to a master or generic program. GPSS and HOCUS were extremely welcome to many potential users of simulation because they offered a route to simulation without the need to learn the detail of a general-purpose programming language. Nor did the users need to understand precisely how the executive was handling and controlling the events within the simulation. That could be safely left to the master program. Inevitably, the flow diagram systems were limited in their scope, but inventive users were often able to find ways round the shortcomings. As with all successful packages, they were successively enhanced. HOCUS, in particular, has now been embedded in an interactive support environment and provided with a much wider range of features.

For most of this period computing and simulation were still batch-oriented. Usually the simulation programs were run on machines which spent much of their time working on commercial transaction processing. 'Scientific' computing was allotted little time in most commercial organisations. Thus, development time for simulation programs could be extremely lengthy. Programs and flow diagram descriptions, too, had to be written on standard coding forms. From these, punched cards were produced and normally there were punching errors. The cards were then fed to the computer as a batch job and the resulting list of syntax errors filled many an hour for simulation analysts. Batch working combined with limited computer time for 'scientific' work meant that it could take an awfully long time to produce a fully debugged program.

1.5.3 Power to the user

During the late 1960s simple batch computing began to be elbowed out by two developments. The first was multi-programming and the second was time-sharing. In a multi-programming environment, several programs can simultaneously share the machine's resources. Thus a large computer could be used for a single large job, or to attend to two or more smaller ones at the same time. This made for a more efficient use of computer resources and thus reduced the turn-round time on batch jobs. This was a slight help to the development of computer demands on a computer as compared to routine transaction processing.

Of even greater significance was the development of time-shared computing, initially on mini-computers via remote terminals. The first commercial time-sharing service in the UK appeared in 1967, based on a DEC PDP 8. Time-sharing had two significant advantages for management scientists and for simulation in particular. Firstly, it put the user or programmer back in the driving seat. There was no longer a need to beg a small amount of scientific time on a computer which was designed and installed for commercial transaction processing. The user could access the machine when and where required — phone bills permitting. Thus the turn-round time on jobs could be drastically reduced. Also there was no longer the risk that a machine operator might abort a program just because there had been no output for a while!

The second advantage of time-sharing was that it brought interactive computing with it. Not only could the user quickly produce working programs, but these programs could incorporate interactive input and output. Thus programs could be run on a conversational basis. This led to rapid developments in financial modelling during the early 1970s.

From a simulation perspective, interactive computing opened up three possibilities. The first was that programming could be simplified and made less formal. The need to write in 80-column FORTRAN format was an obvious candidate for an early departure. Also, Clementson (1982), Mathewson (1977) and others produced the first versions of their interactive progam generators (see Pidd, 1988, Chapter 8). Using these, the programmer could rapidly produce working skeletons of simulation programs as described by Mathewson in Chapter 2.

The second payoff for simulation was the realisation that programs could be run interactively. Using, a display screen, workers such as Bell (1969) were able to display graphical output from a simulation program as it ran. Thus there was no need to plough through pages of printout to analyse the results of a simulation. Many of the effects could be observed on the screen as the program ran. A few years later, Hurrion developed the ideas of interactive graphical simulation which he describes in Chapter 4.

The third possibility was that simulation programs could now be run by users rather than programmers. If a friendly shell could be written to protect the user from the operating system (and vice-versa!) then simulations could be made menu-driven. This of course may not always have been a good idea; not all users wish to run their own programs and not all can properly interpret the results. Nevertheless, this trend to delivered software is with us today — though mainly on personal workstations rather than time-shared machines.

1.5.4 Software consolidation

Whilst this new emphasis on remote, interactive computing appeared, mainframe-based simulation was becoming respectable. During the 1960s and early 1970s, as the IBM 360/370 series became ever more widespread, compilers and translators appeared for most of the well-known simulation languages. CSL grew into ECSL under Clementson (1982) and SIMSCRIPT became SIMSCRIPT II.5. Using these and other similar systems it became possible to write large simulation programs in a fairly efficient manner. The flow diagram languages also came of age. GPSS and HOCUS were available, and used worldwide for applications of which their originators could never have dreamt. Both enjoyed great success in their target markets and beyond.

Thus simulation came of age. Standard computers and standard software were now available. The task of developing useful simulations was still far from straightforward, but at least the analyst no longer had to do battle with unreliable and remote computers via unsuitable software.

1.5.5 Personal computer power

The 1970s saw the emergence of micro-computers and the 1980s have seen the consolidation of personal computer power. The power available on a desk top to a single user is sometimes greater than that available to an entire set of terminals on a mini-computer of the 1970s. The power may be packaged as a stand-alone machine such as an Apple Macintosh or some IBM-compatible computer running MSDOS™, OS/2™ or Xenix™. Alternatively, it may be provided as a networked personal workstation such as those provided by Sun Microsystems and running Unix. Most importantly, the computing resource is under the direct control of the user.

It is thus possible to offer many more facilities in commercial simulation software. In whatever form the power is provided, there is no doubt that the power exists and can be exploited in discrete simulations. At the time of writing (1988), a typical powerful personal machine offers the following facilties at low cost.

1. *Main processor*: usually a 16/32-bit chip able to address many megabytes of memory with no need for explicit bank switching. Most commonly the main processor is based on the Intel 80286/386 or Motorola 68000 series, and frequently a numeric co-processor is used to speed up floating-point calculations. Relatively cheap personal computers now rival third-generation mini-computers, such as the VAX series for raw computing power. In some cases the memory is still addressed in segments as small as 64K, which can be inconvenient. Such limitations will certainly disappear completely before 1990.
2. *Backing store*: usually based on floppy disks and Winchester technology. The Winchesters offering off-line storage of between 20 and 100 Mbytes. The floppy disks are usually of a capacity of between 360 Kbytes and 1.2 Mbytes and are used for

back-up and for secure storage. Before long it is likely that rotating media, with all their reliability problems, will be replaced by cheaper and more reliable media.

3   *User interaction*: most commonly by a QWERTY keyboard, but often supplemented by a mouse or tracker ball. Voice input has been tried, but with very limited success.

4   *Operating system*: most commonly based on a version of MSDOS™, OS/2™ or Unix™.

5   *Output devices*: most commonly a printer and screen. For high-quality print effects, laser printers dominate the scene. High-density dot matrix printers have virtually removed the need for daisy-wheel and thimble printers. Both types of device will accept graphic and text screen dumps. Most screens are bit-mapped with a resolution of 640×350 pixels of better, and for higher resolution and colour it is usually straightforward to avoid a special intelligent graphics device as an additional card to the workstation.

Thus there is no particular reason why the type of simulations carried out by management scientists should be limited by a shortage of computer power at a reasonable price. Needless to say this power offers opportunities either for improving the practice of simulation or for lazy and ill-founded work.

On the software side the simulation analyst is faced with a number of developments, detailed by Mathewson in Chapters 2 and 3, which can be expected to continue. The first is that the long-standing packages have been further enhanced to take at least some advantage of this personal computing power. Systems such as SIMSCRIPT and SLAM now include versions for personal computers and offer at least some graphical facilities. Others such as HOCUS have been embedded in support environments which make model creation, reporting, graphical output and analysis a much less time-consuming task than in the past. In most cases the underlying simulation language remains more or less unchanged. Effort has, however, been applied to adding extra facilities to the packages. Part of this effort is aimed at producing packages which are simple enough for non-specialists to use directly.

In addition, newer systems designed from scratch for use on personal workstations have appeared; Mathewson gives details in Chapters 2 and 3. Some of these are no more than generic models with a fairly wide problem domain. Others are fully fledged simulation systems designed to cope with most simulation problems. All have in common an ease of use which could scarcely have been imagined by the pioneers.

The second thrust on the software side is that, for those who must do so, it is now much easier to develop and use software in-house. The operating systems and editors available on these computers make the production of specialised libraries a relatively easy task. Modules can be written in general-purpose languages such as FORTRAN, Pascal or C. Pidd explores the use of Pascal in Chapter 7, and Crookes does likewise for C in Chapter 8. The modules can be strung together either as source or object code for particular purposes. In some cases in-house modules can be incorporated into programs produced by the commercial simulation packages. This facility can be useful for simulating the effects of complicated control algorithms.

Packages such as SEE-WHY have also appeared. These are libraries of simulation subroutines, written in a subset of FORTRAN in the case of SEE-WHY. These are thus similar in concept to long-standing packages such as GASP, but they include useful routines for interaction and graphical display. To write a simulation program the user strings together the provided subroutines and writes any others which might be needed for particularly tricky parts of the model. The strong point of SEE-WHY and its ilk is that routines are provided for colour graphical output and for on-line interaction by the user. The detail of such systems is explored by Hurrion in Chapter 4.

Generic extensions to existing packages are also popular, and with good reason. WITNESS is a generic model written in SEE-WHY, which aims to ease the modelling of certain types of manufacturing system. SIMFACTORY is written in SIMSCRIPT II.5 with similar applications in mind. Despite selling at prices way above the norm for PC software, these types of packages have found a ready market at a time when manufacturing companies are investing heavily in automated plant.

Powerful and relatively friendly statistical software is also available on these personal computers. These include established suites such as SAS™, SPSS™ and MINITAB™, which have been ported from mainframes and super-minis. Others are available which were especially written for personal computers. Combined with the low cost and wide availability of spreadsheets and database management systems, this means that it can be simple to carry out analyses on simulation results or on input data. All that is required is that the data for analysis be in a suitable file format for the relevant analysis package. The standard use of text files is one way of enforcing this. Ideally these facilities would be fully implemented with modelling and programming facilities in proper integrated simulation support environments. These are discussed by Mathewson in Chapter 3.

Alongside these progressive developments has come the realisation that the rule-based modules which make up the bulk of simulation models have much in common with some of the ideas of artificial intelligence. Thus there may be considerable scope for mutual learning between AI and simulation analysts. There may also be scope for the use of some AI methods in simulation modelling, and in the analysis of results. Paul discusses these developments in Chapters 5 and 6.

1.6 References

Bell, T. E. (1969) *Computer Graphics for Simulation Problem-Solving*. RAND Corporation, Santa Monica, California.

Buxton, J. N. and Laski, J. G. (1962) Control and simulation language. *Computer Journal*, **5**.

Clementson, A. T. (1982) *Extended Control and Simulation Language*. Cle.Com Ltd, Birmingham, UK.

Curran, S. and Curnow, R. (1983) *The Penguin Computing Book*. Penguin, Harmondsworth, UK.

Greenberg, S. (1972) *A GPSS Primer*. John Wiley & Sons, New York.

Hastings, N. A. J. and Peacock, J. B. P. (1974) *Statistical Distributions*. Halstead Press, New York.

Markowitz, H. M., Hausner, B. and Carr, H. W. (1963) *SIMSCRIPT: A Simulation Programming Language*. RAND Corporation, RM-3310 pr 1962. Prentice/Hall, Englewood Cliffs, New Jersey,.

Mathewson, S. C. (1977) *A Programming Language for SIMON Simulation in FORTRAN*. Imperial College, London.

Pidd, M. (1988) *Computer Simulation in Management Science*, 2nd edn. John Wiley & Sons, Chichester.

Poole, T. G. and Szymankiewicz, J. (1977) *Using Simulation to Solve Problems*. McGraw-HIll, London.

Tocher, K. D. (1963) *The Art of Simulation*. English Universities Press, London.

von Neuman, J. (1951) Various techniques used in connection with random digits: 'Monte Carlo method'. *National Bureau of Standards Applied Mathematical Series*, **12**, 36–38.

Computer Modelling for Discrete Simulation
Edited by M. Pidd
©1989 John Wiley & Sons Ltd

2
The Implementation of Simulation Languages

S. C. Mathewson

2.1 Introduction

2.1.1 Interrelated products

Simulation software falls into two broad categories: that which is provided for the expert management scientist and that which is provided for the expert end-user. However, with a few exceptions the domain-specific software is built upon the foundations of a general simulation language. This chapter therefore reviews the broad objectives of a simulation experiment, and looks at the general facilities that have been provided. The subsequent chapter focuses on the narrower field of problem-oriented software tools — largely those concerned with manufacturing and production — and then broadens the discussion to investigate how the modelling aids which have been provided for this narrower application area can be more widely made available.

2.1.2 An overview of developments

This chapter is intended as a guide through the complex market for simulation software. It illustrates that behind the plethora of new products lie three major developments in simulation software.

1   *Powerful languages*, which utilise library submodels and are supported by software development tools which ensure program integrity and adequate software documentation.

2 *Generic models*, which are easy to use and are enhanced with graphics and animation, thus aiding general comprehension of underlying assumptions and operating implications.
3 *Integrated packages* for decision support with access to statistical tools and database management facilities.

Recent general developments in computing have also changed the practice of simulation as follows.

1 *Supercomputers*, and indeed distributed computing on super-micros, permit large problems to be modelled. These large models, written by a team, have problems which require specialist project management techniques.
2 *More computers* are available, and this leads to the development of more models.
3 *Delivered software*, written (sometimes) by management scientists but used directly by the decision-makers on their own workstations or personal computers. These managers are unlikely to be simulation experts and consequently some designers of software packages now aim to develop systems which are more convenient to use (for example SIMSOFT 1986). Such packages are convenient in the sense that the model-building is easier, and that the logic of the physical system can be translated more rapidly into computer code.

Moreover, while technology has created its own changes, there have also been developments in the management of simulation projects. In particular, the emphasis laid upon the individual elements of a modelling project has changed. Much of this change arises from parallel development in the field of software engineering. Figure 2.1 (Balci, 1986) puts simulation software into the broad context of problem-solving and beyond the somewhat limited range of model coding. 'The model development processes portrayed in the figure emphasis the role of the analyst or simulation software development manager and de-emphasise that of the programmer.'

The rest of this chapter explores various application areas and identifies, from the literature, the desirable features that are advocated for a simulation support environment. Subsequently it makes a comparative evaluation of the solutions that are proposed—languages, generic models, program generators and simulation systems. Finally it reviews the software in terms of the original goals and looks to the gaps which the future might fill.

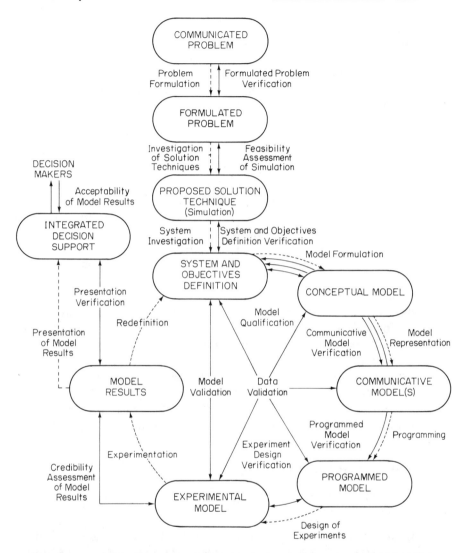

Figure 2.1 The life cycle of a simulation study. (From Balci (1986) Credibility Assessment of Simulation Results. Proc 1986 Winter Sim Conf.)

2.2 The Implementation of Simulation

Figure 2.1 shows only three broad steps in simulation: problem definition, model development and decision support. However, the details in the figure stress the inherent complexity which arises from the many interactions. It therefore provides a useful structure to explore the processes involved in starting with a problem, perhaps specified incorrectly, translating this into a machine-based model and ending with an acceptable aid to the decision-maker. The internal connections are numerous, and if such a process is to be managed effectively the software must be integrated with the task. Before discussion of the software tools for simulation, consider the objectives of the simulation exercise. Much recent work in management science has emphasised the 'system', and it is important to understand why this is so. Simulation is motivated by the need for problem solution. In the past this has often been defined in a very narrow manner. Sometimes the restricted computer power has limited the applications of the method. More often the nature of the software has made it impossible for the simulation model to play a full part in decision-making. Thus the model often lagged and became an endorsement of a policy after the fact. At other times the application area, for example computer operating system design, was one where the success of simulation reflected the skill and experience of the user group and the specific and restricted nature of its enquiries. As the user base widens, a more realistic set of performance criteria is needed. These criteria are not always met, but they do provide the motivation for much of the current work, and are therefore important to review. For each step the following list of desirable features has been suggested. (The points which are made below come from work by many authors including Birtwhistle, Nance, Pidd, and Zeigler. The work will be directly acknowledged in the context of the solutions that they offer.)

2.2.1 Problem definition

(1) Open communication

Commercial decisions need to be understood and debated by all involved so as to avoid overlooking important factors. Hence there is a need for an effective non-specialist channel of communication. In determining effectiveness it is important to bear in mind that the initial representation of the model may serve to focus the experience of a group of people with very dissimilar skills. Ideally a model should be understood by all those affected by the analysis, from the most senior manager to the shopfloor worker.

The benefits of this are demonstrated by the case of a model of a new layout for a hospital accident and emergency department. Here it was a hospital porter who identified the fact that the new operating theatre trolleys would not fit through the redesigned operating theatre doors. Simulation projects carried out in strongly unionised environments have often proceeded more smoothly than might have been expected. Possibly this is because the simulation model provided a very accessible representation of managment proposals and one, moreover, with which the shopfloor representatives could interact.

Various ways of achieving this open communication have been attempted. The first is the idea that simulation models be expressed in a natural language form. Early examples are the papers of Kiviat *et al.* (1968) on SIMSCRIPT, which sought to use an 'English-like language', and the later work at IBM (Heidorn, 1975) into programming via a natural language dialogue. A comparison between recent examples (Paul and Doukidis 1986) and the work of Heidorn shows little change in the past ten years, so progress has been rather slow.

Another approach is to conceive of the model as a specialised flow chart using a small set of symbols, what Pidd (1988) terms 'flow diagram languages'. The successes of Hocus (Poole and Szymankiewicz, 1977) and SLAM (Pritsker, 1979) illustrate that such flow diagram systems have a broader appeal than the text-based ones. Recently developments in raster graphics mean that there are now numerous graphical systems both for the development of the models and the presentation of results.

(2) Speed: modularity, feedback and sensitivity analysis

In practice, problem definition is an iterative process which is constrained by commercial considerations that impose a rigid timescale on the task. Thus speed of model development is important and can sometimes be reduced by the re-use of previous modules. Another approach is to provide a flexible modelling environment with the opportunity for early feedback.

The provision of effective feedback is of value because it prevents expensive investigations into insensitive areas of model performance. In a complex model the degree of detail required is seldom clear from the outset. Collecting detailed data on operating rules or time variations is expensive and time-consuming. For example, in a model of an airport there are many variables, even for single events, say a flight arrival. At the outset it is valuable to know whether model performance is affected by the time to disembark from an aircraft. If it is, then perhaps data must be collected by aircraft type, seating arrangement, aisle width, number of exit doors used and route — or anything else that may increase congestion at the exit. If disembarkation time is not relevant, then data collection can be much more casual, perhaps restricted to the mean, maximum and minimum disembarkation rates. An early indication of sensitivity from the model, combined with the possibility of easily increasing complexity, is an important aid to model development.

(3) Completeness

The diagram also shows a long path between the origin of the investigation and the interface with the decision-maker. To manage this gap, the concept of completeness requires discussion of the total requirements of model output at the initial step of problem definition. Consider a factory model which is concerned with the throughput of a job-shop. When the technical evaluation is complete a set of operating rules, which minimise the machine waiting time, may have been identified. But the user may subsequently wish to consider the costs of the solution. Such costs include the work-in-progress, and it is conceivable that this information is not produced by the model if the original goals were too narrow. In this case the focus of development has been on the physical flows, although the required output is financial indicators. The ability to relate the financial measures to the physical values at the outset, and then have these relationships managed by the program as the physical model develops, is valuable.

2.2.2 Model development

In an era of knowledge-based systems, the boundaries between problem definition, model development, and coding are not well defined. In an advanced integrated system one can envisage that the language in which the conceptual problem is defined will also serve to specify the model. In the absence of such a language it is still feasible for the model definition to relate directly to coding mechanisms and the problems of project management.

(1) Conversion from concept to code

The ease of conversion from concept to code is important because this implies both speed in model-building and error-free computer-based representation of the model. Program generators permit automatic encoding from a reduced vocabulary of modelling concepts. There is therefore a trade-off between the detail permitted and the generality of application.

(2) Problem-specific structures

In application areas where common problem structures predominate, it is beneficial to have a specialist portfolio of conceptual tools tailored to particular tasks. An example of this is found in the area of flexible manufacturing, where a major concern is the behaviour of the system when machines break down while work is in progress. This requires that the data associated with the interrupted activity is sensibly handled by the system. It is a feature which is not easily modelled in many languages. DSSL (Chaharbaghi and Davies, 1986) demonstrates a research system which emphasises these facilities and so seeks to bring benefits to the FMS designer.

(3) Modularity

Modularity permits the user to build on past efforts and to achieve effective control of model logic. In effect the model is constructed, as far as possible, from a library of existing modules. As new modules are required they are added to the library.

(4) Logical consistency checks

If a model has a clear underlying structure it is possible to provide consistency checks on the model logic. For example the system can ask whether jobs which are queued for processing by a machine are in fact removed by the machine when processing starts. If a queue exists in front of a machine, are entities fed into the queue? Before an activity is scheduled, is there a check that every necessary resource is available?

(5) Controlled increase in complexity

Many models start with logical skeletons, reflecting the physical flows within the system, and develop as the control mechanisms are superimposed upon the physical logic. Has the system the required interfaces to permit such a development from simple prototypes?

A project manager needs to keep track of and co-ordinate the work of the members of his team. Automatic documentation is desirable to inform the manager of the progress of the work and inform the programming cells of the requirements of the other groups. If each programmer is working on his own module, a system which identifies all linkages between every other module is useful. In the job-shop example mentioned previously it is assumed that the financial implications of the model were reviewed after the technical decisions. In the concurrent model development of a project team, a system can be envisaged which knows that work in progress is required by the financial module, and ensures it is flagged as required output from the physical flow module.

Database features are also required. A large project will have many versions of the model, some developing the same theme in a more complete manner, others expanding into new areas. The ability to recall and execute a previous model, perhaps in the context of debugging a current program, would be invaluable. The database might also hold a module library and permit synthesis of the models based on old work. With more applications of simulation there is a growing realisation that the present practice of writing specific models for single goals, which are then discarded, is not effective. It is valuable to have a facility which enables the user to carry over some of the experience and benefits of prior models.

2.2.3 Decision support

Simulation users are drawn from a wide cross-section of professionals who are frequently unused to the application of statistical tools in decision-making. Given that most discrete simulation models are highly stochastic, then it is plain that many users will need some support. This must be rather more than simple access to standard statistical methods, but should aid the *interpretation* of results which are stochastic. Thus, a support environment might provide knowledge-based systems to aid the interpretation of statistical models. Other desirable features are database management tools, computer graphics, and interaction, all of which permit a low-cost exploration of an approximate solution space.

(1) Statistical help

Classical statistics are seldom appropriate to the analysis of output

The Implementation of Simulation 31

from computer simulations. For example, congestion is a prominent feature of simulation, and proper analysis requires access to autoregressive models and regenerative processes. The ability to manipulate the random variates is also peculiar to computer modelling and users should have access to control variate analysis as a means of variance reduction.

Unfortunately, general users will usually be unaware of the finer points of using statistical techniques. They may not know of the significant errors incurred by ignoring correlation, or the fact that using more control variates does not necessarily go on reducing the output variance. A number of levels of assistance can be envisaged from simple warning messages to a knowledge-based system that leads the user through the analysis process and selects the best technique for the problem posed.

(2) Database management tools

A database is very useful for managing output data. Results from the simulation model can be archived and indexed by run, and could later be fed to external packages for more detailed analysis. For large systems it has been suggested that a facility be provided which enables the decision-maker to interpolate between two known sets of resource allocation and thereby estimate the system behaviour for some intermediate level.

(3) Computer graphics

Computer graphics provide an effective window into the model activity. Are they easily constructed? Can the user vary the level of detail displayed?

(4) Low-cost exploration of the solution space

Many models are built from approximate data and are designed to increase management insight. In this context the manager will wish to explore the solution space, often in a sense that was not anticipated by the modeller. It is a great asset if the support system is flexible enough to permit some alterations to the model. It can be useful to vary features that have not been specified as variable at model definition or print out model state parameters without the necessity of adding output statements and then re-compiling.

Dubois (1980), of General Electric, made a pertinent point when he said 'in practical situations detailed data . . . is frequently not available . . . therefore in the early stages it is unwise to build detailed simulations.' Following this argument he advocates analytic techniques as an effective means of narrowing a large set of options, and suggests that hybrid software—providing simulation and/or analysis—is appropriate to the decision-making environment. In practical terms an analytic solution, though perhaps lacking in detail and presenting expected values rather than transients, is very much faster to derive. Simulation is, after all, an experimental process which can require large samples and long runs to achieve reasonable confidence intervals.

2.2.4 Approaches to providing such facilities

This review of the facilities which would be attractive to a simulation user has covered a very wide range. Some of the help is strategic and some is tactical. Solutions which have been suggested embrace the same range of complexity.

At the simplest end of the spectrum a modeller can be provided with specialist templates or building blocks which represent typical objects within the modelling environment. These can be assembled to provide a simple model, perhaps generating standard reports. At this level one can imagine the user to be an industrial engineer concerned with the correct number of tool-setters within a proposed group of NC machines. He builds his own model of the shop floor, using a menu of templates, and automatically creates a company standard report form of machine efficiency based on a work schedule held in a production database.

At the other end of the spectrum an integrated system could support a team involved in building a complex and flexible model of a large industrial plant which might be used over several years. This system must be able to cope with changing personnel and possible difficulties over communication. Further complications are that the company divisions may have a complex set of competing goals, and the requirement could be confused by a need for access at several levels within the firm. Thus a fully integrated support system needs to be of some complexity itself, if it is to be of use.

2.3 The Robot Cell

To compare the available software tools in terms of a common problem, consider a robot cell. This is a small manufacturing unit consisting of a numerically controlled mill, with two work tables each holding an identical jig. Either table may be moved under the milling head, but only one at a time. The unused table is available for access. This permits simultaneous milling and set-up or tear-down operations. The machine is serviced by a robot. Jobs arrive in the form of raw castings which queue at the machine. The robot loads castings onto a work table whenever there is a vacant jig. After loading the jig the robot becomes idle. If the machine head is free and a job is loaded on a work table, the table is positioned under the machining head. After the casting has been milled the table is automatically cleared from the vicinity of the head. It will be unloaded as soon as the robot becomes idle. The robot places the casting onto a roller conveyor and the casting slides away under gravity. Assume this conveyor cannot be blocked.

The model can be described graphically, and there are a number of standards available. This text uses the 'entity cycle diagram' approach described in Pidd (1988), Chapter 3. It may be helpful to imagine that with the passing of time the entity moves along the axis of the active state, finally emerging from the end of the rectangle. This is the EVENT associated with the activity, and the time at which the resources held by an activity are released is called the EVENT time. Activities which rely on one resource start when the required resource is released from a preceding activity.

The active states in the system are COMES, LOADS, CUT, UNLOAD and CLEAR. The queues are QUEUE, ROUGH and SMOOTH, the physical queues where castings are actually waiting to move, and the conceptual queues IDLE, FREE and EMPTY which hold the available resources of the robot, mill and tables. The resources required for operation of the cell are: CASTINGS, TABLES (two per mill), MILL, ROBOT, DUMMY. Each resource flows through a cycle which consists of activities and queues. Each resource can be taken in order, for example:

CASTINGS: WORLD COMES QUEUE LOADS ROUGH CUT SMOOTH UNLOAD CLEAR WORLD.

The resource cycle is presented as a closed cycle. This is an artificial presentation which envisages a limitless WORLD outside the immediate environment of the model. If the target simulation language has the required facilities, this can be replaced by an open loop. With such languages, COMES would imply that the casting is CREATED at the beginning of the loop and CLEAR that the casting was DESTROYED. A representation of the model in, say, SIMSCRIPT or SIMULA would reflect this approach.

Considering the other resources.

TABLES: EMPTY LOADS ROUGH CUT SMOOTH UNLOAD EMPTY.

The model may have as many tables as required loaded into the queue EMPTY.

MILL: FREE CUT FREE.
ROBOT: IDLE LOADS IDLE UNLOADS IDLE.

The robot returns to a state of IDLE whenever it has completed a task.

DUMMY: COMES

If the arrival of castings is generated by a random distribution of the inter-arrival times, then the DUMMY resource can be used to schedule the arrival of a new casting, given that a casting has just arrived. Other options are possible.

When all individual cycles are aggregated into one diagram, the result is Figure 2.2. The diagram, with the addition of information on the arrival and service distributions, can be automatically coded in a simulation language. It is a complete definition of the simple system.

2.4 Simulation Language Features

Simulation languages are designed to support the mechanics of modelling. They are tools for the use of the specialist modeller. In consequence they are of restrictive use in the support of industrial decision-makers unless they are embedded in a 'user-friendly' environment. Program generators may be used to produce models coded in specified simulation languages. Application-specific systems provide pre-written templates specified in languages and, as SLAM, frequently permit the user to write extensions in the native code. Simulation languages, or their common constructs, underpin all software environments.

The features provided by a simulation language are typically a subset of the facilities discussed earlier. They are mainly concerned

The Robot Cell

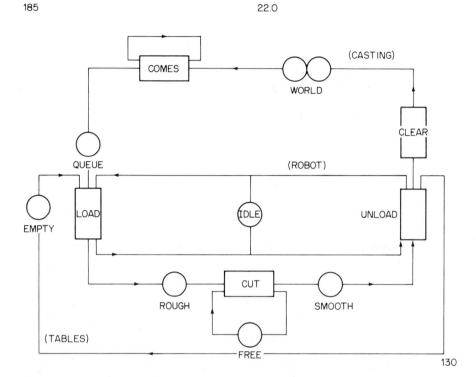

Figure 2.2 Entity cycle diagram for a robot cell.

with the mechanics of modelling and with the simple reporting of the model operation. This list is a shortened version of that due to Kiviat (1969):

1 model a system's static state,
2 provide extensive list processing facilities,
3 model dynamic interactions of data objects,
4 provide statistical sampling,
5 collect data,
6 provide reporting facilities and analyse data, and
7 monitor the model and debug the program.

Today the implementations are different from those suggested by Kiviat; however, the functions are the same.

2.4.1 Modelling a system's static state

This refers to provision of the features which are common to other languages—ALGOL, FORTRAN, or Pascal—through the provision of storage in arrays, conditional branching and simple arithemetic. One other language, SIMULA, extends the handling of data, as represented by attributes, by the mechanisms of CLASS. This is an important facility which is discussed later in the chapter.

2.4.2 Provide extensive list processing capability

As many discrete event simulations are used to investigate resource constrained queuing problems, it is natural that queues as ordered lists should be important. The simplest form of ordered list is the linked list. Each element in the list has an associated pointer. This points to the predecessor or successor of the element and so a simple chain is created. There are variations on this simplest structure. The list can be circular with an exterior pointer to the first element, or it can be a linear structure with a terminator as the final pointer. As the ability to access the list in different ways becomes important so the list structure can be extended to a double linkage, with a successor and a predecessor pointer. More advanced structures are also available—binary trees and multi-level lists. A good discussion can be found in Chapter 2 of Mitrani (1982). The usual trade-off is between the fixed overheads associated with maintaining the list structure and the speed of access to particular points in the list. In the majority of simulations large queues seldom form, and so the benefits of the more sophisticated methods are not realised.

Empirical comparisons indicate that for small queues (<20), the fixed costs associated with the more complex structures—say maintaining two pointers instead of one—outweigh the simplicity of simple lists. For larger lists the benefits are significant. The event list, the means by which most programs maintain control of the time advance, can become large, and it can be beneficial to tailor the list processing method if that implemented in the particular language is slow. If the event list is of the order of 1000, experiments have shown that the access times of commercial software running on the same machine can vary by a factor of four. An example arose in the

Simulation Language Features 37

simulation of passenger movements using a set of lifts in a large building. Here, implementing an improved mechanism was most easily accomplished by adding a user-controlled events list and feeding from the top of this into the event list provided in the software. Thus the implicit list was always short and the effect of poor implementation was reduced. This is analogous to the physical separation of the event lists on a multi-processor computing environment. Comfort (1984) has described the benefit that may arise from the use of a master–slave event set processor. Indeed, the article forms a general tutorial on which to base particular field modifications.

2.4.3 Modelling the dynamic interactions of data objects

The most common time advance algorithms are the event, activity and process approaches summarised in Pidd (1988). It can be shown that any time structure can be mapped into any other. In many ways the time structure is not as significant a difference as is the data structure.

Consider a shorthand notation for the two essential features of any simulation language — the scheduling mechanism and the queue handling instructions. Suppose that the simulation program is coded in BASIC, then control could be directed so as to permit the execution of the instructions in a sequence which manipulates the state of the model as required.

E.N   The entry point for the code describing the outcome of EVENT N. Thus E. COMES is the label for the code describing EVENT COMES.

N'   The set of queues feeding activity N.

T.N'   If resources exist in each queue of the set N' then schedule the start of activity N, otherwise jump to the end of the code segment.

S.N'   Schedule the activity N, employing the resources held in the set of queues N'.

F.N   Find the end of the next scheduled activity — activity N. This is EVENT N. Advance the simulation time to the end of EVENT N and transfer control to the relevant logic.

>QUEUE Put the relevant member in the queue called QUEUE.

QUEUE> remove the relevant member from the queue called QUEUE.

(1) The event-based structure

The procedure is to:

> Identify the next event and complete all changes that are dependent on that event. Review the subset of activities who use resources released by that event, and where possible schedule future events using the newly available resources.

Thus an event-based program must include blocks of code which correspond to the system events and the activity which might follow at the events.

For the robot cell example there are system events whenever a new casting arrives, a table is loaded, a cutting operation is finished, a table is unloaded or all work on a casting is complete (table is clear). Each of these events has activity which may follow, depending on the state of other variables and entities in the simulation. Using the shorthand introduced above, an event-based program could be coded as in Figure 2.3. If two events are

```
                     SET INITIAL CONDITIONS
                         'MAIN PROGRAM'
                            F.EVENT

           SELECT THE APPROPRIATE MODULE OF EVENT CODE

       E.COMES    E.LOADS    E.CUT      E.UNLOAD   E.CLEAR
       >QUEUE     >ROUGH     >SMOOTH    S.CLEAR    >WORLD
       S.COMES    >SMOOTH    >FREE      >EMPTY
       WORLD>                           >IDLE

       T.LOADS    T.LOADS               T.LOADS
       S.LOADS    S.LOADS               S.LOADS
       EMPTY>     IDLE>                 EMPTY>
       IDLE>      IDLE>                 IDLE>
       QUEUE>     QUEUE>                QUEUE>

                  T.CUT      T.CUT
                  S.CUT      S.CUT
                  FREE>      FREE>
                  ROUGH>     ROUGH>

                  T.UNLOAD   T.UNLOAD   T.UNLOAD
                  S.UNLOAD   S.UNLOAD   S.UNLOAD
                  IDLE>      IDLE>      IDLE>
                  SMOOTH>    SMOOTH>

       RETURN TO MAIN
```

Figure 2.3 Event-based program: robot cell example.

Simulation Language Features   39

scheduled for the same time then consideration must be given to some preferred sequence of operation so as to reflect the priorities of the system being simulated.

Each block of event code is internally consistent. Our knowledge of the system would permit some simplification. For example, the model has only a single milling head and thus the EVENT CUT has some redundancy. The test which determines whether or not CUT may re-start includes both FREE or ROUGH, but as there is only a single MILL which is released by the EVENT CUT then we know it is available. However, were the event one which released a block of resources into the system then it would be sensible to cycle around the test head. This attitude is really one of defensive programming, and is taken another step further in the three-phase method.

(2) The three-phase approach

The three-phase structure is a less constrained version of the event-based program. The event-based program requires explicit identification of the subset of activities which use resources released by the event. In an initially complex model, or a model which has been modified over a period of time, it is difficult to keep track of this information. A job-shop simulation with variable routes for the parts, and with program maintenance over several years, and thus the modification of code, is a practical example. The three-phase structure tests all activities whose start is conditional on the state of a preceding queue, such activities being known as Cs. Those which can be directly scheduled are known as Bs and are treated as event notices. This is more costly in terms of the execution overheads, but less so for the programmer.

In the robot cell example there are five events. These are whenever a new casting arrives, a table is loaded, a cutting operation if finished, a table is unloaded or all work on a casting is complete (table is clear). Three of them are conditional activities, or Cs, to represent starting to load a table, starting to cut and starting to unload a table. The Bs are shorter than the corresponding events in the event-based model because the model conditions sort out the conditional activity. The flow of control in the robot cell example would thus be as shown in Figure 2.4. The three-phase time structure is robust because the conditional tests are independent of the

The Implementation of Simulation Languages

```
                        SET INITIAL CONDITIONS
                               F.EVENT

        E.COMES      E.LOADS     E.CUT       E.UNLOAD    E.CLEAR
        >ROUGH       >ROUGH      >SMOOTH     S.CLEAR     >WORLD
        S.COMES      >SMOOTH     >FREE       >EMPTY
        WORLD>                               >IDLE

                                 T.LOADS
                                 S.LOADS
                                 EMPTY>
                                 IDLE>
                                 QUEUE>

                                 T.CUT
                                 S.CUT
                                 FREE>
                                 ROUGH>

                                 T.UNLOAD
                                 S.UNLOAD
                                 IDLE>
                                 SMOOTH>

                        RETURN TO FIND NEXT EVENT
```

Figure 2.4 Three-phase programs: robot cell example.

resource flow within the model. On the other hand it has redundancy. In the 'robot cell' model, for example, the event 'New casting arrives' can never give rise to the start of activity Cut. The more extended the entity flow, and the fewer the feedback mechanisms, the greater the degree of redundancy. In practice this is a small price to pay for the convenience of ignoring the model structure when determining the position of the tests. If the overhead is significant, tests can be written in more efficient ways, or the programmer can adopt a mixed strategy.

(3) The process approach

The event and three-phase approaches each reflect a particular world-view by which the program sits, like a central controller, over the activity of the model. There is an alternative, which is conceptually akin to a decentralised state. This requires a changed concept of control, and physically can be likened to giving each entity a route card on which, at any one time, is indicated the current position. Each event is now replaced as the focal point by

Simulation Language Features 41

```
PROCESS CASTING
IF A TABLE  IS NOT IN EMPTY OR THE ROBOT IS NOT IDLE PASSIVATE
REMOVE 'ROBOT' FROM IDLE
REMOVE 'TABLE' FROM EMPTY
REMOVE 'CASTING' FROM QUEUE
HOLD FOR DURATION OF LOAD
PLACE 'CASTING' IN ROUGH
PLACE 'ROBOT' IN IDLE - ACTIVATE 'ROBOT'
PLACE 'TABLE' IN EMPTY - ACTIVATE 'TABLE'
IF THE MILL IS NOT FREE PASSIVATE
REMOVE 'MILL' FROM FREE
REMOVE 'CASTING' FROM ROUGH
HOLD FOR SAMPLED DURATION OF CUT
PLACE 'CASTING' IN SMOOTH
PLACE 'MILL' IN FREE - ACTIVATE 'MILL'
IF A ROBOT IS NOT IDLE PASSIVATE
REMOVE 'ROBOT' FROM IDLE
HOLD FOR DURATION OF UNLOAD
PLACE 'ROBOT' IN IDLE - ACTIVATE 'ROBOT'
HOLD FOR THE DURATION REQUIRED TO CLEAR
DESTROY 'CASTING'

PROCESS ROBOT
IF A CASTING IS IN QUEUE AND A TABLE IS IN EMPTY
   THEN ACTIVATE FIRST 'CASTING' IN QUEUE AND PASSIVATE ROBOT
IF A CASTING IS IN SMOOTH
   THEN ACTIVATE FIRST 'CASTING' IN SMOOTH AND PASSIVATE ROBOT
PASSIVATE

PROCESS CUT
IF A CASTING IS IN ROUGH
     THEN ACTIVATE FIRST 'CASTING'IN ROUGH
PASSIVATE 'MILL'

PROCESS TABLES
IF A ROBOT IS IN IDLE OR A CASTING IS IN QUEUE
     THEN ACTIVATE FIRST 'CASTING' IN QUEUE
PASSIVATE

PROCESS INPUT
HOLD FOR A DURATION
CREATE A NEW 'CASTING'
PLACE 'CASTING' IN QUEUE AND ACTIVATE 'CASTING
REPEAT

CREATE 'ROBOT 'AND PLACE IN IDLE
CREATE 'MILL' AND PLACE IN FREE
CREATE 2 'TABLES' AND PLACE IN EMPTY
CREATE 'INPUT' AND ACTIVATE 'INPUT
```

Figure 2.5 Process interaction program: robot cell example.

the 'process' of events undertaken by any one entity. The process structure of SIMULA was the original implementation.

The function of the programmer is now to prepare for each entity a route template—PROCESS, showing the actions that must occur at each point along the life of the entity. Each process will interact with some others. To code interactions is not easy, and is simplified by limiting the authority over a particular activity to one process. When two or more processes are involved we have the facility of 'passivating' one or more

42 The Implementation of Simulation Languages

of them. In this way control of an activity can be given to a single process who, as it were, holds the passports of his colleagues until a particular sector of the route is complete. Then the processes are released, activated and resume control of their own destinies. In this new scheme the computer has the task of issuing each process, at its inception, with a route card copied from the master process template. Subsequently the computer maintains a pointer to the current position for each card. Particular representations of a process are shown in quotes; thus 'CASTING' is a specific example of the process CASTING. Written in an English-like form, the program for the process structure has the appearance of the listing in Figure 2.5.

Following the example through, the system creates an INPUT process whose task is to create the arrival of castings. The first casting is created and activated. It finds that a ROBOT and a TABLE are available and so it takes these and starts to LOAD. When LOADING is complete the casting moves into the ROUGH queue. It releases the ROBOT as an ACTIVE process. The ROBOT therefore checks to see if there are any other castings waiting in the QUEUE. This can happen if a second casting has been generated while the first casting is being loaded. This casting would have found an empty table but no robot. It would therefore become passive. The ROBOT activates the second casting and passivates. The first casting has meanwhile found that the mill is available and will hold for the cutting duration. An

```
CASTING NUMBER ONE

PROCESS CASTING
IF A TABLE  IS NOT IN EMPTY OR THE ROBOT IS NOT IDLE PASSIVATE
REMOVE 'ROBOT' FROM IDLE
REMOVE 'TABLE' FROM EMPTY
REMOVE 'CASTING' FROM QUEUE
HOLD FOR DURATION OF LOAD
PLACE 'CASTING' IN ROUGH
PLACE 'ROBOT' IN IDLE - ACTIVATE 'ROBOT'
PLACE 'TABLE' IN EMPTY - ACTIVATE 'TABLE'
IF THE MILL IS NOT FREE PASSIVATE
REMOVE 'MILL' FROM FREE
REMOVE 'CASTING' FROM ROUGH
HOLD FOR SAMPLED DURATION OF CUT   <---- Present status of casting 1
. . . . . . . .

CASTING NUMBER TWO

PROCESS CASTING
IF A TABLE  IS NOT IN EMPTY OR THE ROBOT IS NOT IDLE PASSIVATE
REMOVE 'ROBOT' FROM IDLE
REMOVE 'TABLE' FROM EMPTY
REMOVE 'CASTING' FROM QUEUE
HOLD FOR DURATION OF LOAD <--- Present status of casting 2
. . . . . . . . . .
```

Figure 2.6 Two copies of the casting process.

```
          PROCESS CUT
          IF THE SIZE OF FREE > 0 AND THE SIZE OF EMPTY > 0
               THEN
                    'CASTING' IS THE FIRST CASTING IN ROUGH
                    REMOVE 'CASTING' FROM ROUGH
                    'HEAD' IS THE FIRST HEAD IN FREE
                    REMOVE 'HEAD' FROM FREE
                    HOLD FOR DURATION OF CUT
                    'CASTING' INTO SMOOTH
                    'HEAD' INTO FREE
               END    ACTIVATE MAIN
          END
```

Figure 2.7 Activity-oriented process view.

instantaneous picture of the system would show two copies of the CASTING process as in Figure 2.6.

The proper control over the two processes is complex. It would be easy to overlook the fact that a ROBOT when freed may be able to restart a LOADING or UNLOADING activity. There is also a degree of arbitrariness in the way in which a programmer allocates control over a particular activity to a particular process. The choice of the casting, as a process, reflects the philosophy that it is 'most natural' for a programmer to specify the simulation by following entities in the system. It supposes that the 'most natural' presentation of the model will be the easiest to code and debug. It is also possible to adopt another different style of definition for the process, one in which the focus is on the activity itself.

When each activity has been defined as a process, the model is run by a routine which cycles through all activities and activates each in turn. In this model the test to start the activity CUT is part of the PROCESS CUT, as in Figure 2.7. This formulation will spread the conditional tests among elements of the code. It would be possible to re-write the segment so that the conditional elements were all grouped together in the MAIN program which only branched to activate the process if this was feasible. If the function of the model is to investigate various control strategies then grouping the start conditions would be valuable. These various formulations are discussed by Hills (1973).

(4) Time structure—general discussion

The preceding discussion shows that there are several styles for treating the passage of time, but apparently no intrinsic difference between their information requirements. The CUT activity, as an example, is associated with the same data in all versions of the time control structure. The information is:

the time of the end of the activity;
the resources used (casting, mill and table);
an event identifier, which is a pointer to the appropriate code to be executed subsequent to the event.

In this chapter we call this the 'Active data set'. The distinction between languages is often made on the basis of how the software author perceives this set of data.

If the event identifier is explicit, then the code structure is that of the event, three-phase or activity scan. If the event identifier is implicit, then the code appears to have the features of the process approach. That is without outside specification a system-controlled re-activation pointer returns the program control to the correct code segment, that immediately subsequent to the 'HOLD FOR DURATION' whose completion represents the next event.

A similar difference arises as an outcome of the information used to identify the set of activity-related data. This set can be identified by the EVENT or by any one of the ENTITIES. If the event identifier is used to identify the end of the activity, the program is said to be machine-based. If one of the resources is used to identify the end of the activity, the program is material-based. If there is the possibility of many simultaneous representations of one event, there must be as many event identifiers as there are possible simulataneous representations. This number is determined by the maximum number of the smallest of the class of shared resources. It is clearly feasible to use one of these resources as the key of the activity data set. Early simulation languages made much of the difference between machine- and material-based programming. It is, however, a very practical difference and not one of a philosophical nature. A model of a canning line, which has thousands of cans per minute through one machine, would clearly benefit by having the event 'fill can' associated with the machine rather than the can; there would be fewer overheads. Indeed if there was no requirement to track individual filling, it would be preferable to redefine the events as STOP and START the filling machine, and calculate the throughput whenever required. In this context the resource 'cans' is replaced by the concept of 'can availability' and the count of cans processed becomes an attribute of the entity machine.

Thus although the time structure, and the associated 'active data set' is usually handled in a specific way by a particular language, the choice is arbitrary. There are many alternatives and the emphasis on one or another is, in some senses, a weakness. On the other hand a clear structure is helpful to the programmer as it gives a framework

Simulation Language Features 45

on which to build the model. Hooper (1986) has recently published a discussion which includes a summary of the comments which have been made about the various control structures. In brief these suggest that event scheduling is flexible and efficient but requires programming effort, activity scan is neat but inefficient and process interaction is closest to the 'real world' but demands the greatest degree of support from the simulation executive.

2.4.4 Provide statistical sampling

Most samples from probability distribution are generated by transforming a uniform (0–1) distribution (Pidd, 1988; Law, 1983). The psuedo-random number generator is therefore the kernel of the sampling system. The majority of simulation languages have properly tested generators. A number of machines, however, have system generators which are not tailored to simulation and statistical experiments. For example, some initialise random number seeds from internal clocks, thus preventing variance reduction by way of common random numbers.

2.4.5 Collect data

Data collection during a simulation run can be expensive on computer resources. Collecting time-series can lead to high storage overheads, as do languages which offer indiscriminate data collection facilities on all resources. However, in the context of interactive simulation it can be a great convenience to be able to collect data on any activity or queue. Thus the language provisions reflect a compromise.

2.4.6 Data analysis and reporting facilities

The analysis of simulation results is a special source of concern, whether the concern is with the full range of users or with those who require special statistical techniques. Some facilities can be provided by an overall support environment (see Section 2.2), but others are provided at the language level. The latter includes histograms, plotting routines, distribution fitting, confidence interval analysis and variance reduction techniques.

2.4.7 Monitoring the model and debugging the program

Whatever the desired final output, it is important to be able to trace the model operation during the verification and validation period. The emphasis on error-checking at execution time should become less important as the model-building exercise becomes more structured. It is unlikely that it will become redundant, as even computer-assisted programming may well leave areas for manual modification and thus possible errors.

2.5 Simulation Language Implementations

The major differentiation between languages is on the basis of their preferred time structure (event, three-phase or process), even if the language has sufficient flexibility to permit its use in other modes. This section reviews the popular implementations of each style.

2.5.1 Event-based

SIMSCRIPT II.5

SIMSCRIPT was developed in 1964 by Markowitz at RAND as a translator which produced FORTRAN statements from the SIMSCRIPT source. Subsequently a compiler for native SIMSCRIPT was produced and this, after a number of intermediate owners, was sold to CACI who market it as SIMSCRIPT II.5, now the standard implementation.
   The language is represented as having a number of levels which enable it to form an easy introduction to computer programming.

Levels 1 to 3 cover feature which would be found in the majority of high-levels languages, with considerable emphasis on the removal of FORTRAN-type restrictions.
Levels 4 and 5 introduce the modelling concepts required by simulation. For example, classes of permanent or temporary entities with attributes, say AGE and HEIGHT as attributes of MAN. The set handling features provide for automatic management of all common set disciplines or combination. For example,

Simulation Language Implementations   47

DEFINE QUEUE AS A SET RANKED BY HIGH PRIORITY, THEN BY LOW DUE.DATE.

Level 5 contains the representation of simulation time and includes very attractive features for data collection. Once the user has defined the variables to be monitored, the system will collect all the required statistics without the explicit addition of extra code by the user.

SIMSCRIPT has a single commercial developer and the language development reflects market forces. Two additions exemplify this. Firstly, PROCESSES permit sequences of events to be specified — thus approaching more nearly to the transaction flow of process-based software. Secondly, SIMANIMATION lets the user add graphics animation commands to the SIMSCRIPT II.5 text.

CACI are based in the USA, as are most users of SIMSCRIPT. In 1980 there were 400 installations, 250 university users and seven machine-compatible versions. Since then an IBM PC version has been introduced and also UNIX SIMSCRIPT for use on Gould computers. SIMSCRIPT II.5 has a large number of users within the military, but other users are well supported by documentation and other information. CACI produce a newsletter called *simsnips*, which is a useful abstracting service for papers on simulation in addition to listing books and conferences on the topic.

GASP

GASP is a library of FORTRAN subroutines which provide simulation facilities. GASP II was the first well-documented release (Pritsker and Kiviat, 1969), followed by GASP IV, which provides mixed discrete/continuous simulation. It is popular in US universities because of its cheapness and its FORTRAN base. A further process orientation is GASP VI (Rimvall and Cellier, 1982).

2.5.2 Three-phase

ECSL

The Extended Control and Simulation Language is derived from CSL which, like SIMSCRIPT, first emerged in 1960–61 as a translator to FORTRAN. After various developments, CSL became ECSL, written

```
Zero all data
For each Data Block do Load Data Block
Zero Clock
Obey Initialisation
While Clock < final value do
    Begin
        If RE-CYCLE switch is off then select next Clock value
        Turn off RE-CYCLE switch
        For each integer from oldvalue+1 to new value do
            Obey Dynamics Block
        If ADD switch is on then obey recording blocks
        Update Queues
        Obey each activity in turn
    End
Obey Finalisation block
End.
```

Figure 2.8 The dynamic operation of ECSL.

by Alan Clementson (Clementson, 1985) of Birmingham University. ECSL is written in FORTRAN and is thus available on any machine with a FORTRAN compiler. However, the user is not required to know FORTRAN, nor is the code translated into FORTRAN.

The language has several features which are significant extensions over the original. The authors claim that it successfully implements the 'cell structure' developed at Lancaster University (De Carvahlo and Crookes, 1976) and also incorporates visual interactive modelling. The recent implementations of ECSL have been on MSDOS™-based systems. Further developments envisage an ECSL provided interface for current packages such as FRAMEWORK, SYMPHONY and MINITAB.

An ECSL program is organised into the following five sections:

definition statements
initialisation routine
activities section
finalisation section
data section

The dynamic operation of a program is as shown in Figure 2.8. This shows the way in which the program can cater for experiments by varying the Data Block, and gives an insight into how a continuous process can be built into a next-event structure. If a DYNAMICS section is included, the code will be obeyed for each integer within the step to the next event. The activity is yet another variation of that displayed earlier. In a three-phase simulation the B-phase precedes the C-phase but in real time the C-phase (the start of the activity)

Simulation Language Implementations   49

```
                    T.LOADS
                    S.LOADS
                    EMPTY>
                     IDLE>
                    QUEUE>
               HOLD FOR DURATION
                    >ROUGH
                    >SMOOTH


                    T.CUT
                    S.CUT
                    FREE>
                    ROUGH>
               HOLD FOR DURATION
                    >SMOOTH
                    >FREE
```

Figure 2.9 An ECSL view of part of the robot cell example.

occurs first. An ECSL program takes this natural progression and, for example, part of the Load Table activity would appear as in Figure 2.9 for T.LOADS and T.CUTS. Thus there is no explicit B activity to end the Load Table operation because the A-phase and B-phase are implicit in ECSL. Readers should note the similarity between this implementation and the Process structure.

SIMON

SIMON is a library of simulation routines originally implemented in ALGOL, but developed in FORTRAN since 1966. The basic routines are in their sixth revision. They provide facilities for queue handling and for activity scheduling and event identification. The 'preferred' structure is three-phase but, as indicated earlier, it is simple to use a pure event scheme. The routines include analysis tools for variance reduction and interval estimation.

A number of specialist packages have been based on the routines including early versions of Istel's SEE-WHY. The most recent library— SIMONG—has been extended to incorporate graphics drivers for model animation (Mathewson, 1985). The SIMON and ECSL routines are supported by program generators, DRAFT and CAPS repectively.

2.5.3 Process

SIMULA

The original language to implement the process approach was

SIMULA, designed in the early 1960s. The standard text is SIMULA Begin (Birtwhistle *et al.*, 1979) and the language has an active user group, the ASU (Association of SIMULA Users). SIMULA owes its origins to ALGOL but contains a considerably enhanced structure in the CLASS facility. Whenever a CLASS definition is invoked a copy of the CLASS program, together with space for all the variables required and any other associated routines, is created in core. Control can be transferred to the copy of the program immediately or at any subsequent time. Each clone of the CLASS definition may be uniquely referenced and may have its own set of attributes. A class declaration may be prefixed by another class, which shares common properties.

Thus within the machining cell, a class could be identified to collect reliability data. It takes the form outlined below, although this is necessarily a great simplification.

    CLASS MACHINE; begin
           real breakdown frequency;
           end;

If this class is then used as a prefix to a second class, that second class inherits all the features of the prefix class. Thus

MACHINE CLASS ROBOT; MACHINE CLASS MILL;

would inherit all the general features of a machine. This facility can be used to model the common physical phenomena associated with the machines, but it could also be used as a technique of model management. A class could be defined to collect and process data associated with the model execution, for example queue sizes of waiting times.

The SIMULA language itself operates by defining system CLASSES which provide event scheduling (PROCESS CLASS) and queue manipulation (HEAD, LINK). The difficulty experienced by new programmers in coding the interaction between processes led to the development of new classes.

SIMON 75, by Hills and Birtwhistle, included a model structure more closely allied to the entity–cycle diagram. It also provided predefined resource types for abstracting away minor components, automatic data collection and report generation, automatic scheduling by way of a generalised WAITUNTIL statement and full or selective event tracing.

Simulation Language Implementations

These ideas were further developed (Birtwhistle, 1979) in DEMOS (Discrete Event Modelling on Simula). This is a new class which has extensive features for the synchronisation of activities. The structure is very different from the standard SIMULA. In general terms it reflects another use of 'active data sets'. The system is structured so that the 'active data' set includes the queues where the required resources are found. Any change in the queue status can flag a test mechanism which attempts to activate the process. An activity is associated with an active ENTITY CLASS and a number of passive ENTITY CLASSES, these are described as a master/slave combination. The new features for synchronization include COOPT and WAITUNTIL.

```
ENTITY CLASS CASTING                ENTITY CLASS MILL

                                    MILL ENTERS FREE
COOPT 'MILL' FROM FREE              (Control passes to CASTING)
HOLD FOR THE DURATION OF THE CUT
RELEASE 'MILL'
```

Figure 2.10 The use of COOPT in DEMOS.

COOPT implements the active–passive roles by taking, when available, a process from a queue. Thus the example can be written as in Figure 2.11. A COOPT call delays the caller until the required resource is available. This removes the necessity for activating the CASTING and MILL to ensure that the milling activity can begin when a CASTING arrives or a MILL becomes free.

```
ENTITY CLASS CASTING                ENTITY CLASS MILL

                                    MILL ENTERS FREE
WAITUNTIL (FREE > 0)                (Control passes to CASTING)
ACQUIRE 'MILL'
HOLD FOR THE DURATION OF THE CUT
```

Figure 2.11 The use of WAITUNTIL in DEMOS.

The WAITUNTIL command is similar, but simpler. It holds the flow of control in the ENTITY until the specified conditions are met.

Two further features of DEMOS are RES and BIN. RES permits activities which require a portion of RES, should sufficient RES be available. BIN applies when producers make quantities which are to be used by consumers but a consumer is blocked if a quantity is not available on request. A later relinquishing of the resources not only updates the amount free, but also tests the queue of blocked entities.

In 1985, SIMULA compilers were available for a wide range of machines including IBM, DEC-10, UNIVAC 1100 Series, Data General Eclipse, ICL2900, PERQ, VAX (VMS and UNIX), Honeywell Bull DPS8, Cyber, Simens 7.5, Sperry and Prime computers.

Pascal

As SIMULA was derived from ALGOL, so there are many extensions to Pascal. The current literature includes MICRO PASSIM (Barnett, 1986), Pascal-Sim (O'Keefe, 1986), SIMCAL from Malloy, SIMPAS (Bryant, 1980), SIMTOOLS (Seila, 1986) and SOLE developed at the Technische Hogeschool, Twente by Rooda. Clearly Pascal forms a powerful framework for the creation of simulation derivatives. The topic is taken further in Chapter 7.

SIMSCRIPT II.5

As noted earlier, later versions of SIMSCRIPT (CACI, 1983) have a PROCESS feature. The PROCESS is viewed as an ACTIVITY which may have more than two de-limiting events. It has the capacity of suspending execution and of being re-activated by another PROCESS or EVENT.

2.6 Object-oriented Simulation Languages

2.6.1 Object orientation

The previous section reviewed procedural languages; recent software developments have shifted this emphasis and simulation interests have followed. Object-oriented languages focus on individual objects which relate to each other via message passing, and which have the ability to inherit the features of other objects— much like the processes and prefixes of SIMULA. The benefits of object-oriented programming lie in the ability to generate re-usable code. Although in the context of simulation, and SIMULA in particular, this is not a new idea the importance of the approach to the general programming community will ensure growth in this area.

Early object-oriented software required significant hardware support, and this slowed down the acceptance of the technique. However, new implementations and more powerful micros will accelerate the growth of this technique by increasing the availability of the tools.

Object-oriented Simulation Languages 53

Additionally it is possible to interface PROLOG with Smalltalk, and researchers have designed a tool which contains a hierarchical system description, graphical system entry, performance prediction algorithms and knowledge-based diagnostic capabilities. This gives substantial reductions in development costs (Pazirandeh and Becker, 1987).

Associated with objects are inheritance, methods, messages and data. Ulgen and Thomasma (1987) give examples of a Smalltalk-80 simulation environment for a manufacturing cell environment — here the system was chosen because '[Smalltalk] . . . enables the user to develop much of the model in a programming-free environment. The input to the simulation is based on the graphics layout of the model and the user's settings of a number of parameters.' Smalltalk is an interpretive language and naturally execution is slow. However, the concept of re-usable code implies that once code has been written to describe an object — say a machine — the object can be filed within a library for later use.

It is natural that DEMOS should have been a popular model for the provision of simulation facilities within some object-oriented languages. Particular examples are SIMTALK — a version of Smalltalk written by Bezivin (1987) — and POSE (Stairmand et al., 1988) — a SCHEME-based queuing network. The ROSS system, used by the RAND corporation, is also based on the object-oriented paradigm. Developments of ROSS are reviewed by Cammarata et al. (1987) in an exceptionally interesting paper on the particular problems of designing a graphical interface for an object-oriented simulation language.

2.6.2 Parallel processing

Recent developments in transputer technology have provided the capability for concurrent processing on the micro. Boards with more than seven transputers are available for the IBM PC. Object-oriented programming becomes significant because the most important problem of distributed simulation is how to partition the physical system among a fixed set of processors, and the object represents an appropriate unit of the physical system. A general policy which assigns logical processes to physical processors such that the message traffic is as low as possible seems sensible, but it still leaves unanswered the question of how the simulation is operated. As each processor simulates its own part of the logical system, each processor will have its own virtual local time (VLT). These may differ, and the system management problem is how to cope with the logic of, say, a machine shop, where the lathe is working at 2.00 pm while the grinder has finished work because it thinks it is 6.15 pm!

There are two systems which have been suggested in the literature. One is TimeLock (Bezivin, 1987) and the other is TimeWarp (Jefferson and Sowizral, 1985). TimeLock can be envisaged as a system which circulates messages giving global time, and forbids any process to proceed beyond this moment. A process may not anticipate. TimeWarp, in contrast, permits each process to run ahead as though it were not constrained by the time of its neighbours. If a system then receives a message which should have been processed earlier it stops and backtracks, sending anti-messages to undo the activity at other processes which have been 'misled' by its previous actions.

A problem in such a distributed processing system is one of 'coherence' whenever the system is graphically displayed. At this instant we would wish all processes to be at the same time. However, parallel processing hardware runs far too fast for animation, and consequently this problem is only one of 'snapshots' rather than continuous animation. Coherence is, however, advocated as a benefit of Timelock, although one cannot imagine how the interactive user could keep pace with a network of transputers!

Transputer power does lend itself to a new range of research topics. Among likely topics are: the use of the transputer's speed to examine alternative model management rules; investigation into the proper use of parallel processes — should the model be split into modules loaded on individual processors or should the model functions (simulation, animation, statistical processing optimising strategies) be split over processing centres?

2.7 Conclusions

This chapter has followed the development of simulation languages and closed with the application of new software philosophies to simulation environments. Object-oriented programming is a recognised tool within specialist software development environments. Within the simulation community the concept of a specialist environment is not new, and next chapter is a natural exploration of these ideas.

2.8 References

Balci, O. (1986) Credibility assessment of simulation results, *Proc. 1986 Winter Simulation Conference*, pp. 38–43.

Barnett, C. C. (1986) Simulation in Pascal with Micro-PASSIM. *Proc. 1986 Winter Simulation Conference*, pp. 151–155, Washington, DC, 8–10 December. IEEE, Piscataway, New Jersey.

Bezivin, J. (1987) TIMELOCK: A concurrent simulation technique and its description in Smalltalk-80. *Proc. 1987 Winter Simulation Conference*, A. Thesen *et al.*, pp. 503–6.

Birtwhistle, G. M. (1979) *DEMOS*—discrete event modelling on SIMULA. Macmillan, London.

Birtwhistle, G. M., Dahl, O.-J., Myhrhaug, B. and Nygaard, K. (1979) *SIMULA Begin*, 2nd edn. Van Nostrand Reinhold, New York.

Bryant R. W. (1981) *SIMPAS User Manual*. Technical Report, Computer Science Department, and Madison Avenue Computing Center, University of Wisconsin-Madison, Madison, Wisconsin.

CACI (1983) *SIMSCRIPT II.5 User Manual*.

Cammarata, S., Gates, B. and Rothenberg, J. (1987) Dependencies and graphical interfaces in object-oriented simulation languages. *Proc. 1987 Winter Simulation Conference*, pp. 507–17.

Chaharbagi, K. and Davies, B. L. (1986) Manufacturing systems simulation using DSSL. *Computer-Aided Design*, **18**, 6.

Clementson, A. T. (1985) *ECSL—Extended Control and Simulation Users Manual*. CLE.COM Ltd. Birmingham, England.

Comfort, J. C. (1984) The simulation of a master–slave event set processor, *Simulation*, **42** (3) 117–24.

De Carvahlo, R. S. and Crookes, J. G. (1976) Cellular simulation. *Journal of the Operational Research Society*, **29** (1), 31–40.

DuBois, D. F. (1980) *Distributed System Simulator (DSS) for Computer Networks*. General Electric Technical Information Series No. 80C1S004. Sunnyvale, CA 94086.

Heidorn, G. E. (1975) Simulation programming through natural language dialogue. *Studies in the Management Sciences*, Vol. 1: *Logistics* (ed. M. A. Geisler) North-Holland, Amsterdam.

Hills, P. R. (1973) *An Introduction to Simulation using SIMULA*. NCC Publication S-55. Norwegian Computer Centre, Oslo.

Hooper, J. W. (1986), Strategy-related characteristics of discrete event languages and models. *Simulation*, **46**(4), 153–9.

Jefferson, D. R. and Sowizral, H. (1985) Fast concurrent simulation using the time warp mechanism. *Proc. Conference on Distributed Simulation*, San Diego pp. 63–9.

Kiviat, P. J. (1969), *Digital Computer Simulation: Computer Programming Languages*. RM-5883-PR, The RAND Corporation, Santa Monica.

Kiviat, P. J., Villanueva, R. and Markowitz, H. M. (1968) *The*

SIMSCRIPT II Programming Language. Prentice-Hall, Englewood Cliffs, New Jersey.

Law, A. M. (1983) Statistical analysis of simulation output data. *Operations Research*, **31**(6), 983–1029.

Mathewson, S. C. (1985) Simulation program generators: code and animation on a PC. *Journal of the Operational Research Society*, **36**(7), 583–9.

Mitrani, I. (1982) *Simulation Techniques for Discrete Event Simulation*. Cambridge University Press, Cambridge.

Nance, R. E., Balci, O. and Moose, Jnr R. L. (1984) *Evaluation of the Unix Host for a Model Development Environment*. Technical Report No. CS84009-R, Systems Research Centre and Department of Computer Science, Virginia Polytechnic and State University.

O'Keefe, R. M. (1986) Simulation with Pascal-Sim. *Winter Simulation Conference, 1986*.

Paul, R. J. and Doukidis, G. I. (1986), Further developments in the use of artificial intelligence techniques which formulate simulation problems. *Journal of the Operational Research Society*, **37**(8), 787–810.

Pazirandeh, M. and Becker, L. (1987) Object oriented performance models with knowledge based diagnostics. *Proc. 1987 Winter Simulation Conference*, pp. 518–24.

Pidd, M. (1988) *Computer Simulation in Management Science*. John Wiley & Sons, Chichester.

Poole, T. G. and Szymankiewicz, J. (1977) *Using Simulation to Solve Problems*. McGraw-Hill, London.

Pritsker, A. A. B. and Kiviat, P. (1969) *Simulation with GASP II: a FORTRAN-based Simulation Language*. Prentice-Hall, Englewood Cliffs, New Jersey.

Pritsker, A. A. B. (1979) *Introduction to Simulation and SLAM*. John Wiley & Sons, New York.

Rimvall, M. and Cellier, F. E. (1982) The GASP-VI simulation package for process-oriented combined continuous discrete system simulation. *Proc. 10th IMACS Congress on Simulation and Scientific Computation*. Montreal, Canada, 8–13 August.

Seila, A. F. (1988) SIMTOOLS: A software tool kit for discrete computer simulation in Pascal. *Simulation*, **50**, 93–9.

SIMSOFT (1986) *PCMODEL Manual*. SIMSOFT San José, California, USA.

Stairmand, M. C. and Kreutzer, W. (1988) POSE: a Process-Oriented Simulation Environment embedded in SCHEME. *Simulation*, **50** (4), 143–53.

Ulgen, O. and Thomasma, T. (1987) Graphical simulation using Smalltalk-80. *Proc. SAE/ESO International Computer Graphics Conference* (eds N. Spewock *et al.*). Society of Automotive Engineers, Detroit, Michigan, pp. 317–26.

Computer Modelling for Discrete Simulation
Edited by M. Pidd
©1989 John Wiley & Sons Ltd

3
Simulation Support Environments

S. C. Mathewson

3.1 An Overview

The simulation languages and approaches described in Chapter 2 have developed gradually since the early days of discrete simulation. More recently, software developers have written more complete systems which are more closely tied to particular areas of application. Additionally, they aim to provide support for many, if not all, the phases identified in Figure 2.1. This chapter highlights some of these simulation support environments and suggests likely future developments.

Before discussing specific application-oriented software it is worth reviewing the range of packages currently available. Table 3.1 lists the common packages. It reveals the complex interrelationship between products, and the great variation in the maturity of those which are on sale. Some software packages originated over twenty-four years ago: others have only months of use. The list also illustrates the relative level of recent activity, with a number of new products which equate in many ways to the 'spreadsheet' philosophy of simulation software. Just as LOTUS 1-2-3™ and VISICALC™ revolutionised the use of computers in financial analysis, so these new products hope to carry simulation modelling to a far wider audience.

This chapter will discuss these tools, following the sequence of their introduction. The chapter starts with the earliest concept — graphic building blocks.

Table 3.1 Simulation languages and packages: a partial 1988 portfolio

Language	Date (approx.)	Derivations and associated products
AUTOMOD	1985	AUTOGRAM,
GASP	1969	MAST, GCMS
GPSS	1961	AUTOMOND, GPSS/H(TESS), GPSS/PC
ECSL	1965	CAPS
MAST		
MODELMASTER	1986	
PCModel	1986	PCModel/GAF
SAME	1987	
SEE-WHY	1978	WITNESS
SIMAN	1982	CINEMA
SIMON	1966	HOCUS, SEE-WHY, DRAFT
SIMPLE-1	1985	
SIMSCRIPT	1963	SIMFACTORY, SIMANIMATION
SIMULA	1970	DEMOS
SLAM II	1981	TESS, MHEX
XCELL	1986	

3.2 Generalised Graphical Building Blocks with Transaction Flow

Rather than requiring the programmer to write a full computer program, various systems have evolved in which the 'program' is a stylised description of a flow diagram. The diagram represents the flow of transactions through some, possibly simple, network. The earliest attempt at graphical specification was GPSS, in which a simple block diagram specifies the system. Subsequently this was integrated with the underlying structure which produced SLAM and SIMAN, two other block-oriented languages.

3.2.1 Simple building block systems

GPSS

GPSS represents a system by blocks which are linked by TRANSACTIONS. Transactions are the active elements of the system,

Generalised Graphical Building Blocks   59

and whenever one enters a block, the commands associated with that block type are executed and alter the system status.

Block types are numerous; they can GENERATE and TERMINATE transactions, HOLD transactions for durations, SEIZE and RELEASE facilities and ENTER and LEAVE storage. Statistics are automatically created whenever transactions QUEUE or DEPART from waiting lines. Transactions can branch at TRANSFER blocks and be SPLIT and ASSEMBLE. Facilities are single units of capacity and the transaction obtains a facility by way of a SEIZE block which flags the capacity as 'in use'. The facility is then blocked to other transactions and only available on its RELEASE. STORAGE, used to represent the two TABLES in the cell, is a multiple resource. The graphics flow chart is translated into text for computer input, one line per block. If F() represents a general sampling routine, the ROBOT CELL appears as in Figure 3.1. The lines have been annotated on the right-hand side. With the flow of the castings, and the simple lives of the resources, the program reflects a PROCESS-like structure. The model includes a run-in period of 100 transactions, to take the simulation from an artificial state of 'empty and idle' to some more realistic state. The data collection's statistics are then reset and the simulation processes another 1000 castings.

```
*ROBOT CELL SIMULATION IN GPSS
      SIMULATE
*PROGRAM DEFINITION BY BLOCKS
      STORAGE     S$TABLE,2      Define two tables
      GENERATE    20,2           Generate a transaction U(18,22)
      QUEUE       QUEUE          Join the queue
      ENTER       TABLE          Take a table
      SEIZE       ROBOT          Obtain the robot
      DEPART      QUEUE          Leave the queue
      ADVANCE     F()            Duration of load
      RELEASE     ROBOT          Release the robot
      QUEUE       ROUGH          Join the rough queue
      SEIZE       MILL           Coopt the mill
      DEPART      ROUGH          Leave the rough queue
      ADVANCE     F()            Duration of cut
      RELEASE     MILL           Release the mill
      QUEUE       SMOOTH         Join the smooth queue
      SEIZE       ROBOT          Take a robot
      DEPART      SMOOTH         Leave the queue
      ADVANCE     F()            Duration of unload
      RELEASE     ROBOT          Release a robot
      CLEAR       TABLE          Free the table
      ADVANCE     F()            Duration of CLEAR
      TERMINATE   1              Increase count of castings
*CONTROL CARDS
      START       100,NP         Process 100 castings, no output
      RESET                      Reset statistics
      START       1000           Process 1000 castings
      END                        End simulation.
```

Figure 3.1 Robot cell example: GPSS program.

The explicit definition of a queue provides automatic generation of run-time statistics. A transaction can simultaneously be in a number of queues, so that the device can be used to collect several simultaneous measures of performance. It may join a notional queue 1 when it enters the system and leave queue 1 when it leaves the system. Thus the time spent in this notional queue 1 would give statistics for the overall delay, in addition to the duration of stays in actual physical queues.

The above listing is the closest to a real program of any shown in this chapter. It illustrates the virtue of GPSS. A complete program with the standard output data including average and maximum queue contents, average time spent by the castings and utilisation of the facilities or storage capacity has been written in under thirty lines. This is, of course, a very simple example. For instance, the resources used, for example the mill, have not had 'private lives' of their own in which they break down or are reset or used by totally different tasks.

An unfortunate feature of GPSS is that the number of the blocks is large, certainly greater than fifty. Sadly, this loses many of the advantages of having a simple diagrammatic representation due to the effort of remembering precisely what action in the model is undertaken by which block. The software has developed over the years. For example, each transaction has a priority level to indicate the order in which transactions are served. Early versions of GPSS offered eight levels of priority; modern implementations offer as many as 128. This indicates one aspect of the growth of the language over a very long period of development.

GPSS is an IBM-developed interpretative simulation programming language first discussed in 1961 (Gordon, 1961). GPSS II was available for the IBM 7090 in 1963 and was developed through a number of releases to GPSS V (IBM, 1970). Companies outside IBM also developed versions of the program. For example Norden wrote a CDC version for the US Navy. There are also versions which permit the user to add PL/1 or FORTRAN routines (GPSS/360 Version 2) for handling difficult decisions. This helps overcome the problems which occur when the language features are not powerful enough to represent situations which fall outside the very structured concepts. Use of the generality of a high-level language prevents small, peripheral parts of the model from growing to a disproportionate size as the programmer struggles to express the problem in a very unnatural way. The concepts of GPSS can also be transferred into other languages. The block

Generalised Graphical Building Blocks 61

ideas have been implemented in certain other languages including GPSS-FORTRAN, APL GPSS (IBM, 1977) and PL/1 GPSS (IBM, 1981).

Unlike other languages introduced in this chapter GPSS is supported by many companies. An MSDOS™ version, GPSS/PC, is available from Minuteman Software for use on personal computers. Version 2, the current release, introduces graphics and animation (Cox, 1987). The system can interact with a FORTRAN-coded segment (using RM FORTRAN), called via a HELP block, which enables the user to access or reset block parameters. GPSS/H from Wolverine Software is a compiler for IBM and Amdahl systems which operates about six times faster than the traditional interpreter implementation. A general comparison of languages applied to a variety of job-shop models indicated that GPSS/H compiled about fifty times faster than SIMSCRIPT and about ten times faster than SLAM. GPSS/H executed better than three times faster than either (Abed *et a.*, 1985). GPSS implementations for machines as diverse as Data General, DEC, NCR Tower (UNIX), PDP and VAX machines are available from Simulation Software in Ontario. Enhanced features in these versions include animation and dynamic histogram displays in GPSS/PC, integration in TESS for GPSS/H and Autosimulation's AUTOGRAM, which post-processes output to provide animation, and AUTOMOD, an automatic modeller for producing GPSS/H code from higher-level descriptions. Wolverine have recently announced a version of GPSS/H for MSDOS™. This is not a true compiler, but compiles for a virtual machine, written in C, which is run under MSDOS™. The processing speed, measured in microseconds per block, of a 6 MHz AT with a co-processor is approximately nine times slower than a VAX 11/785.

Good introductory texts on GPSS, such as O'Donovan (1979) and Schriber (1974), are widely available. The softward developer's market for the product is very competitive (Schriber, 1987) and consequently the preceding paragraph is very much a guide to development and progress.

3.2.2 Queuing networks

Several languages use network concepts as their building blocks, usually by defining specific symbols for nodes or arcs. These include a family (Q-Gert, SAINT, SLAM) from one source and SIMAN from another.

Q-GERT, SLAM and SAINT

Alan Pritsker, one of the authors of GASP, is responsible for this family of products which address the problem of modelling queue networks. The earliest of these is Q-GERT, the title being an acronym for Queues—Graphical Evaluation and Review Technique. The package is written in FORTRAN IV and provides a system much like GPSS but with a very different symbolism. Transactions flow within the network from node to node along arcs. Nodes represent queues and decision or data collection points. The arcs represent delays or activity durations. Arcs and nodes have various attributes which are set. For example the Q-node has:

node number
initial number of transactions in the queue
maximum number of transactions permitted in the queue
procedure for ranking transaction.

Branches have:

an activity number
probability of taking the activity
distribution type for delay on branch
parameter set number for branch
number of parallel servers on the branch.

There are only eight basic symbols, and the language is presented as a parameterised list of the nodes and branches, much as GPSS. When all features are considered, including blocking, assembly, statistics gathering, transaction matching and dynamic node redefinition, there are twenty-eight node types. To give power to the language the parameter fields are potentially very long. Some nodes have twenty possible parameters and others, with repetitions, may go up to fifty items.

Pritsker (1979) gives a full history of the languages and any examples of its use. Engi (1985) demonstrates an application of the languages to problems of nuclear reactor reliability. A derivative of Q-GERT, SAINT, was developed by the USAF at the Wright Patterson Airforce base (Wortman *et al.*, 1978) and applied to problems of human task analysis, for example in the management of ECM equipment by operators on aircraft. A micro-computer

Generalised Graphical Building Blocks 63

derivative has been published (Laughery, 1985) and is commercially available.

SLAM II

SLAM was designed and programmed by Dennis Pegden, who based it on GASP IV and Q-GERT, and was subsequently supported by Pritsker and Associates. It is a superset of Q-GERT with three structures: process, event and continuous. The process structure is closely analogous to Q-GERT, with some minor revisions to the appearance of the blocks but essentially the same functions. The event structure is analogous to GASP IV. The modeller defines EVENTS as FORTRAN subroutines, and a FORTRAN subroutine library provides simulation housekeeping routines. The continuous representation permits the user to supply difference or differential equations.

SLAM II is a language which has been continuously revised. MHEX appeared in 1986 as an extension to SLAM II with facilities for materials handling, especially for modelling AGVs. Typical commands are VFLEET and VSGMENT—which allow for the definition of the AGV fleet (number of vehicles, size and performance) and the guidepaths (number of control points, length of each segment and direction of travel). SLAM II is also the base language for the TESS simulation system, which will be discussed in more detail later.

SIMAN

SIMAN was also written by Dennis Pegden, and reflects his experience with the earlier software. In some senses it marks a transition between the idea of a simulation language as a tool for simple model representation and a simulation language as a problem-solving technique. SIMAN introduces concepts to be discussed in later sections—the system theoretic approach and the specialist tool. SIMAN employs block diagrams as the primary means of modelling discrete systems. The blocks, whose shapes indicate their functions, are assembled with arrows indicating the direction of entity flow. There are fewer basic blocks than the earlier languages, ten in all. The blocks are multi-functioned and have facilities for searching files, removing transactions and arithmetic calculations.

SIMAN offers the facility for an EVENT structure, in which entities are manipulated by events. This is supported by a subroutine library

```
BEGIN;
PROJECT,ROBOT CELL,S.C.MATHEWSON,9-5-1986
DISCRETE,100,2,3,0;
TALLIES:1,CASTING IN SYSTEM;
DSTAT:1,NQ(1),ENTRY QUEUE:2,NQ(3),SMOOTH QUEUE:   :3,NR(1),ROBOT
UTIL.:4,NR(3),MILL UTIL.;
RESOURCES:1,ROBOT,1:2,TABLES,2:3,MILL,1;
PARAMETERS: REPLICATE:
END;
```

Figure 3.2 Robot cell example: SIMAN experimental frame.

which approximates to GASP. FORTRAN event subroutines can be integrated with the block structure though the EVENT 'N' block, which calls the user written routine 'N'. Entities may be returned into the block diagram representation by a FORTRAN subroutine call which enables transfer in and out of queues or 'stations'.

'Stations' are a specialist SIMAN tool feature for representing materials handling facilities. Motivated by research which shows that 50–70% of activity within the production area is caused by movement, the language includes blocks which can represent the common transport devices. Thus it embeds special-purpose manufacturing constructs within the framework of a general language. Stations are defined such that movements, by AGVs which TRANSPORT or belts which CONVEY, can be made from station to station. The travel time between stations is calculated as a function of distance and device speed, both of which are set by the user.

Ziegler (see Section 2.10) has long argued that the model and the experiment are part of an integral process. Pegden has adopted this idea by separating the use of SIMAN into two elements, the model frame which mimics the function of earlier packages and the experimental frame which adds an integrated environment for experimentation. Taken together the two elements form the input to SIMAN. Imagine that the GPSS is the SIMAN model frame. The SIMAN experimental frame will take the form shown in Figure 3.2.

The PROJECT card gives a title to the SIMAN summary report. The DISCRETE card allocates the number of entities/transactions in the system (100 maximum), with three attributes defined for each entity. The model has three queues in the system (QUEUE, ROUGH, SMOOTH) and no stations (There are no material handling features specified.)

TALLIES defines the name of report identifiers which have been previously tagged by a TALLY block. In the GPSS example a notional queue was used to discover the time of the transaction in the system. In SIMAN the transit duration is calculated by noting, in an entity attribute, the entry time and comparing this with the departure time. This TALLY activity, the first defined, can be associated with a particular title on the SIMAN output sheet: 'CASTING IN SYSTEM'.

DSTAT switches on the generation of time-persistent statistics associated with the system. The first DSTAT is the ENTRY queue, which is the first queue defined in the system. SIMAN uses queue indices so the statement ensures an appropriate title for what the system knows as QUEUE 1. NQ(1) refers to the number of entries in the queue 1.

RESOURCES allocates the required number of robots, tables and mills.

PARAMETER lets the user change the parameter values. If the GPSS example had hold for DURATION F( ), then in SIMAN F( ) might be x(3,1) which specifies the program is to use parameter set 3 with random number stream 1. Parameter set 3 would be specified on the parameter card. REPLICATE has parameters which specify the number of simulation runs and the way in which data collection is to be managed.

The idea of the experimental frame could be further developed. It might be used to specify the sampling distributions rather than just providing parameters for distributions specified in the modelling frame. Similarly, another development might allow decision rules to be specified (e.g. queue disciplines) for comparison. Finding a way to avoid having to tag the transaction with the TALLY block to permit data collection would be another step forward. Whatever the present restrictions in the presentation of software, this separation of frames is a relative, and in practice real, improvement: 'the SIMAN experimental processor was most helpful in varying model parameters without recompilation' (Schroes *et al.*, 1985).

SIMAN has additional features for interactive model building. BLOCKS, a menu-driven package, allows graphic entry of the model. Blocks are drawn on the screen as selected and the syntax of the block parameters are simultaneously checked for validity. ELEMENTS is a menu-driven pre-processor to construct the experimental frame. The presentation can be animated via PLAYBACK, which is a post-processor to animate simulation results by changing heights and colours in bar graphs, reflecting, say, queue lengths and resource utilisations. A graphic animation CINEMA has also been recently released.

Further comparisons between GPSS/H, SIMAN, SIMSCRIPT II.5 (as a process language) and SLAM II can be found in Banks and Carson (1985). This presents the detailed coding of a simple two-machine problem.

3.3 Application-specific Systems

In an early comparison of simulation languages Krasnow and Merikallio (1964) wrote that 'The earliest generalised simulation packages were not, in any real sense, languages. They were, rather, generalisations of simulation models of specific problem areas having considerable economic or military importance. The insights gained in their development contributed substantially to several languages'. The wheel has now turned full circle, with languages being tailored to specific problem areas. By restricting the area of application to a known environment the software can have a limited set of assumptions and so benefit in ease and directness of application. Many of these systems are not languages but generic models which are 'data-driven'.

3.3.1 PCModel

PCModel (SIMSOFT, 1986), written in IBM's macro-assembler, runs on an IBM personal computer with a minimum of 256 Kbytes of storage. It uses the colour monitor display to provide a direct, character-based, graphics animation of the model. The working area is drawn, in schematic form, on a grid co-ordinate overlay of 32,767 column — row cells. A graphic editor is supplied to build the overlay. Transactions are represented by any one of the 256 IBM displayable characters (standard colour coding features can be set, sixteen foreground colours and eight background colours). The model is set up with statements describing the route of the modelled object and its delays. The logic of the conditional transaction movement is specified as a mnemonic. The system provides a help menu, identifying the key assignments which access model data, statistics, control functions and the editors. During execution the user may collect statistical data, save or restore the model state at a particular moment in time, and vary the animation speed.

The robot cell model was prepared in just twenty minutes by Simcon Ltd., and is shown as Figure 3.3. The required layout was painted onto the screen using the graphic editor. The screen acts as a window onto the modelling surface which can be scrolled past the user. The text editor was then used to define the logical flow instructions. Available commands include positional information, movement speed, conditional delays and time delays. This permits the transaction route to be wholly specified. A development in the

Application-specific Systems 67

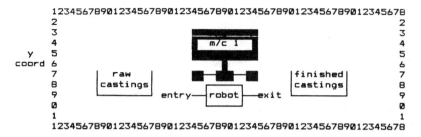

Using PCModel, the above model would be defined as follows:

Step 1

Create the graphic overlay as in above figure.

Step 2

Define the model routing :

```
        BR(1,XY(9,9),5)                      :P2   JB(1,XY(34,7),5)
        MR(6,5)                                    MA(XY(29,9),5)
:P1     ST(1) JB(1,XY(25,7),:P2)                   PO(XY(34,7))
        MA(XY(29,9),5)                             MA(XY(33,7),5)
        PO(XY(24,7))                         :P22  ST(1)
        MA(XY(25,7),5)                             JB(1,XY(29,7),:P22)
:P11    ST(1)                                      MA(XY(29,9),5)
        JB(1,XY(29,7),:P11)                        MA(XY(29,7),5)
        MA(XY(29,9),5)                             ST(100)
        MA(XY(29,7),5)                             MA(XY(29,9),5)
        ST(100)                                    MA(XY(33,7),5)
        MA(XY(29,9),5)                             MA(XY(29,9),5)
        MA(XY(25,7),5)                             CL(XY(34,7))
        MA(XY(29,9),5)                       :END  MA(XY(33,9),5)
        CL(XY(24,7))                               MR(5,5)
        JP(:END)                                   ER
```

The model is defined using 9 of the standard PCModel instructions:

BR-begin route; CL-clear location; ER-end route; JB-jump if blocked;
JP-jump; MA-move absolute; MR-move right; PO-post location; ST-set time.

The approach taken was to represent the robot as an XY screen location -
XY(29,9). All objects must pass through this point singularly as they
are exchanged too and from the pallets and the machining head.

Total building time = 20 mins   Simcon Limited

Figure 3.3 Robot cell example: PCModel instructions.

form of PCModel/GAF uses enhanced graphics hardware to provide better animation with bit-mapped icon images as and alternative to character graphics. This system also interfaces with AUTOCAD. In general, then, PCModel is a good example of the software which can be supported on a simple desktop machine. It overcomes the limitations of the user by providing simple tools for model building.

3.3.2 SIMFACTORY, MAST and SAME

There are a group of similar products whose interface with the model builder appears as a common concept. Essentially this describes the model as a series of blocks, whose parameters are specified via forms which are presented as pull-down menus. These blocks pull parts from one set of queues and push parts, sometimes renamed, out to another. Within the block are concepts of efficiency, maintenance, set-up times and all the other particular features of a production environment. The most widely known of these products is SIMFACTORY.

SIMFACTORY is a product of CACI aimed at the teaching of factory design and production analysis. It runs on IBM PC-ATs or mainframe computers. Factory layout and production parameters are entered through the SIMFACTORY user interface, one of two system components. Modelling concepts include those shown in Figure 3.4.

```
CONCEPTS                      COMPRISES
---------------------------------------------------------------
Processing stations           efficiency, setup, resource requirements
                              maintenance information
Queues                        permissible contents, capacity
Transporters                  speed, maintenance
Factory layout                flow information
Production schedule           schedule details, simulation time
Process plans                 raw material requirements, operational
                              distributions, rejects
Maintenance                   mean times to failure and repair
Reporting                     standard      reporting      options.
---------------------------------------------------------------
```

Figure 3.4 Some SIMFACTORY modelling concepts.

As a data-driven system each modelling run must contain a full data set. For the robot cell this contains files with:

cell layout
product description
production schedule
report specification.

These files of information are linked with libraries holding:

Application-specific Systems

the set of processing stations referenced by the cell,
the set of queues referenced by the cell,
the set of all process plans referenced by the production specification
the set of all maintenance actions referenced by the processes and transporters.

The data is organised into a hierarchy. System-level data is globally available but factory level data is specific to particular problems. Alternative scenarios may be proposed for every factory.

The user interface is provided as a menu-driven editor. There are twelve functional menus with on-line help. Through these menus the data set can be assembled. The display is similarly created by selecting elements and positioning them under cursor control. Execution is supervised by the SIMFACTORY model segment. An animated representation of the factory is provided and this may be used for debugging. Animation has a significant overhead and can be removed for production runs. Trace switches may be set and reset during execution. An interrupt facility is provided for this purpose — the snapshot menu. With this menu the user can interrogate elements within the simulation. Standard reports can be provided at intervals or on completion of the run. These include information on production, processing station and transporter performance, queues, resource utilisation and material consumption.

SIMFACTORY is, as are a number of specialist routines, a 'data-driven simulation'. The generic model is written in SIMSCRIPT II.5 and the application-specific features are selected by input data. This approach enables the software provider to tailor his package to the particular requirements of a limited group, and it simplifies the interface between modeller and software. Features in SIMFACTORY which permit one part to be broken up into others, as a metal sheet may form the basis of several pressings, are very valuable and pertinent to the majority of production modelling tasks.

As the parent language develops, so will SIMFACTORY. For example, it is forecast that later versions of SIMSCRIPT will provide animation via specific combinations of graphic terminals linked to mainframes. This will also give a development route for SIMFACTORY.

There are other simulators for the modelling of flexible manufacturing systems. Conceptually they are akin to SIMFACTORY. GCMS and MAST (Lenz, 1980) are typical. Lenz did much of the work on GCMS whilst a graduate student at Purdue, and later revised it as MAST. Both were originally written in GASP, but this code base has been superseded. Lenz (1983) gives an example of the use of MAST which emphasises the particularly detailed specification of factory shop-floor practice which can be achieved. MAST is written in FORTRAN and accepts free formated data instructions which describe the manufacturing system — thus no FORTRAN knowledge is required. A PC-based implementation is SPAR, MAST and BEAM. SPAR prompts the user to define the system, MAST simulates it and BEAM provides output animation. The property of CMS Research Inc., the package is marketed in the UK by Citroen Industries UK. An additional feature is that not only does SPAR accept the basic model data, it also performs a static capacity analysis and thus ensures that the proposed resource level, say the number of AGVs, is reasonable.

Another automobile company, Renault Automation, is responsible for the third of these packages. SAME is available in a number of modules, SAME/AGVS, SAME/FAS and SAME/FMS, also on personal computers.

What these three packages have in common is the sequence in which the animation represents a final polish to the model-building exercise. In contrast WITNESS, perhaps more naturally, focuses on the representation of the system and, as icons, are defined so the appropriate menu is presented.

3.3.3 WITNESS

Other software designers have followed this path, for example WITNESS is a data-driven system originally written in SEE-WHY. This is a menu-driven simulation created for the study of manufacturing systems. WITNESS can also be integrated with SEE-WHY submodels if its internal capabilities are insufficient for a particular task. The modelling elements of WITNESS are related to the factory — parts, machines, buffers, conveyors and labour. In this aspect, the system is little different from others that have been discussed, or which follow. The interface design can progress in parallel and independently of the parent model. This itself is attractive to the management of system design houses, as it gives them more flexibility in the provision of enhancements to the system. Not all data-driven systems are obviously so, as the XCELL package illustrates.

Application-specific Systems 71

3.3.4 XCELL

XCELL (Conway *et al.*, 1986) attempts to make simulation available to the non-professional by matching the ease of use of the spreadsheet. The modeller has a simple rectangular grid of uniform-sized cells, into which he can place a component selected from a set of five types; WORKCENTER, BUFFER, RECEIVING AREA, SHIPPING AREA, MAINTENANCE FACILITY. The software has a set of function key controls and the model-building process is controlled by selecting the appropriate function from the following options.

NEW FACTORY (clear the current workspace),
DESIGN (a new factory),
ANALYSIS (complete a consistency check and compute flows),
RUN (the current model),
FILE MANAGER (store or retrieve a model),
CHANGE DISPLAY (alter the contents of the display screen).

The model-building sequence might be to create a new factory, initially clearing the screen. The pointer may be moved around the grid and icons placed on cells. The parameters of the icons are set, service time for work centre, for example, or the stock level of a particular part within a buffer. The paths through which jobs flow are then defined. The ANALYSIS option checks the model for inconsistencies, caused by omission, and estimates the capacity of the system in the absence of variability. RUN executes the model. The execution can be interrupted to set TRACE, CHART or PLOT options associated with the icons. RUN time can be stepped, the speed varied and the duration reset at any time.

Without access to a manual the author has found it possible to fumble through a model definition and execution. This is a strong endorsement for the simplicity of the concept and the execution of the interface. It will be one of the touchstone packages for the standard of the end-user interface.

Like SIMFACTORY this is really a generic, data-driven model. When the user lays components on the grid he is, according to Conway *et al.* (1986), identifying existing entities. Each component is already populated with default attributes. The user will subsequently selectively change these, but will do this in an attribute table under the control of an editor so that the system can ensure the validity of his actions. Not only will this create a model that will always run, but it will permit the user to change the parameter values during a pause in execution.

XCELL is still in its development phase. XCELL+ is an enhancement that includes materials-handling features via two new element types: PATH — a connected sequence of elements over which a carrier can move, and CONTROL POINT — the interconnection of the path and the other XCELL elements. CARRIERS move the jobs over the path and the control rules of carrier action are set by the user.

3.3.5 ModelMaster

General Electric have launched the ModelMaster factory modelling system as a PC-based graphical modelling tool for the flow of parts through a manufacturing facility. The software originates from GE's Automation Controls Operation in Charlottesville, VA. The system is also menu-driven and designed for the inexperienced user. It has a two-phase problem definition stage: a menu-driven graphical layout section and a forms-entry data entry section. The layout is drawn on a dot matrix, selecting features from a pop-up window. The keyboard cursor movement keys permit the user to move over the matrix. After the graphical representation a series of context-dependent forms-entry screens prompt the user for data. No programming commands or memorised responses need be used. A help key gives full explanation of the possible responses. Output is in the form of summary statistics reports using pie charts or bar charts, graphs of queue contents and animation.

General Electric claim that the model has been of great value in the design of more than a dozen of their plants, despite the fact that it is very limited in scope. For example, queue disciplines are limited to FIFO or earliest due date, work centres are limited to twenty, jobs may only have twenty operations and the total number of resources is fiteen. This emphasises that there is no one correct detail of modelling. Where a system is very complex an approximate model, based on conceptual aggregation of detail, may be sufficient to guide an engineer towards the robustness that he is seeking, rather than the optimisation that his experience rejects as infeasible.

3.3.6 Other systems

In addition to the block oriented packages presented here, chosen for their wide application, there are other simple systems. INSIGHT (Roberts, 1983) is one of these which has been designed in the building block format and which has special strengths in the statistical tools which are available. The latest version is interactive and includes a section which quizzes the user to ensure a consistent and complete model formulation. Similarly SIMPLE 1 (Cobbin, 1985) is another system which provides a working environment to support both the modelling and the experimental tasks. The models are also specified through blocks, about 25 in all, and the system has the ability to run both discrete and continuous elements. The system's intention is to turn the XT or AT into a complete 'toolbox' for the modeller.

3.4 Simulation Pre-processors

Simulation language pre-processors are called program generators. They are interactive software tools that translate the logic of a model, described in a relatively general and simple symbolism, into the code of a simulation language or the appropriate list of building block definitions. The resulting program listing should be well structured and clearly annotated. The software gives the user the benefits of a simple symbolic input (especially valuable for use by those who are not conversant with programming practices) combined with the power of a high-level language in which to develop models of complex systems. Although it can be claimed that the first program generator was the Query/Answer interface for SIMSCRIPT, present tools originate from work in the early 1970s — CAPS/ECSL (Clementson, 1985) and DRAFT/DRAW (Mathewson, 1974). Subsequently a wide range of programs have been produced (Subrahmanian and Cannon, 1981; Luker, 1986). More recently researchers have sought to front-end other systems; e.g. RESQ (IBM) and TESS for SLAM II, MAP/1 and GPSS/H (Pritsker & Associates).

The program generator shields the user from the intrinsic difficulties of general simulation languages. Although allowing only a restricted set of structures and concepts, the program generator can often entirely replace the host language for a large subset of common problems. With such systems any errors that occur in the generated code are reported in terms of the target language. Although this can be a real problem to the naïve user, who is otherwise kept at arms length from the target code, faults in code are rare and the integrity of the generated code is customarily high.

There are two approaches which serve to minimise error — the structured generator and the generator with an integrated interpreter. It is also true that, for expert users, superimposing a rigid check on the integrity of the generated code can be counterproductive. Such users have found that it can be very efficient to use a program generator to prepare a skeletal framework of a program, even though the code contains logical faults and inconsistencies. Subsequently the code can be extended and developed to represent special and unusual models. In this context it is sufficient to alert the user to errors. For the robot cell this might take the form of a message 'No robot initially set in idle', and the programmer would write in the robot allocation rule at a later time.

3.4.1 DRAFT

The program generator is customarily structured as a group of functional modules linked as shown in Figure 3.5, which is specific to DRAFT but is generally representative. The model expressed as an entity cycle diagram is input via a terminal. The input/editor module identifies minor or semantic errors (e.g. use of reserved variable names, duplicate use of names) and lets the user correct the entry. It also creates a back-up copy of the input on 'scratch' files, which may later be accessed for modification or stored as a compact copy of the model. The analysis module checks the input for errors, which may often be corrected on-line, and prepares a coded internal file of the entity interaction within the model. The file forms a general input to the program writer selected by the user. It is after this stage that the model description is mapped into the particular structure — event, activity, process — associated with the target language. The program generator is able to control operation of the host computer, to provide error-free code which may be used as a model for further enhancement, and offers the advantages and convenience of a shorthand notation.

The input session, shown in Figure 3.6, is a series of responses to prompts from DRAFT. The output is the FORTRAN program of Figure 3.7. See Mathewson (1985) for details of the coding. The sequential input style can be restrictive, especially in the development of large and complex models. In these cases, users prefer to browse over an area involving several resources rather than follow the path of a single entity over the whole model. An alternative input mode using direct specification of the network via a

Simulation Pre-processors

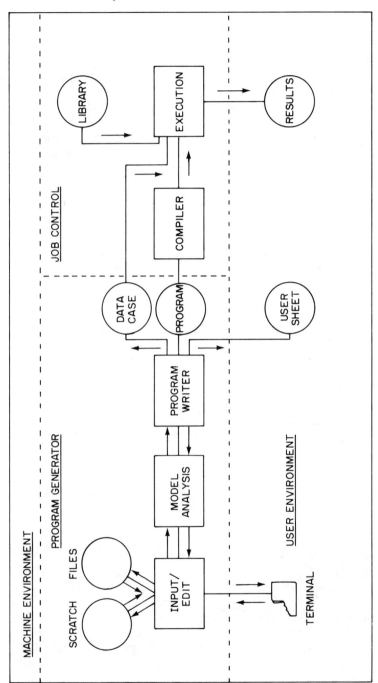

Figure 3.5 The structure of a program generator.

character graphics terminal is an optional alternative to the question-and-answer style of Figure 3.6 (Mathewson, 1987). The grid thus specified is subsequently scanned to prepare standard entry files. Advantages include the possibility of duplicating areas of the grid at other positions so as to common components, and also a macro library may be formed by archiving blocks for later retrieval. Generally the current implementation of DRAFT is far more complex than shown in Figure 3.5, and currently includes support for the spreadsheet-like model definition, complex animation and pull-down forms for the specification of queues, activity and control rule parameters. Figure 3.7 shows the output when the 'three-phase' option is selected. Compare this with the logic flow on p. 40.

```
THIS IS DRAFT. LICENCED TO:-PAXMAN     V. 9/4/86
INPUT IS FREE FORMAT.   DATA IS SEPARATED BY A BLANK OR COMMA.
MODE IS "KEYIN" OR "EDIT". A "SOURCE" FILE MUST BE SPECIFIED
FOR "EDIT" MODE (FIRST OR LAST). NOW ENTER:-  MODE, SCRATCH FILE
(OPTIONAL)

   E.G. "KEYIN" OR "EDIT,LAST" ?k
   PLEASE DEPRESS THE CAPS LOCK
   AND REPEAT THE INPUT IN UPPER CASE
   K(EYIN) OR E(DIT), (F(IRST) OR L(AST)) ?K

   INPUT FILE NAME "XXXXXXXX" FOR PROGRAM.
   IT WILL BE ON THE FILE CALLED "XXXXXXXX.FOR".  ?WILEY

   PLEASE ENTER THE NAMES OF ACTIVITIES IN PRIORITY ORDER
   ",+" INDICATES MORE NAMES ON THE NEXT LINE. * FOR NO DATA
   ?UNLOAD MILL LOADS COMES CLEAR

   NOW THE QUEUE NAMES. * IF NONE
   ?WORLD QUEUE ROUGH CLEAN EMPTY FREE IDLE

   NOW THE FLAG NAMES. * IF NONE
   ?*

   PAGE 3. ENTER THE DURATION FOR EACH ACTIVITY,IN THE ORDER
   THE ACTIVITIES WERE DEFINED. FINALLY TOTAL RUN TIME.
   -1 5 6 7 8 100
      STOCHASTIC VALUES REQUIRED PLEASE ENTER DETAILS
      NORMAL CODE=1,STREAM,MEAN,SD
      NEGEX CODE=2,STREAM,MEAN
      UNIFORM CODE=3,STREAM,LOWER,UPPER
      SAMPLE CODE=4,STREAM
      DEFINE DATA FOR ACTIVITY UNLOA
   ?2 1 10.
```

Figure 3.6a Robot cell example: DRAFT dialogue.

Simulation Pre-processors

```
PAGE 4. NOW ENTER CYCLES.
THE ENTITY NAME "ERROR" WILL ENTER EDIT MODE.

CYCLE    1.
NAME THE ENTITY CLASS, SIZE , AND "H" FOR HISTOGRAM
?INPUT 1
ENTITY CYCLE HISTORY
?COMES

CYCLE    2.
NAME THE ENTITY CLASS, SIZE , AND "H" FOR HISTOGRAM
?CASTING 100 H
ENTITY CYCLE HISTORY
?WORLD COMES QUEUE LOADS ROUGH MILL CLEAN UNLOAD CLEAR
 ENTER HISTOGRAM DATA
 ENTITY   DELAYS   -   GIVE   MEASUREMENT POINTS E.G "END COMES,START
SERVE"
 QUEUE SIZE - GIVE QUEUE NAME
?E COMES E UNLOAD
 NOW ENTER LOWER BOUND AND STEP
?5 5
CYCLE    3.
NAME THE ENTITY CLASS, SIZE , AND "H" FOR HISTOGRAM
?ROBOT 1
ENTITY CYCLE HISTORY
?IDLE LOADS IDLE UNLOAD

CYCLE    4.
NAME THE ENTITY CLASS, SIZE , AND "H" FOR HISTOGRAM
?HEAD 1
ENTITY CYCLE HISTORY
?FREE MILL

CYCLE    5.
NAME THE ENTITY CLASS, SIZE , AND "H" FOR HISTOGRAM
?TABLES 2
ENTITY CYCLE HISTORY
?EMPTY LOADS ROUGH MILL CLEAN UNLOAD

CYCLE    6.
NAME THE ENTITY CLASS, SIZE , AND "H" FOR HISTOGRAM
?FINIS
 ENTER ZERO TO CONTINUE-PAGE NUMBER TO EDIT ?0
 PLEASE SPECIFY:-
 THE TIME STRUCTURE   EVENT:THREE-PHASE ,
 THE CLOCK            REAL:INTEGER   ,AND
 OPTIMISED CODE       YES:NO
?E R Y
 LOADS MAY START FROM UNLOA
 UNLOA MAY START FROM UNLOA
 LOADS MAY START FROM UNLOA
 UNLOA MAY START FROM MILL
 MILL  MAY START FROM MILL
 MILL  MAY START FROM LOADS
 LOADS MAY START FROM LOADS
 UNLOA MAY START FROM LOADS
 LOADS MAY START FROM COMES
 ENTER ZERO TO CONTINUE-PAGE NUMBER TO EDIT ?0

 DATA INPUT OK, PROG ON   WILEY.FOR   -DATA ON WILEY.DAT
  ***********THE MEMORY IS NOW LAST**********
```

Figure 3.6b Robot cell example: DRAFT dialogue, continued.

```fortran
$STORAGE:2
      INTEGER*2 MAST1(1000),MAST2(1000),STATE,TIMES,CLOCK,TAILM
      INTEGER*4 ZZXZZ(40)
      INTEGER*2 SYMVT(96,18),ARCH(96),ARCP(200,5),PV(1600),SETDEC
      INTEGER*2 RFE,RFS,ARCSS(10),ARCDS(10)
      INTEGER*2 WORLD,QUEUE,ROUGH,CLEAN,EMPTY,FREE ,IDLE
      INTEGER*2 BOUND,DFAZE,HEADO,SIZEO
      INTEGER INPUT( 4,2)
      INTEGER CASTI(103,2)
      INTEGER ROBOT( 4,2)
      INTEGER HEAD ( 4,2)
      INTEGER*2 SLAVE( 3)
      DIMENSION ZCASTI(19)
      DIMENSION VCASTI(2,500)
      DIMENSION ISDIST( 5),PARAMA( 5),PARAMB( 5),NRANDY( 5),LEVELS( 5)
      CHARACTER NTITYN(5)
      CHARACTER*5 CODVAR(96),SYMNAM(96),CYCNAM(40)
      CHARACTER*20 AMAST(96)
      CHARACTER*10 XXTIT,YYTIT
      COMMON NIM,TAILM,MAST1,MAST2,ZZXZZ,STATE,NAME,TIMES,CLOCK,MEMBE
      COMMON /SREAL/RMAST(1000),HOURS
      COMMON/GWS/SYMVT,ARCH,ARCP,PV,SETDEC,RFE,RFS,ARCSS,ARCDS,ISGXC,IGX
      COMMON /CDT/ CODVAR,SYMNAM,CYCNAM
      COMMON /TRACE/ AMAST
      COMMON /ATTRIB/ MAST3(1000),MAST4(1000)
      COMMON /PDATA/ VCASTI
      OPEN(2,FILE='WILEY2.DAT   ')
      OPEN(3,FILE='RUN.RES',STATUS='NEW')
C
C     ****** DATA STRUCTURE ******
C     UNLOA HOLDS: ROBOT CASTI TABLE
C     MILL  HOLDS: HEAD  CASTI TABLE
C     LOADS HOLDS: ROBOT CASTI TABLE
C     COMES HOLDS: INPUT CASTI
C     CLEAR HOLDS: CASTI
C     WORLD HOLDS: CASTI
C     QUEUE HOLDS: CASTI
C     ROUGH HOLDS: CASTI TABLE
C     CLEAN HOLDS: CASTI TABLE
C     EMPTY HOLDS: TABLE
C     FREE  HOLDS: HEAD
C     IDLE  HOLDS: ROBOT
C
C     ******READ IN RESOURCE LEVELS******
      WRITE(3,1)
    1 FORMAT(21H      RESOURCE LEVELS)
      DO 2 J=1, 5
      READ(2,3)LEVELS(J),NTITYN
    2 WRITE(3,4)NTITYN,LEVELS(J)
    3 FORMAT(I3,5A1)
    4 FORMAT(6X,5A1,3X,I3)
      DO5 J=1, 5
      READ(2,6)ISDIST(J),PARAMA(J),PARAMB(J),NRANDY(J),NTITYN
    5 WRITE(3,7)NTITYN,PARAMA(J),PARAMB(J),NRANDY(J)
    6 FORMAT(I3,2F8.2,I3,5A1)
    7 FORMAT(6X,9HACTIVITY ,5A1,2X,2F8.2,I6)
      READ(2,8)RUNTIM
    8 FORMAT(F6.0)
      WRITE(3,9)RUNTIM
    9 FORMAT(6X,19HTHE RUN DURATION IS,F8.0)
C
C     ******SET UP SIMON STRUCTURE******
      CALL SIMON
      CALL GROUP(INPUT,LEVELS( 1), 4)
      CALL GROUP(CASTI,LEVELS( 2), 5)
      CALL GROUP(ROBOT,LEVELS( 3), 1)
      CALL GROUP(HEAD ,LEVELS( 4), 2)
      CALL ENTIT(DFAZE, 6)
      CALL HISTO(ZCASTI,   5.00,    5.00)
      NCASTI=0
      VCASTI(1,1)=0
```

Figure 3.7a Robot cell example: DRAFT computer generated FORTRAN code for an IBM PC.

```
              VCASTI(2,1)=0
              CALL SET(WORLD)
              CALL SET(QUEUE)
              CALL SET(ROUGH)
              CALL SET(CLEAN)
              CALL SET(EMPTY)
              CALL SET(FREE )
              CALL SET(IDLE )
              HOURS=0
              CALL HELPI(NNN,WORLD,IDLE )
        C
        C     ******SET IN THE INITIAL  CONDITIONS FOR THE MODEL ******
        C
        C     ******PLACE ENTITES IN SETS******
        C
              N=LEVELS( 2)
              DO 10 J=1,N
           10 CALL ADDLA(CASTI(J,1),WORLD)
        C
              N=LEVELS( 3)
              DO 15 J=1,N
           15 CALL ADDLA(ROBOT(J,1),IDLE )
        C
              N=LEVELS( 4)
              DO 20 J=1,N
           20 CALL ADDLA(HEAD (J,1),FREE )
        C
              N=LEVELS( 5)
              DO 25 J=1,N
           25 CALL ADDLA(J,EMPTY)
              L=LEVELS( 1)
              DO 30 J=1,L
              DELAY=PARAMA( 4)
              CALL SCHED(INPUT(J,1),DELAY,HEADO(WORLD))
           30 CALL BEHEA(WORLD)
              CALL SCHED(DFAZE,RUNTIM,0)
              GO TO 2100
        C
        C     ******SELECT THE NEXT EVENT******
        C
         1000 CALL CAUSE(K)
              CALL HELPC(NNN,K)
              GO TO (1020 , 1040 , 1060 , 1080 , 1100 , 1120),K
        C
        C     ****** THESE ARE THE B-PHASE EVENTS ******
        C
        C     ACTIVITY UNLOA ENDED
        C     MEMBE REPRESENTS ENTITY ROBOT
        C     STATE REPRESENTS ENTITY CASTI
        C     SLAVE( 3) REPRESENTS J OF JTH TABLE
         1020 CALL CREATE(MEMBE,SLAVE, 3)
              AN=HOURS-RMAST(STATE    )
              CALL ADDTO(ZCASTI,AN)
              CALL SGRAPH(VCASTI,NCASTI,HOURS,AN)
              DELAY=PARAMA( 5)
              CALL SCHED(STATE    ,DELAY,BOUND(STATE    ))
              CALL ADDLA(MEMBE    ,IDLE )
              CALL ADDLA(SLAVE(3),EMPTY)
              GO TO 2100
        C
        C     ACTIVITY MILL  ENDED
        C     MEMBE REPRESENTS ENTITY HEAD
        C     STATE REPRESENTS ENTITY CASTI
        C     SLAVE( 3) REPRESENTS J OF JTH TABLE
         1040 CALL ADDLA(STATE    ,CLEAN)
              CALL ADDLA(MEMBE    ,FREE )
              GO TO 2100
        C
        C     ACTIVITY LOADS ENDED
        C     MEMBE REPRESENTS ENTITY ROBOT
        C     STATE REPRESENTS ENTITY CASTI
```

Figure 3.7b Robot cell example: DRAFT computer generated FORTRAN code for an IBM PC, continued.

```
C        SLAVE( 3) REPRESENTS J OF JTH TABLE
 1060 CALL ADDLA(STATE    ,ROUGH)
      CALL ADDLA(MEMBE    ,IDLE )
      GO TO 2100
C
C        ACTIVITY COMES ENDED
C        MEMBE REPRESENTS ENTITY INPUT
C        STATE REPRESENTS ENTITY CASTI
 1080 RMAST(STATE    )=HOURS
      CALL ADDLA(STATE    ,QUEUE)
      DELAY=PARAMA( 4)
      CALL SCHED (MEMBE,DELAY,HEADO(WORLD))
      CALL BEHEA(WORLD)
      GO TO 2100
C
C        ACTIVITY CLEAR ENDED
C        MEMBE REPRESENTS ENTITY CASTI
 1100 CALL ADDLA(MEMBE    ,WORLD)
      GO TO 1000
C
C      ****** THE C-PHASE STARTS HERE ******
C        TEST TO START THE ACTIVITY UNLOA
 2100 IF(SIZEO(IDLE )*SIZEO(CLEAN)) 2200, 2200, 2105
 2105 PA=PARAMA( 1)
      PB=PARAMB( 1)
      IS=NRANDY( 1)
      ID=ISDIST( 1)
      IP=PARAMB( 1)
      CALL DRAW(DELAY,ID,IS,IP,PA,PB)
      CALL RESET(HEADO(IDLE ),  1)
      NCLEAN=HEADO(CLEAN)
      NIDLE =HEADO(IDLE )
      CALL SCHED(NIDLE ,DELAY,NCLEAN)
      CALL BEHEA(IDLE )
      CALL BEHEA(CLEAN)
      GO TO 2100
C
C        TEST TO START THE ACTIVITY MILL
 2200 IF(SIZEO(FREE )*SIZEO(ROUGH)) 2300, 2300, 2205
 2205 DELAY=PARAMA( 2)
      NROUGH=HEADO(ROUGH)
      NFREE =HEADO(FREE )
      CALL SCHED(NFREE ,DELAY,NROUGH)
      CALL BEHEA(FREE )
      CALL BEHEA(ROUGH)
      GO TO 2200
C
C        TEST TO START THE ACTIVITY LOADS
 2300 IF(SIZEO(IDLE )*SIZEO(QUEUE)*SIZEO(EMPTY))1000,1000,2305
 2305 DELAY=PARAMA( 3)
      CALL RESET(HEADO(IDLE ),  3)
      NQUEUE=HEADO(QUEUE)
      NIDLE =HEADO(IDLE )
      CALL SCHED(NIDLE ,DELAY,NQUEUE)
      NEMPTY=HEADO(EMPTY)
      CALL LINKTO(NQUEUE,NEMPTY)
      CALL BEHEA(IDLE )
      CALL BEHEA(QUEUE)
      CALL BEHEA(EMPTY)
      GO TO 2300
C
C      ****** THE D-PHASE STARTS HERE ******
C        WRITE HISTOGRAM FOR CASTI
 1120 WRITE(3, 2900)
 2900 FORMAT(///,20X,16HDELAYS FOR CASTI)
      CALL WRITH(ZCASTI, 2)
      XXTIT='TIME IS  '
      YYTIT='VALUE    '
      CALL EXCELB(VCASTI,NCASTI,40.,10.,XXTIT,YYTIT,0.0)
      CALL HELPB(NNN)
      STOP
```

Figure 3.7c Robot cell example: DRAFT computer generated FORTRAN code for an IBM PC, continued.

3.4.2 CAPS

CAPS is the front-end processor for ECSL, and is discussed in detail in Pidd (1988). For both CAPS and DRAFT, the input is a direct translation of the entity cycle diagram. The level of detail, for example the specification of the FIFO queue in CAPS at the terminal entry level, is indicative of the minor differences between the two products.

EXTENDED CONTROL AND SIMULATION LANGUAGE
COMPUTER AIDED PROGRAMMING SYSTEM

DO YOU WISH TO HAVE INSTRUCTIONAL COMMENTS. n
PROBLEM NAME . cell
DO YOU WISH TO START A NEW PROBLEM. y
ARE YOU GOING TO USE THE IMPLICIT QUEUE MODE. y

LOGIC
TYPE NAME OF ONE KIND OF ENTITY casting,40
TYPE A LIST OF THE STATE THROUGH WHICH THESE ENTITIES
PASS PRECEDE QUEUES BY Q AND ACTIVITIES BY A
qworld acomes qqueue aloads qrough acut qsmooth aunload qclear
IS THIS CYCLE CORRECT. y
. . . .
PRIORITIES
ARE THERE ANY QUEUES WHOSE DISCIPLINE IS NOT F-I-F-O? n
. . . .

3.4.3 The dialog approach

Both CAPS and DRAFT are structured around a network — the entity cycle diagram. The adherence to the rules for mapping the network formulation into a computer program ensures that the program will always execute. In contrast to this approach Birtwistle and Luker (1985), at the University of Calgary, have developed an intermediate interpreter for the dialog approach. Dialogs accept model description in the form of responses to computer-generated prompts. These models are stored in an intermediate form (IF). An interpreter, written in SIMULA, permits model execution for interactive debugging. Once this is achieved the IF can be used to generate compiled code. The first system was Modeller (Luker,

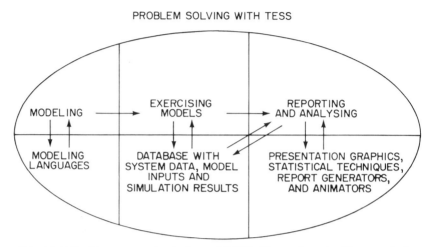

Figure 3.8 The conceptual view of TESS. (Reproduced with permission from Standridge C.R. (1986), A Tutorial on TESS. Proc Winter Sim Conf).

```
DATA ELEMENTS                      FUNCTIONS
                        BUILD      REPORT      GRAPH
                        ------------------------------
MODELLING
    Network              *                       *
    Definition           *           *
    Facility             *                       *
SIMULATION & ANALYSIS
    Control              *           *
    Scenario             *
    Data                 *           *           *
    Summary              *           *           *
PRESENTATION
    Format               *           *           *
    Rule                 *           *
                        ------------------------------
```

Figure 3.9 TESS functions. (Adapted from Standridge, 1986).

1982), designed for continuous simulation. The discrete event system currently under development is ANDES (Animated Discrete Event Simulation Environment). Andes has been implemented with ideas drawn from other research in software prototyping environment. ANDES permits five pre-defined views of the model activity to be selected. The views become increasingly complete (Birtwistle and Carson, 1985). From the program logic view, which depicts scheduled events and associated resource, they develop to include views of the entity cycle diagram, resource allocation, a window on the currently executing code and a statistical display. The work is further discussed in the section on current research.

```
BUILD SCENARIO NAMED(CELLNOW)
    DESCRIPTOR("CURRENT ROBOT CELL OPERATION")
    NETWORK (CELL)
    CONTROL(SIM)
    DATA(OLD.ROBOT,OLD.MILL)
```

Figure 3.10 Use of BUILD SCENARIO in TESS.

```
GRAPH SUMMARY NAMED(CDELAY)
    SCENARIO(CELLNOW,CELLTHEN)
    FORMAT(CDELAY)
    TYPE(BAR);
```

Figure 3.11 Use of SUMMARY in TESS.

3.5 Support Environments

3.5.1 TESS

A complete support system is one which aids all aspects of the use of simulation by providing individual modules for model building, control of experiments, results analysis and results presentation. This is the goal for TESS (Standridge, 1985). Figure 3.8 shows the framework for the language and illustrates the areas covered. Above the centre line are the steps through which the modeller proceeds. Below the line are the support facilities provided by the software tools. The arrows represent the access paths to the tools. The goal is to provide an integrated system.

> Integration hides many of the technical details required to perform a simulation project on a computer but not directly related to problem solving. For example, translation of models from graphically specified forms to forms which can be analysed by the simulation processor needs to be implicit and transparent. Flexible data selection for reports, graphs and animations can be provided with the mechanics of the data selection hidden from the user. In addition, integration allows the user to learn a single software package to perform an entire simulation project (Standridge, 1985).

This package is available as an environment for SLAM II, MAP/1 and GPSS/H. Overall control is through three functions — BUILD, REPORT and GRAPH, which operate on the various data elements within the steps of the modelling task. Permissible combinations are shown in Figure 3.9 (adapted from Standridge, 1986). A TESS user creates the overall structure by calling on TESS BUILD language statements which have been written to provide standard implementations of much of the work required. It permits the user to specify a schematic of the model, to generate a SLAM network and to enter the input data into the TESS database.

BUILD FACILITY permits the user to create a schematic of the model on a screen. This representation can be used for presentation purposes. The model is composed of user-defined icons or simple building blocks, rectangles, triangles and bars. They can be interactively laid out and titled on the viewing screen.

BUILD NETWORK creates the equivalent SLAM II network using the same interactive screen handling facilities. The programmer assembles SLAM II symbols on a large plane surface. BUILD NETWORK NAMED (CELL) would permit the user to define the robot cell. The screen acts as a selective window onto the modelling plane. User-written SLAM programs may be linked prior to execution.

BUILD DEFINITION model input or output data. Each data set can be given its identity for subsequent recall. BUILD DEFINITION NAMED (OLD.ROBOT), for example, sets aside an area to store information about the variables associated with robot performance.

BUILD CONTROL selects the length of the experiment and specifies what parameters are to be monitored. These elements (network, dataset and control) are linked together using the BUILD SCENARI. statement. A robot cell simulation constructed of these modules appears as in Figure 3.10. To re-run the simulation with an alternative scenario, perhaps a new robot with faster response, would require that the new scenario (CELLTHEN) replaces the DATA specification with, say, NEW.ROBOT.

The report is prepared by a BUILD SUMMARY statement. The scenarios have each collected a large number of observations. The presentation of this information will be, of necessity, selective. If one of the measures collected by CONTROL is the casting delay and this is to be presented comparatively then Figure 3.11 shows the use of SUMMARY. FORMAT enables the user to title the graphs, SCENARIO would plot bar charts of the performance of both options. Spike graphs, bar graphs and pie charts are available within the system. Default formats are associated with all reports and graphs so that sensible options are chosen if the programmer omits his own specification.

The animation is created through BUILD RULE. A rule relates the stored event trace to the appearance of the facility, the schematic defined originally. As the system steps through the event trace it is possible to define three types of rules: firstly, to change colours on the facility blocks according to status; secondly, to reset counters to represent queue levels; thirdly, to move entities along the path to reflect the physical movement of castings.

An important feature of this system is the use of database facility to hold the system data, model input and simulation results. The former gives flexibility in model definition and modification while the latter enables results to be recalled and the user to create diverse reports. Broadly speaking the uses can be categorised as follows.

1   Experimental control which includes initial conditions, end-of-run criteria and output variables;
2   model description;
3   model data;
4   and real system data.

3.5.2 SDL

SDL (Simulation Data Language) is a FORTRAN-oriented set of routines which have been used with GASP, Q-GERT and SLAM. They permit the user to manipulate data, to calculate statistics and make plots and histograms of selected information. Later authors have written interfacing routines for spreadsheet packages (e.g. LOTUS 1-2-3™). Whilst these are helpful in preparing selected output they do not serve the broad function of a simulation-specific tool. It is surprising that simulation language designers have taken so long to realise the value of integrated data management techniques. In the general study of decision support systems, data management has always occupied a central position (Ariav and Ginzberg, 1985).

3.5.3 RESQ

RESQ (Research Queuing Package) is a product of IBM Research. It is a general flow network with queues and activities (called passive and active queues in their nomenclature). RESQ builds a simulation program in APLOMB based on the model definition, simulates and produces a statistical analysis of the simulation output. The existence of a structure underlying the simulation model permits other algorithms to 'solve' the model and estimate some parameters of system performance. Normally these parameters are a restricted subset of those available from a full simulation experiment — for example the mean queue size, queue size distribution, or waiting time may be given. This contrasts with the full information available from the trajectory of the queue size which is generated by a simulation. If the network can be mathematically analysed the RESQ package has the facility to do so via the QNET4 numerical solution software.

RESQ provides a set of modelling primitives specific to resource-constrained problems, e.g. computer systems, communication networks and manufacturing processes. Apart from the basic nodes, jobs can arrive and depart via source and sink nodes, split and wait for Boolean conditions to be met. Job routes may be specified as deterministic chains, or be dependent on the system state. These are features that have already been met in the discussions of other transaction flow languages.

A new concept is that of the sub-model. A sub-model is a parameterised template built up of a number of RESQ functions, each of which may be called as though it were itself a node. It is analogous to a macro in a programming language. It is an important tool in the modelling of hierarchically structured systems. RESQ also has a high level of support for analysis, providing simulation specific tools for confidence interval estimation, e.g. the 'regenerative' method.

3.5.4 RESQME

The early versions of RESQ used textual interaction based on the information content of a graphical network. Recently RESQME, a workstation environment, has been written for the package (Kurose *et al.*, 1986). RESQME is the RESearch Queuing Package Modelling Environment, and is an integrated, graphics-oriented system of hardware and software. It is designed to facilitate the use of models for performance evaluation purposes. Graphics are used because the developers believe that the analyst both thinks in terms of a network diagram when constructing his system, and also prefers to review the output in terms of graphical presentation. The hardware is made up of a personal computer connected to the mainframe with both a fully addressable graphics display and a character display. The graphics display uses the IBM virtual display interface provided by the graphics development toolkit. It is the primary user interface and uses a pointer system for the selection of menu items and objects. The character

Support Environments

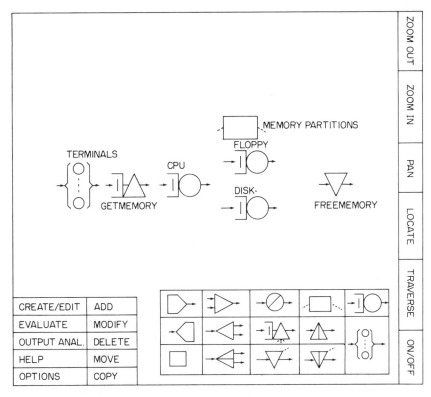

Figure 3.12 The appearance of a partially complete RESQ model. (From Kurose J.F. (1986)).

screen provides the input device for details of element attributes, model run parameters, output control parameters, and tutorial information. The designers believe that two-screen interaction keeps the graphics presentation clear of redundant detail. Combining a personal computer and mainframe system permits an interactive building mode with the benefits of mainframe power at run-time. As with TESS, the user has three phases of model specification or modification, simulation and output analysis and display.

Figure 3.12 shows the graphics screen during a model-building session (note that this is not the robot cell!). The system makes wide use of window displays. The main menu, on the left, has been used to create a model. Other options for help and default windows are possible. The bottom right-hand side window displays the symbol selection that is available. Down the right-hand edge is the screen management menu. This permits zooming in and out and panning across the building plane. The vertical planes, which may be traversed with the 'LAYER' command, permit hierarchical modelling and the use of library facilities. Thus, a macro specified in detail on a lower plane may be used on the main model, it being simply represented by a particular icon. Individual copies of the submodel may be specified with different parameter settings.

The character screen is also separated into working areas. The graphical model is assembled by picking icons from the menu and placing them in the modelling area. The icon is colour-coded to indicate its current 'state': red when picked or when an icon's attribute is incorrectly specified, yellow when placed but without attributes defined, and green when the attributes are correctly set. Attributes are defined on context-sensitive forms which relate prior answers to current questions. Where the responses are limited, the user can scroll through all possibilities and select that required. Routes are defined by grouping sets of 'from' nodes and sets of 'to' nodes which are then automatically connected. Although a system algorithm draws network linkages, the user may define intermediate points to force specific arc shapes. The model is 'evaluated' on the host mainframe but RESQ controls all interaction between the workstation and the host computer. The user is unaware of the external protocols. The output is transferred back to the workstation where graphs and charts can be produced.

The output analysis appears extremely easy. The user points to a node or group of nodes and selects 'Specify Content', which produces a list of available output variables. Selecting a variable and pressing 'PLOT' will automatically generate a graph with, say, confidence intervals. Reflecting the considerable expertise of IBM in the field of statistical analysis, three confidence interval estimation techniques are available to the user — the regenerative method, the spectral method and independent replications.

From the above, abbreviated, description of RESQ and RESQME, it is clear that the systems have a high level of user-friendliness. In its present form, RESQ does not have a database facility, or animation, but these are among promised developments. Other promised enhancements include features for integrating segments of old models into new systems.

3.6 System-Theoretic Representation

So far, the discussion has used a practical example, the robot cell,

System-Theoretic Representation 89

and looked at pragmatic approaches for resolving the problems of model representation and use. An alternative view is recommended by Ziegler (1984). This takes, as a starting point, the abstract representation of a model, and builds towards the pragmatic. Although there are no commercial implementations, the ideas have a strong following in a number of centres. Proponents of the approach argue that a formal language, based on the rigorous tools of logic and set theory, will provide an unambiguous and unrestricted method of model formulation.

The model can be summarised as a system, S, structured so that

$S = \langle T,X,Z,Q,Y,d,g \rangle$

Where T defines the integer or real time base,

X the set of model inputs through which exogenous events are fed,

Z the chronological pattern of inputs,

Q the internal system states,

d the state transition function which transforms Q for a given Z to a new Q,

Y the set of output channels and

g the output function which transforms Q to give Y.

The model is constructed for purposes of an experiment.

Ziegler defines an 'experimental frame' as the limited set of the real system environment which is to be observed or investigated. The formal specification of this, in terms analogous to those of the system, S, ensures that the goals of model formulation are consistent with the model defined. The X and Z of the model must include the X' and Z' of the experimental frame if the experimental proposals are to be valid.

The function of the formal specification is to encourage a rigorous approach. However, to write such a description is not a practical task and so, in the final analysis, the model representation is transformed into various special formulisms, each relating to a specific subclass of all systems. In deriving special formulisms for simulation models, Ziegler has suggested a decomposition tree be used to specify the static structure of the model — the system entity structure. An entity is a part of a system which has been identified as a component. A system can be decomposed in a number of ways; each decomposition is called an aspect. The robot cell can be defined in terms of the components mill and robot. Aspects might be power consumption and reliability. Each component has attached associated variables, which themselves have restricted ranges, and describe the attributes of the entities or aspects. The robot may have reliability between 0% and 100%

The decomposition tree represents a hierarchical system. Rules have been derived for manipulating the tree structure so that it provides an efficient database. Nodes define 'components' or 'component types'. A component type is a macro which becomes a specific component when the variables are defined. Thus all robots as a 'component type' have a reliability variable with its associated range, meaning and units. Once the variables are specified the component becomes a specific machine. Operations on these variables, as members of a set which are structured by their relationships in the tree, will be consistent. In a similar sense a formal specification of the discrete event structure has been proposed.

The realisations of this approach have been limited. The static structure has been investigated. Work by Ziegler (1985) and Leo de Wael of the AI-LAB at Vrije Universiteit Brussels, have investigated the use of a knowledge representation language (KRS) as a vehicle to encode the objects and relationships of Ziegler's multifaceted modelling methodology. This forms a tool to validate models and store and retrieve them from model bases. Rozenblit (1986) has published a technical report describing a conceptual basis for integrated model-based system design. He argues that if the system entity structure is appropriately designed, then for any experimental frame a procedure can be specified which will abstract the substructures of the system which are specific to the goals of the experiment. This is called 'pruning'. In the context of the robot cell it implies that an experimental frame concerned with, say, reliability, could be used to reduce the system to those specific elements concerned with reliability. The frame would determine the aspects required — those concerned with efficiency, the depth of the pruning process and the descriptive variables of components that were relevant. Others, e.g. power consumption, would not be included in the model.

A software tool (ESP — the Entity Structuring Program — Ziegler, 1980) has been designed as an aid to structuring data in a formal way. It has been described as a conceptual scratch-pad and communication tool. Prototype software for experimental frame specification (EXP, Rozenblit, 1986) has also been written.

3.7 Current Research and Progress

'A Simulation environment provides tools for specifying the processes in a simulation and generating debug and production models automatically from these specifications' (Birtwhistle, 1985). The preceding sections have reviewed the diversity of software tools available for discrete event simulation. In an industrial environment the objective of a simulation user is to improve the quality of decision-making. High-level languages, program generators and generic modelling software have only the partial goal of aiding model coding, and so they naturally omit important features. To be specific, they do not adequately direct experimental procedures, they do not invoke the appropriate statistical tools, and they do not provide output in the several styles appropriate to a broad user hierarchy. Such tools shorten the coding cycle, they do not guide the user or reduce the experimental task. In contrast, the survey has also illustrated implementations which serve, in part, to address the broader problems.

The academic and research communities are able to take longer-term views than the practitioner or consultant. As a consequence, there are several research programmes which focus on the full requirements of the modeller. For example, the JADE programme of the Department of Computer Science at Calgary University (Unger *et al.*, 1984), which aims to provide an integrated set of software tools. Another example is the CASM (computer-assisted simulation modelling) project at the London School of Economics. This aims to provide aids for problem formulation, program generation and output analysis. Paul gives some details in Chapters 4 and 5.

Further examples are ROSS (RAND Object-oriented Simulation System) which is an English-like, interactive language implemented in LISP (McArthur and Sowizral, 1986) and is an interesting example of an implemented AI-based system. Another is at the Virginia Polytechnic Institute and State University, which has had a long interest in simulation systems and is currently engaged in the study of simulation environments. The papers published by the group at the Virginia Systems Research Centre show that it is one of the most advanced in the area of integrated system development. They particularly emphasise the basic building blocks of the discipline — as exemplified by Figure 2.1. In their publications these groups have suggested some new aspects and some new solutions to elements of model building. The objectives, as summarised by Nance, are to:

1. offer cost-effective, integrated and automatic support of model development throughout the model life cycle,
2. improve the model quality by effectively assisting in the quality assurance of the model,
3. significantly increase the efficiency and productivity of the project team, and
4. substantially decrease the model development time.

The contributions suggested by research, over and above those elements already demonstrated in commercial code, will close this chapter. The work will be taken in the sequence of a project implementation.

3.7.1 Model specification

Work by Ziegler and others shows promise of successful model building based on selectively extracting information from a structured database. The alternative approach, suggested by Nance, is the conical methodology. This precedes model specification by a model definition phase. The model definition phase requires the modeller to perform an object decomposition, assigning attributes, by type, range and dimensions, to objects based on the system and the objectives under study. This static information is then used to construct a bottom-up specification of the changes in the object states, and thus identify model dynamics. The approach promises to lead to models which are internally consistent and thus eliminate error.

3.7.2 Automatic program generation

Models differ in scope. Simple systems, with well-defined templates, can be represented by generic models, for example SIMFACTORY and PCModel. More complex systems, if they have an underlying structure such as a flow network, can be built with program generators. The program generators that have been demonstrated (DRAFT, TESS and RESQ) have taken their input from a network representation. If the formal specification of the system theoretic approach proves to be practical this will widen the choice of underlying structures. It is a goal of software engineers to define a precise system specification language. Should a mechanism with correctness-maintaining transformations be produced, then code will be generated directly from the model specification language; that is, from the language in which the system extracts the model from a database according to a known set of experimental objectives.

An alternative approach, one which is not excluded by the integrated representation but can exist outside, is the increased use of macro-modules. RESQME is an example of such software. Access to submodel or macro-model libraries will be an important area as the hardware speeds increase to permit more complex models to be written and run. The integration of macro-modules and a modular environment, like TESS, is a sensible broader development.

For even less familiar systems, the group at Virginia Tech. have advocated access to a rapid prototyping system for the purpose of testing ideas or requirements and accelerating the learning process. Meanwhile Birtwistle looks forward to the provision of specialist editors, with a knowledge of the language syntax, which would provide an improved interface with simulation languages.

3.7.3 Program debugging

The automatic coding of a model from a system specification reduces the need for error-checking. However the diversity of systems is such that not all models can be built in this way. Simple trace messages that can be switched on and off without overheads are necessary. It has been suggested that models be tested against known systems—thus a particular project could be simplified to represent an analytically tractable model and the theoretical and simulation results compared. Birtwistle notes that, even if the model is derived automatically from a system specification, it is possible that the original specification is in error. A convenient simulation of the system, accessible during model development, will provide subjective evidence of correctness. The interpretative execution of intermediate files, as in JADE, is thus a possible aid to verification as between the specification and the real world. In consort with the other tools suggested, it should improve reliability.

During debugging, animation is valuable as the screen reflects the model state in a code-free context. Thus it enables model logic to be monitored by independent specialists. In a limited exposure to animation this author identified two problems which would have been otherwise hidden. In one case it showed that an established program which had been hitherto unchallenged, permitted a robot to use the same physical space for two components. In another case it disclosed that upgrading between two program releases had not included proper dimensioning and so stray activity appeared on the screen, reflecting minor mayhem in the factory logic.

3.7.4 Simulation experiments

Simulation requires special statistical tools; these are seldom provided and they are often inadequate when they are. Law (1983) has shown how poorly most analysis techniques estimate the behaviour of even the simplest system — an M/M/1 queue. A system which provides analysis support should include information about the performance of the tools. This is clearly an area where artificial intelligence might apply. Apart from the use of confidence interval estimation, output can take other forms. It is envisaged that the experimental frame could be front-ended with a pre-processor to indicate the nature of the output processing, for example sensitivity analysis, control of parameter ranges and use of a search technique for maximisation or minimisation of particular values.

3.7.5 Project management and documentation

A consideration in managing development teams is the current skills portfolio of the individuals. An earlier section of this chapter spent some time in discussing the essential similarity of most simulation languages. It stressed that for the entity cycle diagram there is no coding tool which is uniquely feasible. It follows, then, that the use of 'high-level' modelling concepts like the entity cycle diagram is more effective over a broader range of programming expertise than is the policy of marrying, *ab initio*, the system to a high-level language. High-level tools remove a real constraint on the use of simulation, the lack of skilled staff and the difficulty of importing, say Pascal programmers, to work in a FORTRAN environment.

Documentation changes its nature throughout the life of a project. Program generators can provide a level of documentation appropriate to the user of a specific model. Complex models require working documents for information interchanges between development groups. This can be another output of the system specification database and its associated procedures. It is a problem which has been addressed by software engineering texts.

3.7.6 Management access

The busy manager wishes to see the output of a model but may only be interested in a restricted set of parameters. The modeller, on the other hand, may have many intermediate results to check. This is an important difference in emphasis. One solution is, as in many of the generic models, to keep all output and provide a friendly selection mechanism, illustrated best by RESQME. The overheads of such a policy may be excessive, but it is possible to provide alternative outputs by way of specialist libraries. One library could be used for the experimental sessions and the long runs, another for the more 'subjective' appreciation by a manager.

Similarly managerial expectations for access to models arises from exposure to graphics and animation, and thus the measure of adequate presentation may differ between decision-makers and programmers. The quality and detail of graphics presentation is not a current topic, largely because few systems offer great flexibility in this regard. However DRAFT/DRAW demonstrates how the entity cycle diagram can be displayed either in its original form, with the software managing the layout, or in a representational form which mimics the perceived system and omits artificial devices used for programming purposes.

Figure 3.13 illustrates the concept with three different pictures, the first two driven from the same program. The first picture is a mapping of the entity cycle diagram, the second shows icons replacing the abstract concepts of 'activity' and 'queue'. It also illustrates how the presentation of management-level information is often most successful if redundant detail is omitted. In this concept the three symbols of a lathe which is idle, being loaded, running, waiting for unloading and being cleared are all represented by one basic icon. In the third picture the icons of a similar application have been replaced by actual diagrams of the factory layout. Thus, the model state can be selectively presented, and it follows that differing presentations could be simultaneously available for different users.

Apart from the different levels of detail, the manager requires information quickly. RESQ, and at a more approximate level XCELL, illustrate how hybrid models can give good results when the model

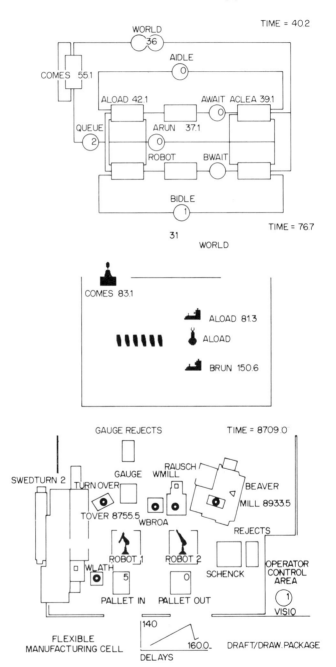

Figure 3.13 DRAFT/DRAW graphics.

Current Research and Progress 97

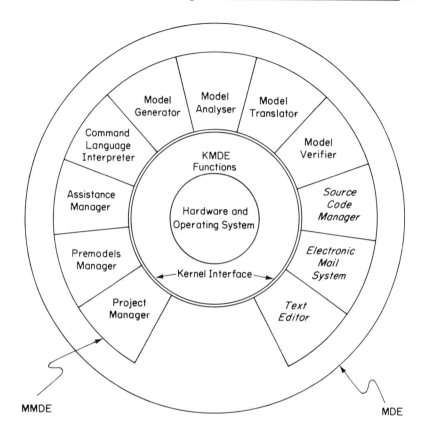

Figure 3.14 The structure of model development environments. (From Nance R.E. (1983) Dept of Computing Science, Virginia Polytechnic Institute).

can be presented in a simplified and analytically tractable form. Alternatively a database management system could be provided to interpolate between the results of prior experiments.

3.8 Conclusions

Most, if not all, of the features which have been discussed exist to some degree in the current software. One should, incidentally, recollect that this chapter has not covered all available software. It has presented excerpts from the current range with a view to illustrating the particular features desirable in a simulation support environment. These features can be assembled in a coherent way, as suggested by Figure 3.14. However, it is not reasonable to assume that every model-builder will have access to such an integrated system. The providers of software are responding at every level from the integrated environment of TESS to the spreadsheet ease of ModelMaster or XCELL. It is probable that, whatever the future developments, the software will focus on the development environment rather than the model representation, and the difference will be in the scope of the decision support environment rather than the 'power' of model representation.

The existence of a structure underlying simulation models leads to an approach whereby other methods are used to 'solve' the model and estimate some parameters of system performance. Normally these parameters are a restricted subset of those available from a full simulation experiment — for example the mean queue size or waiting time may be given. This contrasts with the full information available from the trajectory of the queue size which is generated by simulation.

3.9 References

Abed, S. Y., Barta, T. A. and McRoberts, K. L. (1985). A quantitative comparison of three simulation languages: GPSS/H, SLAM, SIMSCRIPT: *Computers and Industrial Engineerin*, **9**, 45–66.

Ariav, G. and Ginzberg, M.J. (1985) DSS design: a systemic view of decision support. *Comm: AC*, **2**(10), 1045–52.

Banks, J. and Carson, II, J. S. (1985) Process-interaction Simulation Languages. *Simulation*, **44**(5), 225–36.

Birtwistle, G. and Luker, P. (1985), Dialogs for simulation. *Simulation in Strongly Typed Languages: Ada, Pascal, Simula*. Simulation Series, Vol. 13, No. 2, SCS, pp. 90–5.

Clementson, A. T. (1985) *ECSL* — Extended Control and Simulation: System Users' Manual. Cle. Com, Ltd, Birmingham.

Cobbin, P. (1986) *SIMPLE 1: A Simulation Environment for the IBM PC, Modeling and Simulation on the Microcomputer* (ed. C. C. Barnett) Society for Computer Simulation, pp. 243–48.

Conway, R., Maxwell, W. and Worona, S. (1986) *XCELL: Factory Modelling System*. Scientific Press, USA.

Cox, S. (1987) Interactive graphics in GPSS/PC^{TM}. *Simulation*, **49**(3), 117–22.

Engi, D. (1985) Maintainability analysis using Q-GERT network simulation. *Simulation*, **4**(2), 67–74.

Gordon, G. (1962) A General Purpose System Simulation Program, *Proc. Eastern Joint Computer Conference, Washington DC*. Macmillan.

References

IBM (1970) *GPSS V Users Manual*. Form No. SH20–0851, IBM Corporation, White Plains, New York.

IBM (1977) *APL GPSS Users Manual*. Form No. SH20-1942, IBM Corporation, White Plains, New York.

IBM (1981) *PL/1 GPSS Users Manual*. IBM Corporation, White Plains, New York.

Krasnow, H. S. and Merikallio, R. A. (1964) The past, present and future of general simulation languages. *Management Science*, **11**(2), 236-67.

Kurose, J. F., Gordon, K. J., Gordon, R. F., MacNair, E. A. and Welch, P. D. (1986) A graphics-oriented modeler's workstation environment for the RESearch Queueing Package (RESQ). *Proc. ACM/IEEE Fall Joint Computer Conference.*

Laughery, K. R. (1985) Modelling human operators on a microcomputer: a micro version of SAINT. *Simulation*, **44**(1), 10–16.

Law, A. M. (1983) Statistical analysis of simulation output data. *Operations Research*, **3**(6), 983–1029.

Lenz, J. E. (1980) *MAST User's Manual*. CMS Research Inc., Oshkosh, Wisconsin.

Lenz, J. E. (1983) MAST: a simulation tool for designing computerised metalworking factories. *Simulation*, **41**(8) 51–8.

Luker, P. A. and Stephenson J. (1978) Simulation without programs. *Proc. 1978 UKSC Conference on Computer Simulation.* IPC Science and Technology Press.

Luker, P. A. and Burns, A. (1986) Program generators and generation software. *Computer Journal*, **29**(4), 315–21.

Mathewson, S. C. (1974) Simulation program generators, *Simulation*, **23**(6), 181–9.

Mathewson, S. C. (1985) Simulation program generators: code and animation on a PC. *Journal of the Operational Research Society*, **3**.(7), 583–9.

Mathewson, S. C. (1987) Draft/Draw/SSIM—an integrated network based toolkit for simulation. *Proc: 1987 UKSC Conference on Computer Simulation* (ed. R. N. Zobel). UKSC pp. 154–159.

McArthur, D. and Sowizral, H. (1986) An object-oriented language for constructing simulations. *Proc. 7th International Joint Conference on AI.*

O'Donovan, T. M. (1979) *GPSS Simulation Made Simple*. Wiley-Interscience, New York.

Pidd, M. (1988) *Computer Simulation in Management Science*, 2nd edn. John Wiley & Sons, Chichester.

Pritsker, A. A. B. (1979) *Modeling and Analysis using Q-Gert Networks* (2nd edn.). Halstead Press, John Wiley & Sons, New York.

Roberts, S. D. (1983) *Simulation Modelling and Analysis with INSIGHT*. Regenstrief Institute, Indianapolis, Indiana. Distributors: oSystech Inc., USA.

Rozenblit, J. W. (1986) A conceptual basis for integrated, model-based system design. Technical Report, Department of Electrical and Computer

Engineering. College of Engineering and Mines, University of Arizona (January).

Schriber, T. (1974) *Simulation Using GPSS*. Wiley-Interscience, New York.

Schriber, T. J. (1987) Perspectives on simulation using GPSS. *Proc. 1987 Winter Simulation Conference*, pp. 112–125.

Schroes, B. J., Black, J. T. and Zhang, S. X. (1985) Just-in-time (JIT), with Kanban, manufacturing system simulation on a microcomputer. *Simulation*, **45**(2), 62–70.

SIMSOFT (1986) *PCModel Manual*. SIMSOFT, San José, California, USA.

Standridge, C. R. (1985) Performing simulation projects with the extended simulation system (TESS). *Simulation*, **45**(6), 283–91.

Standridge, C. R. (1986) A tutorial on TESS. *Proc. 1986 Winter Simulation Conference*.

Subrahmanian, E. and Cannon, R. L. (1981) A generator program for models of discrete systems. *Simulation*., (March), 93–101.

Unger, B., Birtwistle, G., Cleary, J., Hill, D., Lomov, G., Neale, R., Peterson, M., Witten, I. and Wyvill, B. (1984) JADE: a simulation and software prototyping environment. *Proc. SCS Conference, La Jolla, 198.* (eds R. Bryant and B. W. Unger), pp. 77–83.

Wortman, D. B. *et al.* (1978), *Simulation Using SAINT: A User-Oriented Instruction Manual*. Aerospace Medical Research Laboratory, AMRL-TR-77-61. Wright-Patterson AFB, Ohio (July).

Ziegler, B. P. (1985) System-theoretic representation of simulation models. *IIE Transaction*, **16**(1), 19–34.

Ziegler, B. P. and De Wael, L. (1986), Towards a knowledge-based implementation of multifaceted modelling methodology. *Proc. European Conference on AI Applied to Simulation*. Published as *Simulation*, series **18**(1).

Zeigler, B. P., Belogus, D. and Bolshoi, A. (1980) ESP—an interactive tool for system structuring. *Proc. 1980 European Meeting on Cybernetics and Systems Research*. Hemisphere Press.

Computer Modelling for Discrete Simulation
Edited by M. Pidd
©1989 John Wiley & Sons Ltd

4
Graphics and Interaction

R. D. Hurrion

4.1 Introduction

The use of computer graphics has rapidly expanded over the past few years. Until the early 1980s computer graphics technology was expensive, and was available only on large mainframe computers. It is now possible to buy small home computers that have excellent graphics and animation facilities. Thus computer graphics are replacing the more traditional printed report as a presentation medium. Business graphics use charts, pie diagrams, graphs and histograms to display information, while in education and entertainment computer-generated animation films are becoming common.

This chapter considers the role of computer graphics for discrete event simulation in management science. The use of animated computer graphics is now an integral part of a simulation project. Computer graphics assist in all phases of a simulation project, from its initial problem specification to final project implementation.

Until relatively recently, computer simulation has been confined to large mainframe computers operating in batch mode. The advent of powerful personal computers has meant that substantial computer simulation applications can now be implemented on dedicated inexpensive micro-computer equipment. The use of micro-computing has also meant that it is now cost-effective to use graphics in the form of an animated display to show the dynamics of particular models. It is now common for managers, engineers and decision-makers to run simulation models of complex industrial situations. Instead of relying on printed results at the end of a simulation it is now possible to watch the dynamics of a model unfold in the form of a semi-pictorial silent film. Equally important is the fact that, if experienced users can watch the dynamics of a model, then it is possible for them to stop the running of a model and interact with it in order to try different decision strategies.

The concept of linking graphics with discrete event simulation began in the mid-1970s and became standard practice by the mid-1980s. Different methodologies on the use of simulation graphics have emerged from North America and the UK. The technique adopted in North America is to use high-resolution colour graphics terminals to animate the dynamics of a simulation, but not let the user interact with the model while it is running. This approach is often called post-processing or 'playback' graphics. The method that has become common practice within the UK is known as visual interactive simulation (Hurrion and Secker, 1978). This technique uses graphics to animate a model as it is running, but also allows a user to interact during the execution of the model. This method has distinct advantages during the initial stages of a project when both client and simulation analyst are searching for a suitable simulation model to represent the original problem. But the method can be dangerous if unrestricted use of user interaction is allowed during the experimental design phase of a simulation project.

This chapter will comment on the role of graphics and interaction in simulation projects.

4.2 The Graphics Approach

The basic approach of including graphics within a simulation model is described by Pidd (1988), and consists of an analyst building a simulation model (computer-based) of some problem situation. The model has a graphics component so that the user commissioning the study can observe, in a suitable animated form, the dynamics of the model. The user is then able to use his or her own expert knowledge, experience and judgement of the original problem domain in order to interact with the model and experiment with alternative decision scenarios. The key aspect of the graphics simulation approach is that it incorporates an animated dynamic display to represent the system under investigation.

The improved communication which the animated graphics bring to the simulation is of particular importance at the multiple interfaces between client, analyst and model. The approach has

The Graphics Approach

helped managers gain confidence in the use of a model, because they have then been better able to criticise it, while still contributing to its validation. In most visual simulation applications the simulation technique has become transparent; it is no longer regarded as a 'black-box' method, which in turn has helped the user gain a better insight into the original problem.

4.2.1 Graphics methods for simulation

There are basically two types of graphics animation used for discrete event simulation. Both of these methods are constrained by current graphics hardware technology. As graphics hardware becomes cheaper and more cost-effective it is certain that interactive graphics systems will begin to use three-dimensional and holographic model representation on a routine basis. The current graphics methods for discrete event simulation are known as character graphics and bit-mapped graphics. The specific hardware and software methods for micro-computer graphics are described by Johnson (1987). The two basic representational methods can be summarised as:

1. *Character graphics.* Most common micro-computer screens are text-based. Text can be placed on the screen at locations defined by a grid of 24 rows by 80 columns. The repeated drawing and erasing text at slightly different locations will give the impression of elements moving. This simple technique can give a surprisingly realistic view of a simulation model, especially if colour is used to code elements in a model, for example the status of machines in a manufacturing simulation.
2. *High resolution bit-mapped graphics.* The technology for high-resolution bit-mapped graphics is improving dramatically, and becoming increasingly cost-effective. With a high-resolution bit-mapped screen the display area is also divided up into a grid. The grid will typically consist of 640 rows by 480 columns. The intersection of a row and column is known as a pixel (picture element) and, typically, that point can be displayed by any of one to sixteen different colours. The cost of graphics cards, which can be added to micro-computers, and the cost of graphics workstations, is still reducing in price and even higher graphics resolution for simulation work will be economic. Experimental systems have been developed which use a three-dimensional approach.

Careful consideration should be given to the role of graphics within a simulation. The effort of producing an animated display can be high, and the processing overheads to run the animation may be excessive. Sufficient realism is needed to represent the problem, but excessive graphics may be counter- productive. It still needs to be shown that high-quality displays, usually associated with CAD systems, are necessary for management science simulation applications.

4.2.2 Management science graphics simulation history

The idea of animating and allowing simulation models to be interactive has taken some time to become established in the management science community. Donovan et al. (1968), Harverty (1968), Bell (1969), and Katske (1975) describe early graphical facilities for simulation. Sulonen (1972) documents the use of graphics to build block GPSS simulation models which are then run in a conventional batch manner, and Sohnle et al. (1973) suggest general requirements for interactive simulation. Bazjanac (1976) describes an animated interactive simulation which considers the emergency evacuation of people from high-rise buildings using elevators, and Palme (1977) comments on the advantage of having 'moving displays' generated by SIMULA simulation models. Hurrion (1976) developed interactive simulation and animation methods for operational and production-related problems. This led to applications of visual interactive simulation in batch manufacturing industries (Brown, 1978), process chemical plants (Fisher, 1982) and facilities design in the automotive industry (Fiddy et al., 1981).

The majority of the early management science visual interactive modelling applications used simulation; however, Lembersky and Chi (1984) developed an application technique which they describe as a decision simulator. In one of their examples a dynamic programming formulation is used to develop optimal forestry and tree-cutting strategies. An interactive and animated graphics component was added to the model, which then gave a realistic training environment for forestry staff.

The software used by operational research practitioners to support graphics simulating applications is also becoming extensive. It can vary from small micro-computer menu-driven systems through to the use of high-resolution graphics supported by mainframe computing. Pope (1984), Bell (1984) and Bell and O'Keefe

(1987) catalogue current graphics animation for manufacturing systems and general visual simulation software. A recent set of conferences, 'Simulation in Manufacturing' (Heginbotham, 1985, Micheletti, 1987), also document the role of graphics and animation within manufacturing.

4.3 Visual Interactive Simulation

This section describes the method of visual interactive simulation. A key component, unlike that advocated in the USA, is of allowing interaction during the execution of a model. The technique of visual interactive simulation consists of:

1 developing a simulation model of the system under investigation;
2 incorporating a method of animating the model using one or more colour graphics terminals. The dynamic animated view of the model ensures that the client commissioning the original study can observe the model in the form of a 'video' film. This has been shown to be of considerable help in removing the communications barrier that may exist between analyst and client with regard to the modelling technique and its assumptions. If a client can observe how a model is progressing through time then he/she is in a position to:
3 interact with the model in order to explore alternative decision strategies.

Having a visual dynamic representation of a model, and the ability to interact with it, are the key components.

The major contribution that interactive graphics has had, and probably will continue to have, is the ability to improve the communications and language barriers which exist between different management and professional staff for an application. Visual interactive simulation is like a voyage of discovery (Fiddy *et al.*, 1981). The client/clients have their own perception of the target system. If the simulation approach is perceived to be applicable, then the analyst/analysts will be employed first to develop a formal model. The analyst, via interviews and observations, then establishes his own perceptions of the problem (quite often this will be in a mathematical form). The animated interactive model has tended to act as an interpreter between these different cultures. Thus the main thrust of the visual simulation work has been to improve communications between analyst and user, so that both have an improved understanding of the problem. This improved understanding has led to insights, and has been the catalyst by which new policy rules have been articulated (Fiddy *et al.*, 1981).

4.4 Graphics and Simulation Examples

Some visual interactive simulation applications are now described, to give the reader an insight into the approach. The whole essence of the method is that a visual interactive dynamic model gives a better insight into an application than a static report will ever achieve. The school-teacher's adage, 'a picture is worth a thousand words', is appropriate. With regard to visual interactive simulation this should be extended to: 'a picture is worth a thousand words, but an interactive graphical model is worth a thousand pictures'.

An example of the visual interactive simulation technique acting as a communications catalyst between an OR team and a production manager is documented by Brown (1978). This application is briefly described below.

An OR project team had developed a complex manufacturing simulation which considered alternative batch scheduling rules. The two rules of particular interest were 'Least stock per operation (LSPO) and expect lateness (EL)'. The rules, when used in the simulation model, gave answers which were opposite to what one might intuitively expect. The model and rules were believed to be correct but the OR team had substantial difficulty in convincing the production management staff as to their validity. The project stalled at this phase, and any thoughts of implementation were not considered until the (simulation) model could be demonstrated as valid.

A simplified visual simulation experiment was developed in order to help communicate and understand the dynamics of various scheduling policies. The simplified model was:

> Components enter a flow shop at a fixed rate of one item every six minutes. The flow shop consists of six machines. Each component must be processed in sequence at each machine, i.e. machine 1, followed machine 2, ... concluding with machine 6. A component takes one minute to be processed at each machine and the transfer time between machines is assumed to be zero. An operator is also

Graphics and Simulation Examples 107

needed to assist in the processing of a component at each of the machines.

Suppose the first component arrives at time zero and that there is only one operator, then the question posed, once a suitable visual interactive simulation model had been constructed, was:

If the work in progress at each machine consists of two components, what difference, if any, would occur if the rules,

1 process the next batch with the least number of operations remaining, or
2 process the next batch with the most number of operations remaining were used?

This example problem is reasonably simple and deterministic. Components arrive every six minutes and each component takes exactly six minutes of processing time.

This question was given to simulation analysts and production managers. Participants were given a limited time in order to state their intuitive answer. The answers ranged from 'no difference in work in progress between the rules', to 'some small increase in work in progress'.

Given the initial starting conditions then:

1 using the rule which chooses the job with the fewest operations remaining gives a stable solution of seven components waiting at the first machine with one further component being processed;
2 using the second rule gives a stable solution of forty-three components waiting for their final operation with one component being progressed.

This substantial increase in work in progress (over 500%) was not anticipated.

Clearly a complete prior analysis could have established the correct result; however, this simple visual interactive simulation model was used as a catalyst which helped to unlock one fixed management perception. Most practical industrial problems are far more complex than the example shown above. But if a visual interactive model can help in this small example then the technique is likely to be of use in more complex industrial problems. Current experience of using interactive graphics in simulation suggests that this statement is true.

There is a view that a major difficulty in a simulation study is that of persuading the owner of a problem to change his/her mind (Boothroyd, 1978). If the manager and management scientist came to a problem with no preconceived notions, then this task should be easier. Normally, however, implementation of a project will involve the owner of the problem 'unmaking' his mind. The visual interactive simulation approach tends not to feed the manager with results, but allows him to search for alternative solutions himself.

A further example showing the importance of animation in a training role is given by Lembersky and Chi (1984). They describe a forestry application which involves the optimal cutting of high-value North American West Coast Douglas Firs. Operational decisions with regard to optimal tree-cutting and logging have to be taken on site. A visual interactive model was developed, called a decision simulator, using high-resolution graphics to display trees. An operator, using a joystick, can rotate, turn, or generally view a tree from any angle. The operator can then simulate the cutting of the tree and then immediately compare his answers with the optimal solution available from a dynamic programming formulation. The authors report on the power of the visual model in this training environment. Forestry operators, with considerable practical experience, were exposed to this 'decision simulator' which improved the quality of their operational tree and logging decisions. Savings of $7 million per year are reported.

Both of these examples were described in some detail to indicate to the reader the power, immediacy and learning which can occur from linking interactive graphics with simulation. In both examples the formal mathematical modelling techniques of simulation and dynamic programming are known to management science practitioners; however, the major difficulty of most projects is the transfer of these modelling insights to the client.

Numerous interactive graphics manufacturing simulation applications have been reported. See for example, Goodhead and Mahoney (1985), Looney and Warby (1985), Chan (1982), Nenonen *et al.*(1981), Norman (1984), Udo *et al.*(1985) and Anderen (1984). One particular example considered the storage of car bodies between the spot-welding and finish-welding lines. After a car body has been spot-welded it proceeds to a lift point where a sling transports it to a buffer store. The buffer store consists of a number of parallel conveyors. After leaving the store the sling and car body move to a drop section where a finish-welding operation occurs. The plant layout also contained bypass loops so that slings can re-cycle. The original software which controlled the plant was such that, on occasions, lanes and conveyors became blocked.

A visual interactive simulation model of the store and its proposed control rules was built. Management and analysts were then able to observe an animated view of the plant. Running the model, observing its dynamic characteristics and evaluating alternatives were important stimuli in designing the rules which were finally used to control the plant (Fiddy et al., 1981).

Further examples of graphic animation of the output of a flexible manufacturing system are described by Wortman and Wilson (1984). The application they describe uses colour graphics to model ten horizontal milling machines, which are in turn serviced by a combination of raw material input, conveyor transportation, inspection and robot loading stations. The authors state in conclusion that

> a facility diagram can be animated to allow the engineers to actually see the operations . . . such animations are key elements in the presentation of results to decision makers.

Nenonen (1981) has developed visual interactive simulations with special reference to the mining industry; while Rogers (1978) describes a visual model appropriate to the chemical industry.

The list of visual interactive modelling applications is substantial and growing. Bell and O'Keefe (1987) comment that graphics and animation in the form of visual interactive simulation is the most important advance in discrete event simulation since the introduction of specialist simulation languages in the late 1950s.

4.5 Display and Interaction Methods

Current simulation display methods have concentrated on two types of graphics display, and two approaches to interaction have been employed to provide smooth and safe experimentation.

4.5.1 Schematic display

The majority of visual interactive simulation applications have tended to use dynamic displays which aim to mimic the operational characteristics of the system under study. This is particularly true of the manufacturing/flexible manufacturing systems/chemical applications where the development of suitable visual mimic or blueprint diagrams would seem to be a natural method of displaying the model (Goodhead and Mahoney, 1985; Anderen, 1984; Fisher, 1982; Hollocks, 1983).

4.5.2 Logical display

The second type of animated displays have tended to take the form of logical representations of the system under investigation. These logical representations have taken the form of bar charts, time-series and histogram graphics. They have been used when the main component of the model is financial (Bell, 1984), or for complex models where it is sensible only to show summary measures of performance (Bell and O'Keefe, 1987).

4.5.3 Passive versus interactive graphics

It is important to comment on the different ways that graphics have been incorporated within discrete event simulation. In North America the method tends to use a passive graphics approach so that the user can only watch the progress of a simulation but cannot interact with it and alter its progress. The UK approach will allow user interaction at run-time. This method is much richer, since it allows the experience of the client to be part of the search for an acceptable solution. The danger in allowing a user to interact with a model in an unrestricted manner is that the statistical significance of any results is harder to obtain. It would seem preferable to allow user interaction during simulation execution, since it gives a much richer set of decision policies for the user.

4.5.4 Entity interaction

A model which includes animated graphics puts the client in a position to use his/her experience to alter the execution of the model. The original method of interaction proposed (Hurrion, 1976) was to allow the user to modify any attribute of any entity in the model. This approach was powerful, but it meant that only the

Display and Interaction Methods

analyst, who wrote the original model, could make safe and valid changes because of the complexity and low level of the interaction.

4.5.5 Menu interaction

One way of preventing incorrect use of low-level entity interactions is to use a 'bullet-proofing' method which only allows a user to interact with the model from a model-specific menu. The objective of this menu is to shield the user from the model so that the client can only make predetermined parameter changes to a model. An example of this technique (Fisher, 1982) was developed for a chemical plant simulation model. The model itself was complex, consisting of stochastic arrivals of raw materials, continuous and discrete manufacturing operations occurring over both two- and three-shift operations.

Allowing the user unrestricted access to the model was unsuccessful, and therefore a structure to the interactions was needed. A menu of interactions was developed so that the client could simulate decisions such as changing product feeds, altering product manufacturing sequences or changing possible shift patterns. It was important to build an interaction shell or window that gave controlled access to the model in the 'language of the client', and not using the language of the simulation analyst.

This concept of producing an interaction menu specifically 'owned' and designed for each simulation project is equally as important as the design of unique animation displays for a model. The approach of producing specific interactions which are 'owned' by the model may seem restrictive, but has the advantage of only making pre-programmed valid changes to a model. It is thus much harder for a client to 'break the model'.

This method of 'bullet-proofing' a model with its own set of unique menu options is now common practice. A hierarchy or tree structure menu can be used for complex interactions with a model (Da Silva, 1982). This technique makes it possible to add pre-programmed rules to a model, and thus start to add the user's or client's expertise to the problem. For example, in the chemical simulation model outlined above 'warning' levels exist for each storage tank in the model. If a tank is filled past its warning level an interaction occurs, telling the user, and advising on the methods of dealing with this exception condition. The combination of graphics animation and structured interactions is thus very powerful, since the knowledge and experience of operational staff can be added to the model.

4.6 Phases of a Management Science Simulation Project

This section outlines the different phases of a simulation project and describes the contribution that graphics and interactions can make when linked to a simulation model. The phases of a typical management science simulation project are

1 formulation and model specification
2 model development
3 model verification
4 model validation
5 experimental design
6 implementation

The first four phases are all concerned with the development of a valid model of the system under investigation. With the introduction of the interactive graphical simulation approach the four phases are now more closely linked, and a prototyping method is used to produce an exploratory model which is then continuously refined until a valid model of sufficient complexity is obtained.

The initial phase of a simulation project is concerned with the investigation of the original problem. Consider a manufacturing system: problem investigation consists of working with the client in order to specify a model in sufficient, but not over-complex, detail. The use of similar manufacturing simulation models, if they exist, is a useful method of helping to specify a model of the system under investigation. It is far easier to offer constructive criticism of an existing model than it is to create an abstract specification. Once an outline problem has been formulated the technique is to get an initial visual simulation model developed and working as soon as possible. This prototype can be criticised by the client in order to improve the model specification. Thus an evolutionary process of developing a model is adopted so that both analyst and client can check the validity of the model and the level of detail of it. Progress in the first four phases of a simulation project is thus greatly eased by the use of graphics and interaction facilities. They help both the analyst and

Intelligent Visual Interactive Simulation

client to be confident that the model is a valid representation of the system under investigation.

The next phase of a simulation project, once a valid model has been obtained, is to use the model to try alternative decision strategies or, more formally, to undertake the experimental design. This phase of a visual interactive simulation project has been criticised because an unstructured use of the model's interaction may easily invalidate the results of simulation experiments. A set of well-conducted simulation experiments should not allow user interaction while a model is running. If this occurs the integrity of the simulation experiment is not lost. However, the very process of designing a visual simulation model will stimulate the user into articulating the types of experiment and decision strategies to be tested.

The final phase of a simulation, implementation, is also assisted by using graphics and animation. Changing or leaving a system unaltered will both have operational, organisational and cost implications. A suitable visual simulation model can thus assist in the presentation of alternative decision strategies, which in turn help clarify the implementation of those decisions.

The use of graphics and interaction is now standard practice for most discrete event simulation studies. The powerful technique of simulation does not now remain with the simulation analyst, but is now used by the manager in a search for an acceptable solution. The very fact that the technique is powerful has led to difficulties. The major problem is that interacting with the execution of a model may destroy the statistical validity of that model, and it is possible to obtain misleading results based on sample sizes which are too small. The simulation technique used to be carried out by an analyst who would have had sufficient training for the statistical design of a simulation project. The use of interactive graphics now allows the client to use the visual interactive simulation model themselves. While this approach is highly preferable to that of excluding the client from the analysis phase of a project, care must be taken to ensure the results are valid.

4.7 Intelligent Visual Interactive Simulation

The previous sections of this chapter have described the current practice of linking graphics with discrete event simulation. The benefits of using the method have been described. The main difficulty of the method is the fact that an interactive simulation model will be used by an (experienced) manager but there is no method within the current visual interactive framework by which this expertise can be retained by the model for future use. The interaction facility of current visual interactive models is passive. The user must decide when to interact, what action to take and when to accept the validity of the results. The expertise of the user is lost and not retained by the simulation project.

This section describes the next generation of visual interactive models which allow the model itself to take an active role in a search for a solution. The interactive facility now becomes 'two-way'. The user may interrupt the execution of a model, or an advisory and monitoring function within the model can interrupt its own execution and suggest to the user alternative model parameters or experiments. The possibility of giving visual interactive models a learning and intelligent aspect is due to recent advances in artificial intelligence. Linking simulation and artificial intelligence is described in Chapters 5 and 6 but the concept of giving models intelligent interaction facilities is discussed below.

4.7.1 Monitoring

The concept of adding an expert interactive component to a visual simulation model is described by Flitman and Hurrion (1987), and Taylor and Hurrion (1988). The method consists of adding a PROLOG component to a model. This component acts as a monitoring device. The PROLOG module contains a monitoring facility and can watch the progress of a model. An experienced simulation analyst will have a set of rules which determine if a model is in a steady state and can be used to collect statistically valid results.

A simple example of such a rule is 'run a model for some time and observe one or more key variables; the model can be described as in a steady state if the average of the key variables approach constant values . . .'. There are numerous rules that can be used, which are described by Law and Carson (1979). The PROLOG monitoring module contains a set of rules to determine a steady state. When a user now interacts with a model all recording methods can be turned off until the PROLOG advisory module determines that the state of the model is once again in a statistically valid state for recording to continue.

Intelligent Visual Interactive Simulation   115

4.7.2 Learning

The PROLOG module will also monitor the state and type of interactions carried out by a user. The expert PROLOG component can record the interactions of a user and when they occurred. An example of this approach is described by Flitman and Hurrion (1987). A visual interactive simulation model was used to represent the operations of a depot. The depot had random arrivals of different types of vehicle which needed to pass through the depot with the task of loading and unloading stock.

The simulation model was programmed so that it was devoid of any control logic. Five people were asked to control the model by allocating different resources within the model while it was running. The PROLOG module was able to monitor the type and style of interactions made by each user, and hence learn how each person allocated resources to control the model. Each person received a 'score' on his or her ability at controlling the model. After all five people had run the model the control knowledge of the five trainers was combined and used by the PROLOG module to control the simulation model itself. The combined control knowledge extracted from each user was able to run the original problem equally as well as any of its five trainers, and for one combination did better than any of the original five users. The experiment described above was small in that each of the five human trainers only had to control two resources while the model was running; however, it suggests intelligent components can be added to simulation models which learn by monitoring their own and the user's performance. Once the intelligent component has learnt control strategies it can intelligently interact with the model and pass its advice back to the user.

4.7.3 Simulation experiment advisor

Shannon has commented that up to 700 hours tuition may be required to train a person to become proficient in the practice of simulation (Shannon *et al.*, 1985). Adding graphics and interactive facilities to simulation models has made them accessible to busy managers and executives who probably would not have had the necessary simulation and statistical training. As described above, visual interactive simulation models are very easy to interact with and use. However, this very ease of use can make the results of a simulation project invalid if incorrect simulation analysis and design methods are used. The PROLOG module described above is also used to act as an advisor for a client in helping to determine the correct type of experiments to carry out.

The simulation experimental advisor technique is described by Taylor and Hurrion (1988). The technique uses a PROLOG module which is attached to a simulation model. The PROLOG module learns about the simulation problem in an interactive dialogue with the user. The PROLOG module, also via the dialogue, asks about the type of analysis required, i.e.: Does the user just wish to evaluate a particular simulation configuration, compare two alternatives or try to find the best simulation configuration for a set of objectives? This level of interaction and dialogue with the user can be described as intelligent because the PROLOG component of the model is mimicking the role of an experienced simulation analyst in deciding what experiments to execute, their order, and how to interpret the results. The technique now links an interactive simulation (expert) advisor which controls the execution of a previously validated visual interactive simulation model.

The interactive advisory system will help the user set up simulation experiments such as

1   evaluation
2   comparison
3   prediction
4   sensitivity analysis
5   optimisation
6   functional relations
7   transient behaviour

The approach has been tested on an industrial flexible manufacturing visual interactive simulation model. It guided a non-simulation specialist to the same solution as that obtained by a simulation specialist who only had access to the visual interactive simulation model of the problem.

4.8 Conclusion

This chapter has described the history, role and impact that interactive graphics have had on the management science simulation discipline. Graphics and interactive methods have become an integral part of simulation methodology. The chapter has described the power of interactive graphics simulation and some of its dangers. The final section of the chapter indicates the possible future by making the interactive component of a model intelligent. The addition of interactive graphics to simulation has been a leap forward for the discipline of simulation. The addition of artificial intelligence methods to simulation could well be the next quantum advance for simulation.

4.9 References

Anderen, L. (1984) Animated CAD. *Systéms International*, November, pp. 25–9.

Bazjanac, V. (1976) Interactive simulation of building evacuation with elevators. *Proc. 9th Annual Simulation Symposium*, Florida, March, pp. 15–29.

Bell, P. C. (1984) Benefits and challenges of decision simulator techniques. Paper presented at the ORSA/TIMS Joint National Meeting, Dallas, November.

Bell, P. C. and O'Keefe, R. M. (1987) Visual interactive simulation: History, recent developments, and major issues. *Simulation*, 49(3), 109–16.

Bell, T. E. (1969), *Computer Graphics for Simulation Problem-Solving*. Rand Corp, Santa Monica, California.

Boothroyd, H. (1978), *Articulate Intervention*. Taylor & Francis, London.

Brown, J. C. (1978) Visual interactive simulation: further developments towards a generalised system and its use in three problem areas associated with a high-technology manufacturing company. M.Sc. thesis, University of Warwick.

Chan, A. W. (1982) Interactive computer modelling of conveyor systems. *CIM Bulletin*, November pp. 81–3.

Da Silva, C. M. (1982) The development of a DSS generator via action research. Ph.D. thesis, University of Warwick.

Donovan, J. J., Jones, M. M. and Alsop, J. W. (1969) A graphical facility for an interactive simulation system. *Proc. IFIP Congress*. North-Holland, Amsterdam.

Fiddy, E., Bright, J. G. and Hurrion, R. D. (1981) See-why: interactive simulation on the screen. *Proc. Institute of Mechanical Engineers*, **C293/81**, 167–172.

Fisher, M. J. W. (1982) The application of visual interactive simulation in the management of continuous process chemical plants. Ph.D. thesis, University of Warwick.

Flitman, A. M. and Hurrion, R. D. (1987) Linking discrete-event simulation models with expert systems. *Journal of the Operational Research Society*, **38,** 723–33.

Goodhead, T. C. and Mahoney, T. M. (1985) Experience in the use of computer simulation for FMS planning. *Proc. 1st International Conference on Simulation in Manufacturing*, Stratford, UK, March.

Harverty, J. P. (1968) *Grail GPSS: Graphic On-Line Modelling*, Rand Corp, Santa Monica, California.

Heginbotham, W. B. (ed.) (1985) *Simulation in Manufacturing*, IFS Publications, UK.

Hollocks, B. W. (1983) Simulation and the Micro. *Journal of the Operational Research Society*, **34**, 331–43.

Hurrion, R. D. (1976) The design use and required facilities of an interactive visual computer simulation language to explore production planning problems. Ph.D. thesis, University of London.

Hurrion, R. D. and Secker, R. J. R. (1978) Visual interactive simulation, an aid to decision making. *Omega*, **6**(5), 419–26.

Johnson, N. (1987) *Advanced Graphics in C*. McGraw-Hill, New York.

Katske, J. (1975) User's Guide NGPSS: Superset of GPSS V. Norden Report 4059, R0001, Norwalk, CT 134.

Law, A. M. and Carson, J. S. (1979) A sequential procedure for determining the length of steady state simulation. *Operations Research*, **27**, 1011–25.

Lembersky, M. R. and Chi, U. H. (1984) 'Decision simulators' speed implementation and improve operations. *Interfaces*, **14**(4), 1–15.

Looney, M. W. and Warby, A. H. (1985) Simulation in a high variety small batch FMS project — a case study. *Proc. 1st International Conference on Simulation in Manufacturing*, Stratford, UK, March.

Micheletti, G. F. (ed.) (1987) *Simulation in Manufacturing*. IFS (Conferences), Ltd.

Nenonen, L. K., Graefe, P. W. U. and Chan, A. W. (1981) Interactive computer modelling of truck shovel operations in an open-pit mine. *Proc. Winter Simulation Conference*, pp. 133–9.

Norman, T. A. (1984) Graphical simulation of flexible manufacturing systems. Proc. Winter Simulation Conference, Dallas, November.

Palme, J. (1977) Moving pictures show simulation to user. Simulation, **29**(b), 240–09.

Pidd, M. (1988) *Computer Simulation in Management Science*, 2nd ed. John Wiley & Sons, Chichester.

Pope, D. N. (1984) A review of graphics animation of manufacturing systems. *AUTOFACT 6, Conference Proceedings*, Anaheim, California, October.

Rogers, M. A. M. (1978) Interactive computing as an aid to decision making, in K. B. Haley (ed.), *Operations Research '78*. North-Holland, Amsterdam, 1979, pp. 829–42.

Shannon, R. E., Meyer, R. and Adelsberger, H. H. (1985) Expert systems and simulation. *Simulation*, **44**(6), 275–84.

Sohnle, R. C., Tartar, J. and Sampson, J. R. (1973) Requirements for interactive simulation systems. *Simulation*, **20**(5), 145–52.

Sulonen, R. K. (1972) On-line simulation with computer graphics. *On-Line-72*, Online Computer Systems, Brunel University.

References

Taylor, R. P. and Hurrion, R. D. (1988) An expert advisor for simulation experimental design and analysis. *Proc. Multi-Conference on Artificial Intelligence and Simulation*, (T. Henson, ed.). SCS International, San Diego, California.

Udo, P. W., Graefe, P. W. U. and Chan, A. W. (1985) A production control aid for managers of manufacturing plants. *Proc. 1st International Conference on Simulation in Manufacturing*, Stratford, UK, March.

Wortman, D. B. and Wilson, J. R. (1984) Optimising a manufacturing plant by computer simulation. *Computer-aided Engineering*, September.

Computer Modelling for Discrete Simulation
Edited by M. Pidd
©1989 John Wiley & Sons Ltd

5
Artificial Intelligence and Simulation Modelling

Ray J. Paul

5.1 Scene Setting

5.1.1 Artificial intelligence and simulation

Artificial intelligence (AI) is defined by Barr and Feigenbaum (1981) as 'the part of computer science concerned with designing intelligent computer systems, that is, systems that exhibit the characteristics we associate with intelligence in human behaviour — understanding language, learning, reasoning, solving problems, and so on'.

At first sight this definition does not readily suggest any relationship between simulation and AI. However, researchers and practitioners in both fields have faced quite similar problems in creating models of complex and sometimes partially understood systems. Despite this, solutions to such problems have largely been developed independantly in each discipline. This has led to software tools and techniques which often overlap conceptually if not in terminology. For example, the commonly used representation of a fact in a knowledge base, the IF–THEN rule, is similar to the method of testing for state changes in simulation.

AI researchers have recognised the relevance of simulation. For example, Campbell (1986) remarks about high-level programming in AI: 'workers in object-oriented programming in AI are discovering that techniques and facilities of use to them, e.g. for inheritance of properties, have already been invented by designers of simulation languages'. Campbell also claims that, whilst large programming projects in AI have some components of the mathematical modelling approach, as in simulation, they also possess a richer structure with no analogue in such modelling. One difference is that AI models make essential use of the heuristic level of their subject. A second asserted difference is due to the AI interest in intelligent behaviour. In this case AI applications usually require some explicit concentration on cause and effect in AI applications, while standard mathematical models are passive in this respect. Recognition of these points, and how they might be overcome, is emerging in published papers on AI and simulation, some of which are discussed below.

5.1.2 At the research stage

Researchers in AI and simulation are very enthusiastic about each other's area of expertise. Conference proceedings have been published on intelligent simulation environments (Luker and Adelsberger, 1986), AI graphics and simulation (Birtwhistle, 1985), AI applied to simulation (Kerckhoffs *et al.*, 1986) and AI and simulation (Holmes, 1985). Many papers have appeared in the literature linking the two disciplines, some of which will be discussed later. Many authors discuss proposed enhancements for modelling, intelligent enhancements to known modelling structures, new methods for writing simulations using AI techniques, the use of one approach with the other, the use of one approach to aid the other, etc. However, what is rarely discussed is a real application! Prototypes abound, experiments have been conducted galore, developments profusely develop, but live applications? — not yet.

There are two possible reasons for this lack of application. The first is the increasing cry that the AI emperor is wearing no intelligent clothes. This view has been succinctly put by Parnas (1985) in his critical essays on the proposed US strategic arms defence systems.

> Artificial intelligence has the same relation to intelligence as artificial flowers have to flowers. From a distance, they may appear much alike, but when closely examined they are quite different. I don't think we can learn much about one by studying the other. AI offers no magic technology to solve our problem. Heuristic techniques do not yield systems that one can trust.
>
> The latter point he reinforces by stating that the rules that one obtains by studying people turn out to be inconsistent, incomplete and inaccurate. Heuristic programs are developed by a trial and error

Scene Setting 123

process in which a new rule is added whenever one finds a case that is not tackled by the old rules. This approach usually yields a program whose behaviour is poorly understood and hard to predict.

The message is clear. The hype attached to the promise of AI may be speculative nonsense.

AI is concerned with the methodology and the structuring of software systems that are large, complex and have only recently been tractable with respect to computing memory and speed. Such systems will attempt to handle a wider variety of problems, encompassing a richness of variables, data and relationships. No major breakthrough in the understanding of social/economic problems has come about. But it is possible that the ability to develop larger well-structured systems can help with these problems. Possibly, then, understanding in these areas will improve with the usage of AI systems. Given this situation, the second reason for the lack of applications becomes clear. Progress has not been sufficient for confidence in current developments to be applied. This chapter therefore concentrates on those areas where research is promising, but avoids extravagant claims both current and for the future.

5.1.3 The computer-aided simulation modelling project

Some of the discussion of this chapter is amplified by experiences of the author, who co-directs a group of simulation researchers at the LSE in the computer-aided simulation modelling (CASM) project. An outline of the CASM research is given in Balmer and Paul (1986). The CASM project team has been working upon a flexible plan for developing computer aids to simulation modelling. Here we develop an overview of this plan.

Figure 5.1 illustrates the basic process of simulation model development as envisaged by CASM. The analyst formulates the problem in some structured way, for example as an activity cycle diagram (ACD) or a flow-chart. ACDs are described by Clementson (1982) and Poole and Szymankiewicz (1977), among others. The model logic thus defined is fed into an interactive simulation program generator (ISPG). As mentioned in Chapter 2, several ISPGs exist, such as CAPS by Clementson (1982); DRAFT, by Mathewson (1985); CASM.AUTOSIM, a Pascal emulation of CAPS, by Paul and Chew (1987), and VS6, by sysPACK Ltd (1988). Most ISPGs interactively interrogate the user about the problem ACD, including

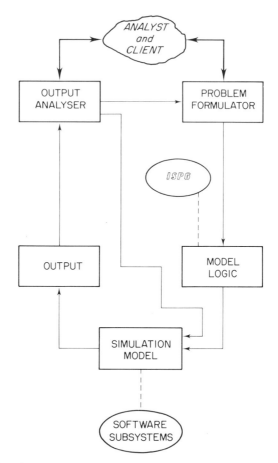

Figure 5.1 The process of simulation modelling.

quantitative questions concerning sampling, arithmetic and initial conditions. VS6 uses pop-up tables to achieve the same effect with greater flexibility and user control. The program generator then automatically writes the simulation model using a host of software subsystems. These latter would include a model structure (in our case, the three-phase method — see Pidd (1988) for a description of this method) and various routines for data sampling, queue manipulation, recording, etc. CASM.AUTOSIM accesses the LIBSIM software subsystem to produce the simulation program. LIBSIM is described by Crookes *et al.*. 1986) and Paul and Chew (1987). VS6 similarly accesses a library of routines, optionally in Pascal, FORTRAN or C. Under control of the analyst, the model is run and output is produced. The output can be used to determine 'correctness' of the model logic, and of the computer program (if the ISPG is not trusted), as well as reruns. Graphics are used to emulate the simulation model output dynamically.

Assuming that the above process works satisfactorily, the labour-intensive activities remaining are problem formulation and output analysis (plus customer satisfaction!). These activities are 'intelligent' contributions of an analyst which tend to improve with experience. In Figure 5.1 problem formulation is depicted with the aid of an AI system which helps the analyst formulate the problem with the customer. The expertise of the analyst can similarly be further captured in an output analyser to help decide what, if anything, is wrong and how to run the model to obtain satisfactory answers. So the modelling environment closely represents practical as well as desirable model development. The simulation environment is not depicted as a single-pass system, but as a continuous loop of activity. This enables gradual model development in small, easily checked stages; model correction in the light of program output; and determination of the running conditions and run lengths of the simulation model. The latter could be determined dynamically as a function of output, and hence the feedback loop from the output analyser to the simulation model. The analyst is in control of, and participates in, this process. A major benefit is that, with fast model development, the customer can also participate in the modelling process. In these ways integration of the system is advanced considerably. The data file of the model logic can also be used to document the simulation model.

Work on the problem formulator has been in progress from an early date, and a first attempt at using an expert system was described by Doukidis and Paul (1985). Expert systems turned out to be inappropriate for handling what was essentially a natural language understanding problem, and a recent paper by Paul and Doukidis (1986) updates the previous publication. A discussion of some aspects of this system follows in a later section. CASM is now researching into a natural language understanding system (NLUS) combined with graphics. The research that led from an expert system to a NLUS is described by Doukidis and Paul (1986).

5.1.4 Artificial intelligence

Bonnet (1985) provides a short but lucid introduction to the practical achievements in AI so far. He suggests that the most important areas at the moment are image understanding, natural language understanding, expert systems and techniques for learning. *Image understanding* has some potential for using simulation, for example by simulating various hypotheses to determine likely images from data, but little has been reported. *Techniques for learning* encompass computer-assisted instruction, a field which embraces a particular form of simulation or simulator not relevant to this book, and programs that learn — a subject in its infancy.

Natural language understanding and *expert systems* are major areas of AI development of interest to simulation, and are discussed in the next two sections. Following this outline of the main practical AI techniques, a discussion of the conceptual similarities, where they exist, follows in Section 5.4. Important though these are, some of the more exciting applications are based on the potential of one discipline to use the other. Chapter 6 examines the combination of AI and simulation.

5.2 Natural Language Understanding

5.2.1 Basic concepts

Recently there has been a growing emphasis on the need to make computers easier to use. This is reflected in innovations such as touch-screens and WIMP environments. It is hardly surprising, therefore, that many people are beginning to discuss, and implement, systems which allow a naive user (or an expert) to use natural language when working with computers.

The fluent use of natural language is an information-processing activity of great complexity. Having computers with this ability has long been a major goal of research in artificial intelligence. The two primary goals of this field are to understand how humans communicate and to create machines with human-like communication skills.

The first is a scientific goal pursued to help us understand ourselves. In particular, although we all are implicitly expert in the use of natural language, we have only a vague idea of the mental processes involved. A clearer insight into their essential nature and functioning might enable us to be better communicators. We might teach our children better language skills, or possibly design more efficient inter-computer communications.

Natural Language Understanding

The second goal is an engineering one pursued for a practical purpose — to create machines that can communicate with people in languages they already know. At present only a relatively small segment of the population can communicate with computers. The advent of machines that understand natural languages could make it possible for virtually anyone to make direct use of powerful computational systems.

Attempts to use computers to understand human language come in two forms; natural language understanding and speech recognition. The two forms are closely related, although the second is more difficult to achieve. The task of natural language understanding is to get the computer to respond appropriately to something in English or some other natural human language. The task of speech recognition is to achieve a more comfortable, natural, and efficient interface using spoken language.

5.2.2 Syntactic and semantic analysis

To understand something is to transform it from one representation into another. The second representation is chosen to correspond to a set of available actions that could be performed. To understand natural languages for a specific task, we need to think of a language as a pair (source language, target representation), together with a mapping between elements of each to the other (see Figure 5.2). The target representation will have been chosen to be appropriate for the task at hand. Natural languages are used in such a variety of situations that no single definition of understanding can account for all of them. In building computer programs that understand natural language, one of the first requirements is to define precisely what the understanding task is, and what the target representation should look like. Having done that, it will be much easier to define, at least for that environment, what a given sentence means.

Natural language understanding systems (NLUSs) designed for specific applications vary considerably. Even so, for most of them the underlying methodology is the same in analysing a sentence. They perform a syntactic analysis on a sentence (with reference to a dictionary) by checking the word sequences against the language's rules, and by transforming linear sequences of words into meaningful phrases. They also perform a semantic analysis which helps to resolve ambiguity and to build the final semantic representation. In other words, a mapping is made between the

```
The ship's cargo of 230 tonnes is unloaded

        ship           ------------------------> entity
        cargo weight   ------------------------> attribute
        unloaded       ------------------------> activity
        230 tonnes     ------------------------> data
```

Figure 5.2 Mapping of an English sentence onto simulation terminology.

syntactic structures and objects in the task domain. Structures for which no such mapping is possible may be rejected.

Syntactic analysis

Syntax is the description of the ways in which words must be ordered to make structurally acceptable sentences in a language. Words are grouped into classes of nouns, verbs, adjectives, and so on. Rules for the proper construction of noun phrases, verb phrases, sentences, and other structures are based on these classes. An acceptable noun phrase, for example, can be composed of any number of adjectives, a noun and perhaps some prepositional phrases. Every NLUS has some form of syntax analyser, which tries to map a string of words onto a set of meaningful syntactic patterns. Hence the syntax analyser determines whether a sentence conforms to the constraints of the syntax of a language. It also builds a representation of the syntactic structure which is meaningful to the purposes of the NLUS.

Syntactic analysis is fraught with problems. As Winograd (1984) points out, 'a given sentence may have hundreds or even thousands of possible syntactic analyses. Most of them have no plausible meaning'. Research into natural language processing has produced many different ways of performing syntactic analysis. For a critical review of the various approaches see Barr and Feigenbaum (1981) and Winograd (1983).

A component that the syntax analyser interacts with very regularly is the dictionary. It consists of lexical categories, often called word classes, such as nouns, verbs, auxiliary verbs, etc. The dictionary is an important part of the syntactic analysis since any NLUS operates on the initial input using some kind of dictionary to assign each word to a set of word classes. For example, if the system accepts sentences which describe actions, then for the sentence:

THE BARMAID —— THE ——

the word in the first blank will be searched in the word class verb, and the one in the second blank will be searched in the word class noun. One extension to a simple dictionary would be to use word endings to indentify the class to which a word belongs. For example, a word ending with '-ing' is probably a verb.

Semantic analysis

Checking a sentence for correct syntax is only the first step towards understanding it. At some point a semantic interpretation of the sentence must be produced. One extreme way to do this is to generate a complete syntactic interpretation and then to hand this structure to a separate semantic interpreter. This approach was mainly adopted by classical linguistic researchers. Designers of specific NLUSs realised that there is a major difficulty with this approach. That is, it is usually not possible to decide on the correct syntactic structure interpretation without considering some semantic information. Approaches which have been developed for this can be classified as semantic grammars, or as semantic filtering of syntactically generated phrases.

Semantic grammars combine all types of knowledge, both syntactic and semantic, into a single set of rules.

Systems which perform *semantic filtering* of syntactically generated phrases begin the analysis of a sentence with a syntactic parse. The entire sentence is not parsed in one process, however. The syntactic analysis continues until a meaningful unit has been parsed; then semantic routines are called to analyse that unit. If there are no objections to the unit on semantic grounds (i.e. it does not violate the semantic representation of the specific problem), the syntactic analyser will continue. Otherwise the semantic routine informs the syntactic analyser that there is a problem and a different parse is tried or the sentence is rejected.

5.2.3 Classification of NLUSs

NLUSs can be classified on three (out of many) properties that they have: their domain, their dictionary and their independence.

Domains can be specific or family in character. *Specific domains* have a very limited domain of discourse. An example of such a system is where the domain is the set of objects that exist in a classroom. Here it is not difficult to represent full knowledge about this world. The knowledge consists of objects and their attributes (interrelationships between objects). An example of such a system is the LUNAR system by Woods (1973). LUNAR has been designed to help geologists access, compare, and evaluate chemical-analysis data on moon rock. Since such NLUSs have a full knowledge of their domain, they can accept and understand a large set of sentences of different structures. Hence their dialogue is very impressive. Their main disadvantage is that they cannot be extended to a larger domain. For example, the objects that exist in a classroom are a sub-domain of objects that may exist in a room.

Family domains consist of many sub-domains which have something in common. For example, if the domain is about objects which exist in a room, then we can distinguish many sub-domains: objects that exist in a classroom, in an office, in a bedroom etc. NUDGE, by Goldestein and Roberts (1977), can be considered as such a system since it accepts informal specifications of scheduling problems. It is not easy to represent full knowledge of these NLUSs, because they can only accept a restricted set of sentences of different structures. As a result of this, the dialogue is typically less impressive.

Dictionaries can be knowledgeable or learning. NLUSs with knowledgeable dictionaries have a comprehensive dictionary of English words. The dictionary does not change, which means that it cannot be updated automatically each time the system is used. It is quite difficult to build such dictionaries except for systems that operate on specific domains. Based on the interaction, the system looks very knowledgeable and the conversation is very impressive.

The basic principle behind the construction of NLUSs with learning dictionaries is that it should be possible to analyse sentences without recourse to a complete dictionary of the language under consideration. The dictionary of English words is initially small, and can be modified each time it is used (new words can be added automatically). Hence the data structure used to represent the dictionary must allow dynamic allocation. We can say that such systems have the ability to 'learn'. Although the conversation is not as impressive as a knowledgeable NLUS, a learning system is more flexible. Its dictionary is easier to build in the first place and, if the appropriate code exists, it is very easy to update (this is done automatically by the system itself).

An interesting use of natural-language processing is as part of a larger computer-based system. For example, imagine devices that not only communicate in English, but also control complex equipment such as industrial robots or furnish expert advice about mechanical repairs. NUDGE can be considered as such a system, since the output of the natural language processor (a formal specification of a scheduling problem) is used as input to a scheduling algorithm. This then provides the answer to the specific problem. Some NLUSs are not designed as part of a larger computer-based system. Even those systems that have been developed as 'front ends' for a variety of data-processing tasks, have to generate programs specifying how the computer is to retrieve the information. GUS, by Bobrow *et al.* (1979), is probably the only system that can be thought as very near to a stand-alone system. It simply converses with a client who wants to make a return trip to a city in California by accessing a small and specially designed database.

5.3 Expert Systems

5.3.1 Basic concepts

Definitions of expert systems vary from an emphasis firmly on methodology to an emphasis on performance. For example, in the first case Basden (1983) states that:

> they are loosely assumed to be computer systems that can hold human-like knowledge of (in theory) any kind and can process knowledge in a more human-like fashion than do conventional computer systems.

In the second case Bramer (1982) defines an expert system as

> a computing system which embodies organised knowledge concerning some specific area of human expertise, sufficient to perform as a skilful and cost-effective consultant. Thus it is a high-performance special-purpose system which is designed to capture the skill of an expert consultant such as a doctor of medicine a chemist or a mechanical engineer.

Stefic *et al.* (1982) give a more complete definition by presenting the relationship between expert systems and AI research:

> Expert systems are problem-solving programs that solve substantial problems generally conceded as being difficult and requiring expertise. They are called knowledge based because their performance depends critically on the use of facts and heuristics used by experts. Expert systems have been used as a vehicle for AI research under the rationale that they provide a forcing function for research in problem solving and reality.

The one thing upon which most writers agree is that expert systems are designed to perform as a consultant for problems that are difficult, and which normally require human expertise for their solution.

In general, an expert system consists of a knowledge base and a control structure. The *knowledge base* contains the knowledge of an expert(s) in an organised way. A *control structure* is a program which tries to solve a problem based on the knowledge base, the user's responses and the status of the conversation.

5.3.2 Knowledge representation

Knowledge representation is handled by a combination of data structures and interpretive procedures. If these are used in the right way in a program, this leads to 'knowledgeable' behaviour. Work on knowledge representation has involved the design of several classes of data structures for storing information in computer programs, as well as the development of procedures that allow 'intelligent' manipulation of these data structures to make inferences. It is possible to experiment with the type of knowledge which can be represented by the system and the ease with which that knowledge can be represented. This aspect takes account of the fact that knowledge is not a concrete entity, it is not easily described and is not tangible.

Of the many ways in which knowledge has been represented in expert systems, four in particular have achieved widespread acceptance (for a critical review see Barr and Feigenbaum, 1981):

production rules, semantic nets, frame systems, procedural representation.

When using *production rules* the basic idea is very simple; there is a database and a collection of production rules each of the form

Expert Systems 133

```
"Jones works in the marketing department"

               works-in
  Jones  ------------------>  marketing department
```

Figure 5.3 A unit of a semantic network.

[situation→action]. The situation part of each rule expresses some condition about the state of the database, and at any point is either satisfied or not. The action part of each rule specifies changes to be made to the database every time the rule is used ('fired'). The system conceptually goes through an evolutionary process. At each cycle, one rule whose situation is satisfied is selected and fired, changing the database and so affecting the rules that could possibly be fired on the next cycle. A further explanation of production rule-based systems is given below.

The basic unit of a *semantic network* is a structure consisting of two points, or 'nodes', linked by an 'arc'. Each node represents some concept and the arc represents a relation between pairs of concepts. Such pairs of related concepts may be thought of as representing a simple fact. Nodes are labelled with the name of the relevant relation. Figure 5.3, for example, represents the fact that:

'Jones works in the marketing department'

'note that the arc is directed, thus preserving the 'subject/object' relation between the concepts within the fact. Moreover, any node may be linked to any number of other nodes, so giving rise to the formation of a network of facts.

In *frame systems* the kernel of the idea is the representation of things and events by a collection of frames. Each frame corresponds to one entity and contains a number of labelled slots for things pertinent to that entity. Slots in turn may be blank or refer to other frames, so the collection of frames is linked together into a network. An interesting, much-discussed feature of frame-based processing is the ability of a frame to determine whether it is applicable to a given situation. The idea is that a likely frame is selected to aid in the process of understanding the current situation, and this frame in turn tries to match itself to the data it discovers. If it finds that it is not applicable, it could transfer to a more appropriate frame.

In a *procedural representation*, knowledge about the world is contained in procedures or small programs that know how to proceed in well-specified situations. For instance, consider a parser for a natural language understanding system. The knowledge that a noun phrase may contain articles, adjectives, and nouns is represented in the program by calls (within the noun phrase procedure) to routines that know how to process articles, nouns and adjectives.

Although there is serious concern about the validity of the various representation schemes, it is not yet possible to prove that one scheme captures some aspect of human memory better than another. As Barr and Feigenbaum (1981) said

> there is no theory of knowledge representation and we do not yet know why some schemes are good for certain tasks and others not.

In the early days of expert systems it was thought that computer-based consultation would be confined to the conventional performance goal of earlier computing technologies. That is, to deliver good answers to the client's input question. This turned out to be the wrong goal for expert systems. As Michie (1980) says, 'the user demands explanation as well as answers'. The ability to explain the line of reasoning in a language convenient to the user is necessary both for applications as well as for system development (e.g for debugging and for extending the knowledge base). Thus most expert systems make available an explanation facility for the user, be it an end-user or a system developer. What constitutes 'an explanation' is not a simple concept, and considerable thought needs to be given, in each case, to the structure of the explanations.

To emulate human thinking, machine intelligence must be flexible and expandable. These are two hallmarks of expert systems. They can be expanded by the addition of new knowledge, and corrections to the knowledge base can be made and immediately assimilated. In this way an expert system continues to build up its knowledge base by adding new information incrementally. Thus the expert system is not static; it can be said to 'learn'. That is, expert systems must be able to add to and refine their knowledge in the light of observations presented by the user or sampled directly. Most expert systems have such facilities in one degree or another.

One interesting set of problems that occurs in expert systems involves finding ways of effectively manipulating incomplete descriptions in the knowledge base, when it is incrementally constructed. Expert systems are consultative and interactive. Users

Expert Systems

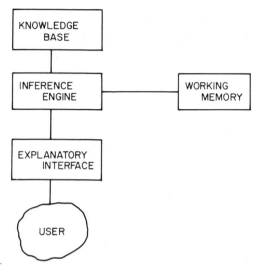

Figure 5.4 The structure of a production system.

of expert systems are bound to make mistakes, especially when the interaction is done through a natural language. Thus deductions may be made which are consistent with the available information but may, in fact, turn out to be incorrect in the light of information subsequently obtained. This problem has not yet been taken into account in many expert systems developments (see for example Bramer, 1982).

5.3.3 Production systems

Production systems are the most popular type of expert system because they are easy to develop. They originate from MYCIN (the most well-known expert system) and are the type of expert system adopted by the British Computer Society. They consist of four main elements:

1. the knowledge base which has the form of production rules;
2. the inference engine which drives the execution;
3. the working memory (or database) which keeps track of the status of the problem;
4. an explanatory interface which explains the line of reasoning.

The architecture of a production system is shown in Figure 5.4.

The knowledge base contains rules, but also needs a mechanism for manipulating the rules to form inferences, to make diagnoses and so forth. In order for a system to reason, it must be able to infer new facts from what it has been told already. The rules have the following general form:

IF ⟨trigger fact 1 is true⟩
⟨trigger fact 2 is true⟩
..
..
THEN ⟨conclusion fact 1 is true⟩
⟨conclusion fact 2 is true⟩
..
..

The facts in the IF part of a rule can be thought of as patterns that can be matched against existing facts in the working memory. The facts in the THEN part of a rule can be thought of as actions that can be performed, or conclusions that can be deduced, if all the facts in the IF part match.

Most of the mechanisms needed for manipulating the rules to form inferences can be regarded as a form of theorem prover. Different designers often use different techniques to produce an efficient system. Problem-solving is carried out by searching through all the possible solutions. But the number of candidate solutions is usually so great that an exhaustive search is not feasible. Three main approaches are used to overcome the difficulties associated with search in complex problems: goal-driven (or backward chaining), data-driven (forward chaining) and the bi-directional control strategy. The choice of one of these depends mainly on the application area of the system.

A *backward chaining* strategy means searching backwards from the goal. In this type of search the system works from goal to subgoal. Using the action side, the system proceeds in a hierarchical search trying to satisfy all the conditions necessary to meet the chosen goal.

A *forward chaining* strategy means searching forward after starting from a given set of conditions (true facts). In forward chaining the system simply scans through the rules until one is found where all the IF-PART facts are true. The rule is then applied, the working memory updated, and the scanning resumed. This process continues until either a goal state is reached, or no applicable rules are found.

To improve the efficiency of the search, sometimes both backward chaining and forward chaining are used. This is called the *bi-directional control strategy*, and involves searching from both ends and (hopefully) meeting somewhere in the middle. Such a combined search is applicable to complex problems when the search space is large.

A typical expert system normally has a working memory in addition to the knowledge base. This keeps track of the current status of the current problem and records the relevant history of what has been done so far. For example: the facts that are true (given at the beginning of the conversation or proved during the conversation), the facts that proved to be false, the rules that we try to prove, etc.

5.4 Comparing the Modelling Approaches

5.4.1 A production system view of three-phase modelling

Vaucher (1985) and O'Keefe (1986a) have outlined some similarities between production rules and blocks of code in simulation programs. Doukidis (1986) has exemplified the similarities using the three-phase simulation approach as an example of a production system. In the three-phase simulation system used and developed by CASM, described by Crookes *et al.* (1986), a library of Pascal routines support the writing of a problem-specific simulation program. The latter program is heavily structured into an executive controlling the three phases of the model, blocks of code for each B and C event, and initialisation and report routines as shown in Figure 5.5. Any three-phase structure would be similar to that shown in this figure. Such a structure can be redrawn as a production rule expert system similar to that shown in Figure 5.6.

The knowledge base contains the set of rules that describe general knowledge about the problem domain. In this example the rules have two compositions. The first, the B events, are the outcome of the end of an activity which occurs when the simulation time reaches the activity end. These events or rules can be considered as 'demons' in AI terminology, since they do not have a conditional part, only an action or series of actions.

138 _____**Artificial Intelligence and Simulation Modelling**

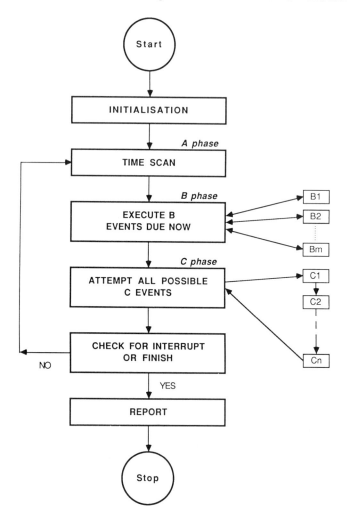

Figure 5.5 Simulation modelling in a three phase structure.

The rule waits to be fired when a certain event occurs, i.e. when the B event is at the front of the simulation timing mechanism. The C events are typical if–then production rules, called active rules by Doukidis (1987). Whenever a certain situation is encountered in the IF part of the rule, the actions in the THEN part are executed. In simulation terminology, when the necessary conditions for an activity to start are met, the necessary actions are taken. For

Comparing the Modelling Approaches

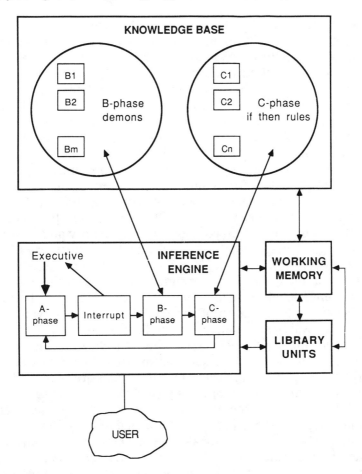

Figure 5.6 The three phase simulation system as a production system.

example, queue manipulation, setting up the appropriate B events in the timing mechanism, sampling activity durations.

The working memory component of the production system in Figure 5.6 stores the current knowledge about the system. Its structures are assembled and manipulated from the inference engine by calls to the library of simulation units. The latter create the requisite data structures and allow their updating or deletion. The main part of the working memory is made up of goals and facts, as in any production system. The facts, the status of the simulation model at any one point in time, are the states of the entities and queues which are used by the rules to make inferences. Goals are the elements of the timing mechanism which represent the scheduled bound or B events. As in any production system model, the goals provide a direction to the processing of the system by giving the status that must be achieved. In a three-phase simulation the properties of the simulation goals that are used are time (when something will happen) and priorities (the relative priorities of activities). An auxiliary part of the working memory holds information about sampling and recording.

The inference engine in Figure 5.6 controls the timing, termination, B event demon calls and testing of all the C event production rules. The simulation system is not typical of production systems in its inferencing. The latter first finds all the rules that are satisfied by the current contents of data memory and then applies a selection strategy to determine which ones to execute; whereas, in a simulation, a simple set of four 'metarules' are executed in turn. The A phase metarule advances time to when something is bound to happen. The interrupt metarule, common to all production systems, checks for termination of the model run. The B event metarule executes all B events identified by the A phase metarule. Lastly, the C event metarule tests each C event production rule in turn and executes those which match the requisite data memory elements in the working memory. These four metarules are repeatedly applied until the interrupt metarule is positively invoked.

The inference engine follows a forward chaining method in matching and executing C event production rules. This is an obvious inferencing mechanism for a situation where there are many equally acceptable goal states and a single initial state. Also, there is no predetermined final state upon which backward chaining could be applied, since the final state is what the model is attempting to uncover. The simplicity of the inference engine and knowledge base could lead to computer run-time inefficiency for complex problems. This could be alleviated using cellular simulation, as described by Spinelli de Carvalho and Crookes (1976), requiring a modification to the inferencing engine and the structure of the knowledge base.

Time handling has not been a strong point in AI programs, being described as a research enterprise by Hayes-Roth *et al.* (1983). Simulation models, by their nature, model time explicitly and a variety of techniques have been used to achieve this, as described by Pidd (1988). Here, then, is one aspect of simulation of potential benefit to AI researchers. A second area of cross-fertilisation for AI is in the advanced development of priority mechanisms to specify

Comparing the Modelling Approaches 141

synchronisation between parallel co-operating activities in simulation.

Vaucher (1985) puts the main difference between the AI and simulation approaches as the stress on logical inference by the former as against the concern with the dynamic behaviour of systems by the latter. As seen above, there is some agreement on the power of the if-then or condition–action rules to describe state transitions. A further area of agreement is in the use of hierarchies of types to describe objects—Pascal records in CASM's simulation systems, for example. Similarly LISP and PROLOG, the two most widely used AI languages, use atoms and lists for data elements in the former, and assertions and rules of deduction in the latter. The AI languages are interpretive systems which provide rapid model exploration and development. Simulation researchers are investigating the power of these languages and some of this research is now described.

5.4.2 AI languages in simulation

The most common AI language for simulation development appears to be PROLOG, which is fast becoming the most popular AI language as well. Futo (1985) discusses a system written in TS-PROLOG that combines simulation and problem-solving. A model in this system is made up of a hierarchy of independent components, for which goals can be defined. The system provides a very flexible communication mechanism, allows the behaviour of any component to be continuous or discrete, and allows backtracking to try several alternatives in case of deadlock in goal-seeking. Futo and Gergely (1986) use a spaceship model to illustrate TS-PROLOG as a sublanguage of colloquial English. This enables the main properties of the conceptual model to be easily and formally represented as a procedure which can be executed at the same time. Another paper from the same research group by Deutsch, Futo and Papp (1986), describes the use of a goal-oriented simulation system written in TC-PROLOG for solving drug administration problems. Cleary et al. (1985) present a preliminary version of a concurrent logic programming language for discrete event simulation written in Concurrent PROLOG. Limited backtracking is supported to enable alternative paths to be explored for acceptable solutions. Some simple examples are given of applications. The ability to backtrack in these systems results in a high level form of interaction, seeking a complete set of solutions for a given question. It is worth observing that backtracking is of limited value in systems which are highly interdependent.

More traditional PROLOG-based simulation systems have been developed by Flitman and Hurrion (1987) and O'Keefe and Roach (1987). The former system uses a three-phase executive as the basis for a production rule system similar to that shown in Figure 5.6. Apart from forming the basis for AI research in simulation, the authors claim that the PROLOG system allows the structure of the model to be modified by data which is then interpreted as code. O'Keefe and Roach, on the other hand, have written a PROLOG system that is an implementation of the transaction flow-based language GPSS. Random variate generation and statistics collection routines written in Pascal are linked in. Other references to PROLOG-based simulation systems are given by Shannon *et al.* (1985).

Birtwhistle and Kendall (1986) argue the advantage of LISP as the implementation language for discrete event simulation environments, based on their experiences prototyping a VLSI CAD environment. Other authors have tended to develop their own special-purpose AI simulation language. Groundwater (1985) reports on a demonstration ocean surveillance information expert system. The system simulates how intelligence analysts solve the problem of determining the probable destinations and missions of selected survey ships. The system was written in the OPS5 production rule language and in LISP. Marsh (1985) also reports on a rule-based modelling system constructed with the same mixture of languages. The model simulates the usage of the flight control rooms for space shuttle flights in order to estimate the resource usage and capacity of the current and new configurations at the mission control centre.

Bauman and Turano (1986) are concerned with the specification and verification of complex systems using the technique of modelling by Petri net. A Petri net is a directed symbolic graph consisting of places (input or output), tokens (movement from an input to an output), transitions (the 'firing' of a token) and arcs (representing the possibility of a transition between an input and an output). OPS5 was used to model a Petri net that simulates the behaviour of a communications protocol. The latter is usually too complex to be modelled by Petri nets, but the OPS5 application provided a simple approach that reduced the complexity of the net, and eased the implementation of the simulation.

Middleton and Zanconato (1986) report on a special-purpose

Comparing the Modelling Approaches   143

language, BLOBS. This is an object-oriented language designed to provide the framework for the design and building of both simulation and reasoning systems involving multiple real-time objects. The system has been used to experiment with the modelling of the decision-making process of a ground controller monitoring aircraft tracks on radar. The problem is to interpret multiple sources of simultaneous input concerning an aircraft(s). BLOBS was written using POPLOG, which contains a block structure language with the expressive power of LISP. Klahr (1986) reports on the object-oriented simulation system and environment called ROSS. This system is designed to improve the intelligibility, modifiability, credibility and performance of large-scale simulations. Two military battle simulations have been implemented in this system, one strategic and the other tactical. The interactions and outcomes of combat between two opposing military forces are simulated. ROSS was written in LISP.

Wilkinson (1986) reports on the development of a language compiler called Stimulus, which produces compiled programs that operate as an intelligent rule base. The purpose of such programs is to simulate production control by emulating the role of a production supervisor.

Ruiz-Mier and Talavage (1987) have developed an experimental network simulation environment which provides explicit constructs for the representation of complex behaviour in real problems. This is achieved by implementing the environment in a library of logic objects that act as the building blocks for modelling. It is claimed that this enables complex decisions to be represented, although relatively simple examples are presented as evidence.

Barton (1987) describes a problem simulated conventionally and then using LOOPS, an object-oriented LISP-based environment. The problem concerned was the sizing of a new central police computer facility to handle the larger major crimes. Major benefits were a substantial reduction in production time, but more importantly, flexibility for changes. The latter was partially achieved by modelling and storing the decision rules explicitly so that they could be altered without touching the code. Disadvantages were the heavy investment in purchase costs and substantial training effort.

McRoberts *et al.* (1985) report on the KBS knowledge-based simulation environment written in LISP supported by a frame-based knowledge representation language. They describe a mechanism by which simulation models can be altered to execute at different levels of abstraction, so that a slow-running detailed model can be made to perform better by focusing on only a portion of the model. Reddy *et al.* (1985) report on the use of KBS to provide a selective instrumentation facility where only the data relevant to a particular modelling goal is gathered and analysed.

Glicksman (1986) describes an environment for simulating an autonomous land vehicle. The system, written in LISP, is composed of many coexisting but independent processes. For example, vehicle motion, sensors, a planning system. Other intelligent simulation environments are described by Robertson (1986), Adelsberger *et al.* (1986), and Zeigler and De Wael (1986).

Many authors have written on the benefits of combining artificial intelligence and simulation, such as O'Keefe (1986a,b), Gaines and Shaw (1985), Shannon *et al.* (1985) as well as Doukidis (1986) and Vaucher (1985). In Chapter 6, applications using various mixtures of AI and simulation are examined, along with their potential.

5.5 References

Adelsberger, H. H., Pooch, U. W., Shannon, R. E. and Williams, G. N. (1986) Rule based object oriented simulation systems. *Intelligent Simulation Environments*, (eds P. A. Luker and H. H. Adelsberger) Simulation Series Vol. 17, No. 1. Society for Computer Simulation, San Diego, USA.

Balmer, D. W. and Paul, R. J. (1986), CASM—The right environment for simulation. *Journal of the Operational Research Society*, **37**, 443–52.

Barr, A. and Feigenbaum, E. A. (1981), *The Handbook of Artificial Intelligence*, Vol. 1. Pitman, London.

Barton, A. (1987) Experiences in expert systems. *Journal of the Operational Research Society*, **38**, 965–74.

Basden, A. (1983) On the application of expert systems, *International Journal of Man-Machine Studies*. 19, 461–77.

Bauman, R. and Turano, T. A. (1986) Production based language simulation of Petri nets. *Simulation*, **47**(5), 191–8.

Birtwhistle, G. (ed.) (1985) *AI, Graphics and Simulation*. Society for Computer Simulation, San Diego, USA.

Birtwhistle, G. and Kendall, J. (1986) A view of LISP. *Intelligent Simulation Environments*, (eds P. A. Luker and H. H. Adelsberger). Simulation Series, Vol. 17, No. 1. Society for Computer Simulation, San Diego, USA.

Bobrow, D. G., Kaplan, R. M., Kay, M., Norman, D. A., Thompson, H. and Winograd, T. (1977) GUS: a frame-driven dialog system. *Artificial Intelligence*, **8**, 153–73.

Bonnet, A. (1985) *Artificial Intelligence:Promise and performance*, Prentice-Hall International, London.

Bramer, M. A. (1982) A survey and critical review of expert systems

References

research. *Introductory Readings in Expert Systems* (ed. D. Michie), pp 3–29, Gordon & Breach. London and New York.

Campbell, J. A. (1986) Principles of artificial intelligence. *Artificial Intelligence: Principles and Applications* (ed. M. Yazdani). Chapman and Hall, London.

Cleary, J., Goh, K. and Unger, B. (1985) Discrete event simulation in Prolog. *AI, Graphics and Simulation* (ed. G. Birtwhistle). Society for Computer Simulation, San Diego, USA.

Clementson, A. T. (1982) *Extended Control and Simulation Language.* Cle.Com Ltd, Birmingham, UK.

Crookes, J. G., Balmer, D. W., Chew, S. T. and Paul, R. J. (1986) A three phase simulation system written in Pascal. *Journal of the Operational Research Society*, **37**, 603–18.

Deutsch, T., Futo, I. and Papp, I. (1986) The use of TC PROLOG for medical simulation. *Intelligent Simulation Environments* (eds P. A. Luker and H. H. Adelsberger). Simulation Series, Vol. 17, No. 1. Society for Computer Simulation, San Diego, USA.

Doukidis, G. I. (1986) An overview of expert systems. Paper presented at 'Computers: Applications in Management and Business', UNESCO International Seminar, University of Patras, Greece.

Doukidis, G. I. (1987) An anthology on the homology of simulation with artificial intelligence. *Journal of the Operational Research Society*, **38**, 701–12.

Doukidis, G. I. and Paul, R. J. (1985) Research into expert systems to aid simulation model formulation. *Journal of the Operational Research Society*, **36**, 319–326.

Doukidis, G. I. and Paul, R. J. (1986) Experiences in automating the formulation of discrete event simulation models. *AI Applied to Simulation* (eds E. J. R. Kerckhoffs, G. C. Vansteenkiste and B. P. Zeigler), Simulation Series, Vol. 18, No. 1. Society for Computer Simulation, San Diego, USA.

Flitman, A. M. and Hurrion, R. D. (1987) Linking procedural discrete event simulation models with non-procedural expert systems. *Journal of the Operational Research Society*, **38**, 723–33.

Futo, I. (1985) Combined discrete/continuous modeling and problem solving. *AI, Graphics and Simulation* (ed. G. Birtwhistle). Society for Computer Simulation, San Diego, USA.

Futo, I. and Gergely, T. (1986) TS-PROLOG Logic programming in simulation. *Transactions* **3**(4), 319–35.

Gaines, B. R. and Shaw, M. L. G. (1985) Expert systems and simulation. *AI, Graphics and Simulation* (ed. G. Birtwhistle). Society for Computer Simulation, San Diego, USA.

Glicksman, J. (1986) A simulator environment for an autonomous land vehicle. *Intelligent Simulation Environments* (eds P. A. Luker and H. H. Adelsberger). Simulation Series, Vol. 17, No. 1. Society for Computer Simulation, San Diego, USA.

Goldestein, I. P. and Roberts, R. B. (1977) Generating project networks. *Proc. Fifth International Joint Conference on Artificial Intelligence*, pp 888–93.

Groundwater, E. H. (1985) A demonstration of an ocean surveillance information fusion expert system. *Artificial Intelligence and Simulation* (ed. W. M. Holmes). Society for Computer Simulation, San Diego, USA.

Hayes-Roth, F., Waterman, D. A. and Lenat, D. B. (eds) (1983) *Building Expert Systems*. Addison-Wesley, Reading, Mass.

Holmes, W. M. (ed.) (1985) *Artificial Intelligence and Simulation*. Society for Computer Simulation, San Diego, USA.

Kerckhoffs, E. J. H., Vansteenkiste, G. C. and Zeigler, B. P. (eds) (1986) *AI Applied to Simulation*. Simulation Series, Vol. 18, No. 1. Society for Computer Simulation, San Diego, USA.

Klahr, P. (1986) Expressibility in ROSS, an object-oriented simulation system. *AI Applied to Simulation* (eds E. J. R. Kerckhoffs, G. C. Vansteenkiste and B. P. Zeigler). Simulation Series, Vol. 18, No. 1. Society for Computer Simulation, San Diego, USA.

Luker, P. A. and Adelsberger, H. H. (eds) (1986) *Intelligent Simulation Environments*. Simulation Series, Vol. 17, No. 1. Society for Computer Simulation, San Diego, USA.

McRoberts, M., Fox, M. and Husain, N. (1985) Generating model abstraction scenarios in KBS. *AI, Graphics and Simulation* (ed. G. Birtwhistle). Society for Computer Simulation, San Diego, USA.

Marsh, C. A. (1985) RBMS—an expert system for modeling NASA flight control room usage. *Artificial Intelligence and Simulation* (ed. W. M. Holmes). Society for Computer Simulation, San Diego, USA.

Mathewson, S. C. (1985) Simulation program generators: code and animation on a PC. *Journal of the Operational Research Society*, **36**, 583–9.

Michie, D. (1980), Expert systems. *Computer Journal*, **23**(4), 369–76.

Middleton, S. and Zanconato, R. (1986) BLOBS: an object-oriented language for simulation and reasoning. *AI Applied to Simulation* (eds E. J. R. Kerckhoffs, G. C. Vansteenkiste and B. P. Zeigler). Simulation Series, Vol. 18, No. 1. Society for Computer Simulation, San Diego, USA.

O'Keefe, R. M. (1986a) Simulation and expert systems—taxonomy and some examples. *Simulation*, **46**(1), 10–16.

O'Keefe, R. M. (1986b) Advisory systems in simulation. *AI Applied to Simulation* (eds E. J. R. Kerckhoffs, G. C. Vansteenkiste and B. P. Zeigler). Simulation Series, Vol. 18, No. 1. Society for Computer Simulation, San Diego, USA.

O'Keefe, R. M. and Roach, J. W. (1987) Artificial intelligence approaches to simulation. *Journal of the Operational Research Society*, **38**, 713–22.

Parnas, D. L. (1985) Software aspects of strategic defence systems. *Communications of the ACM*, **28**(12), 1326–35.

Paul, R. J. and Chew, S. T. (1987) Simulation modelling using an interactive simulation program generator. *Journal of the Operational Society*, **38**, 735–52.

References

Paul, R. J. and Doukidis, G. I. (1986) Further developments in the use of artificial intelligence to formulate simulation problems. *Journal of the Operational Research Society*, **37**, 787–810.

Pidd, M. (1988) *Computer Simulation in Management Science*, 2nd edn. John Wiley & Sons, Chichester.

Poole, T. G. and Szymankiewicz, J. Z. (1977) *Using Simulation to Solve Problems*. McGraw-Hill, London

Reddy, Y. V., Fox, M. S. and Husain, N. (1985) Automating the analysis of simulations in KBS. *AI, Graphics and Simulation* (ed. G. Birtwhistle). Society for Computer Simulation, San Diego, USA.

Robertson, P. (1986) A rule based expert simulation environment. *Intelligent Simulation Environments* (eds P. A. Luker and H. H. Adelsberger). Simulation Series Vol. 17, No. 1. Society for Computer Simulation, San Diego, USA.

Ruiz-Mier, S. and Talavage, J. (1987) A hybrid paradigm for modeling of complex systems. *Simulation*, **48**, 135–41.

Shannon, R. E., Mayer, R. and Adelsberger, H. H. (1985) Expert systems and simulation. *Simulation*, **44**(6), 275–84.

Spinelli de Carvalho, R. and Crookes, J. G. (1976) Cellular simulation. *Operational Research Quarterly*, **27**, 31–40.

Stefic, M., Aikins, J., Balzer, R., Benoit, J., Birnbaum, L., Hayes-Roth, F. and Saceroti, E. (1982) The organization of expert systems: a tutorial. *Artificial Intelligence*, **18**, 135–73.

sysPACK Ltd (1988), *VS6 User's Guide*, London.

Vaucher, J. G. (1985) Views of modelling: comparing the simulation and AI approaches. *AI, Graphics and Simulation* (ed. G. Birtwhistle). Society for Computer Simulation, San Diego, USA.

Wilkinson, D. G. (1986) Computers and manufacturing at the NEL. *Computer Bulletin*, **2**(4), 3–5.

Winograd, T. (1983) *Language as a Cognitive Process*, Vol. 1: *Syntax*. Addison-Wesley, Reading, Mass.

Winograd, T. (1984) Computer software for working with language. *Scientific American*, **251**(3), 90–101.

Woods, W. A. (1973) Progress in natural language understanding: an application to lunar geology. *AFIPS Conference Proceedings 42*, National Computer Conference, Montrale, NJ, pp. 441–50. AFIPS Press.

Zeigler, B. P. and De Wael, L. (1986) Towards a knowledge-based implementation of multifaceted modeling methodology. *AI Applied to Simulation* (eds E. J. R. Kerckhoffs, G. C. Vansteenkiste and B. P. Zeigler). Simulation Series, Vol. 18, No. 1. Society for Computer Simulation, San Diego, USA.

Computer Modelling for Discrete Simulation
Edited by M. Pidd
©1989 John Wiley & Sons Ltd

6
Combining AI and Simulation

Ray J. Paul

The use of artificial intelligence (AI) techniques could improve many aspects of the process of simulation modelling outlined in Figure 5.1. This chapter outlines a natural language understanding system (NLUS) developed to aid simulation model formulation, and then considers other examples of the benefits of combining AI and simulation.

The complexity of the problems faced in real applications enables simulation to use AI in two ways. First, the art of simulation modelling itself can possibly be enhanced by adding AI software applications to the analysts' tools. Second, parts of a simulation might be modelled by an AI application. The next four sections of the chapter illustrate both cases with examples.

Similarly, AI applications face large, complex problems, for which simulation models could provide help. The inference process used in AI applications could include a simulation model. Alternatively, the input or output of an AI application could be produced or analysed, respectively, by a simulation model. Section 6.6 pursues these ideas, again with examples.

The final section of the chapter looks ahead to future developments between AI and simulation.

6.1 Natural Language Processing Concepts in CASM

6.1.1 Fundamentals of the CASM NLUS

Paul and Doukidis (1986) reported on developments with a natural language understanding system that aids the analyst and decision-maker in formulating a simulation model in the form of an ACD representation. The system operates within the 'family domain' of defining problems for simulation analysis. The sorts of problem it is concerned with are largely queuing problems, arising in many walks of life such as hospitals, banks, ports, assembly lines, etc.

It is a 'subsystem' since it is considered as part of a larger computer-based system. Its semantic representation can be used as input to a simulation program generator, such as that described by Paul and Chew (1987).

It is a learning system for two reasons. First, the vocabulary is potentially infinite depending upon the application. The initial dictionary is specific to simulation modelling and is expanded as the problem tackled is processed. Second, the dictionary is flexible. Sometimes different verbs which represent the same action have to be grouped together. The dictionary allows for the manipulation of such specific cases.

Most of the conversation is controlled by the computer which asks the user to describe a specific activity or activities in the problem under investigation. When a new problem is started, the user has to describe an action that takes place. Based on this information, the system starts the investigation from this initial action and the main entity. From now on, the computer tries to build its own description of the problem bit by bit, by following one entity at a time and asking what this entity does next after a specific activity. In the early stages of development an 'open' approach was used whereby the user initially described various actions that took place. Then the computer would ask questions to fill in the gaps. By experimentation it was found that this approach was not very helpful, especially when the problem was a complicated one.

The informal specification of the problem is in a restricted form of English sentences. Because of the nature of such problems, the system accepts a specific set of sentencese called 'action sentences'. A discussion of the types of sentences accepted by the program is given below.

6.1.2 Syntactic and semantic analyses in the CASM NLUS

As in all NLUSs, there are syntactic and semantic analyses which are not isolated from each other. The analysis starts by going through the words sequentially and checking if the word sequences violate the preordained structure. The syntax analysis does not need to

Natural Language Processing Concepts in CASM   151

build a syntactic structure, since the sentences that the system accepts are simple and have only one structure (action sentences). A syntax error could arise if the user does not start with a noun phrase, or a verb is not found when the search has moved to the second part of the sentence.

At the same time the analysis checks that the input is semantically correct. This is undertaken when an important word is expected in the sentence, such as a noun or a verb. For example, an error occurs if an action is supposed to be described for entity A, and instead an action for entity B is input. Another semantic error occurs if the first sentence of the interaction starts with a pronoun instead of a noun. If there is an error reported by the syntactic or semantic analysis, the parsing stops and an explanation is given. Otherwise, the analysis continues until the end of the sentence is reached. At this point the semantic analyser attaches meanings to verbs and nouns by storing them into the appropriate places in the semantic representation. This is the end of the syntactic and semantic analysis cycle for a specific sentence.

Finally, the semantic analyser checks the entire semantic representation to see if it is logically correct. If it is not, it reports the error. Otherwise it checks if the semantic representation is complete for the entity under investigation. The interaction is then appropriately guided by asking the user to describe a specific action, or by stopping the cycle.

As the dialogue progresses, the system uses the information it obtains from the English dialogue (sentences, option-choices or true–false answers) to build a semantic representation of the problem. This representation, which is called the computer representation of the problem, provides the basis for generating questions that are to be answered by the user, protects the user from getting away with meaningless answers, points out fallacies and gaps in his thinking, provides an ACD-like description and eventually, if required by the user, creates a data file.

One of the basic principles behind the construction of the NLUS is that it should be able to define many discrete event simulation models, without recourse to a complete dictionary of the problem under consideration. Thus there is an initial small dictionary, and the system is capable of handling sentences from a potentially infinite vocabulary. For example, new nouns or verbs can be found and analysed. The dictionary is not totally isolated from the computer representation of the problem. Sometimes different verbs are grouped together, since they specify the same action.

6.1.3 Validation and successive refinement in the CASM NLUS

To validate the model, the client and the analyst must be provided with an English-like description which should be familiar to both of them. The description that the system provides consists of information about activities (the entities involved in each activity). Also, all the activities that an entity was mentioned in, and the various paths that an investigated entity followed in its life cycle, are given. If a 'life-path' description is not appropriate (as for a facility entity or an entity involved in only one activity), then the system provides alternative ways of representing the life cycle.

It is unlikely that a problem description (or a life cycle description) will be completely successful at the first attempt. Hence a debugging facility is available to the user which enables changes to be made to the already described (or partly described) problem. Such changes can be made on a local or a global basis. Local changes concern the life cycle of a specific entity (delete an activity, start a new path, delete the current partially described life cycle and start a new one). Global changes concern the whole problem (delete an entity which has been investigated or partly investigated, define a new entity which has not been mentioned so far, delete the life cycle of an entity and start a new one). In all cases the conversation is moved accordingly in order to fill the 'gap' that may have been created.

The user can save the complete (or incomplete) problem in a data file. This file can be recalled later for changes to the existing description, for continuing the conversation from where it was interrupted or just refreshing the user's memory about a problem that has been described (or partly described) previously.

6.1.4 Trapping ambiguous and meaningless responses in the CASM NLUS

Because it is an interactive system, special concern is given to trapping ambiguous or meaningless responses. The mistakes that a user might make can be classified into two categories: on the natural language part and on the discrete event simulation domain. Although the natural language input is in a reasonably 'free' format, there are certain restrictions that ensure viability. If

Natural Language Processing Concepts in CASM 153

the user violates these boundaries the program is capable of stopping the parsing, of describing the mistake and of asking the user to try again. It is also able to identify wrong answers to true–false or option-choice questions. The system is used in the initial part of the formulation phase, hence it is of fundamental importance to point out and elaborate mistakes and gaps in the user's understanding of the problem. Mistakes can vary from describing an action for a wrong entity, to describing an incomplete life cycle for an entity.

Most of the sentences used to describe queuing problems share a common structure. They typically have an agent and a recipient, and they contain a time inference (the action described follows another action). They may involve an instrument and may involve a movement. They may well include a condition that must be satisfied for the action to start. Sometimes they describe more than one action. Examples of the variety of sentences are:

1   The minder repairs the machine.
2   The ship arrives at the depot.
3   The crane will leave if its weight is less than 100 kilograms, otherwise it will be loaded.
4   The machine is loaded by the operator.
5   The petrol pump is used to fill the car.

A common component of all these sentences is the activity phrase, which consists of two (sometimes three) parts:

1   The main entity phrase, which describes the main entity (the entity under investigation). The main entity can be an agent or instigator of the action (e.g. sentence 1 and 2); an object or entity affected by the action (e.g. sentence 4); or an instrument, an entity used in causing the action (e.g. sentence 5).
2   The action phrase, which describes the action that the main entity is involved in.
3   The additional entities phrase, which describes the additional entities (if any) involved in the action. This phrase may not exist, as in sentence 1. An additional entity can be an agent, object or instrument of the action. Usually there is only one additional entity but sometimes there is a combination of additional entities.

6.2 Simulation Program Debugging using an Expert System in CASM

At the heart of the CASM simulation system depicted in Figure 5.1 is a suite of Pascal routines that provide the support for writing discrete event simulation programs using the three-phase simulation structure (Crookes *et al.*, 1986). This system is supported by an interactive simulation program generator (ISPG) that, based on information taken from an activity cycle diagram description of the problem, produces a Pascal simulation program using the suite of supporting routines (Paul and Chew, 1987). Powerful though this type of ISPG is, some complex problem decision rules cannot always be handled directly, requiring the amendment of the generated code. Also, re-evaluation of the problem being modelled gives the analyst the choice of using the ISPG again or amending the code.

From experience of teaching students at the LSE, and of applied work with the systems, a variety of amended program errors, both run-time and in the output, have been determined. These errors are typically diagnosed by a limited number of 'experts' in the simulation system, and whose availability is usually restricted. A number of solutions to this problem of scarcity of expert advice have been devised, and the expert system debugger SIPDES (Simulation Program Debugger using an Expert System) described by Doukidis and Paul (1988) is one of them.

6.2.1 An outline of SIPDES

SIPDES is a stand-alone expert system designed to help an analyst discover where his simulation program written with the CASM systems has gone wrong. The error may be a run-time error (for example, attempting to move an entity from an empty queue) or it may be an obvious mistake in the output (for example, nothing happened, or an entity disappears completely over time). The SIPDES system provides messages to facilitate the nature of the hypothesis being tested, as well as the normal help facilities. SIPDES can be defined (Shannon *et al.*, 1985) as an 'expert simulation system' since its goal is 'to make it possible for engineers, scientists and managers to do simulation studies correctly and easily without such elaborate training'. SIPDES can also be considered as an 'advice-giving simulation expert system'; these are defined (O'Keefe, 1986a) as systems 'that assist the simulation scientist and simulation user'.

Simulation Program Debugging   155

Since SIPDES can be applied to a simulation program that models any of this class of simulation problems, it is domain-independent. Its knowledge base concerns simulation in general, the CASM systems in particular, and relevant aspects of Pascal as well.

The reasons why SIPDES was developed as a debugging tool are as follows. The problem of debugging simulation program code has all the hallmarks of an expert system. The availability of an expert system development environment made the task of writing SIPDES feasible. Crucially, the CASM software systems are under constant development. Whilst the systems could be updated for potential user mistakes, these are difficult to determine before the system modifications have been made. Empirical evidence is required to determine new problems that arise. Only run-time errors can be detected within the system. Mistakes that can only be detected at the reporting stage cannot be determined by an inbuilt error system.

With the development of the CASM systems the incorporation of run-time error detection expands disproportionately with the size of the system, consuming more computer memory and/or slowing the system down. Since an ISPG program will work, and efficiency is a major objective, the incorporation of an expensive and frequently updated run-time error-detecting system into the simulation system is an expensive aberration. Run-time errors should be few if the systems are used correctly, and can readily be sought from the expert system. The latter can also aid the determination of mistakes detected at the report stage.

SIPDES is not a purely diagnostic expert system. It includes detailed step-by-step instructions for trouble-shooting when the cause of the problem cannot be identified precisely. It is intended to serve both as a training tool and as a debugging aid for inexperienced (and sometimes experienced) CASM users. When a hypothesis has been proven a course of action is recommended to the user. When it is appropriate, the system provides extra information on what that action may entail, after giving examples of the correct code required.

6.2.2 System control in SIPDES

The overall system control starts with data-driven forward chaining followed by goal-driven backward chaining. When SIPDES is run, the user is presented with a top-level set of goals, as shown below.

At which stage was the error noted?

1 Before all bound-events had been completed at least once.
2 Sometime in the simulation run.
3 At the simulation final REPORT.

The user, by choosing any of these options, can narrow the search by indicating the subgoal to focus on. Once the specific rules are evoked, SIPDES works as a regular back-chainer. Hence SIPDES can be seen to operate at two levels. In the higher level, SIPDES uses easily observed information about the initial symptoms of the problem to identify a subset of possible bugs. SIPDES then proceeds to the second level were step-by-step instructions about bug-finding for the identified subset are provided.

SIPDES can explain its line of reasoning at any point of demand. This capability enhances both its ability to serve as a trainer to the inexperienced user, and its credibility as an expert consultant to the more experienced user. SIPDES uses both the general explanation facility provided by the skeletal expert system ASPES (Doukidis and Paul, 1987) and one specially designed for this domain.

6.3 Other Examples of AI Tools in Simulation

Hill and Roberts (1987) have developed a prototype knowledge-based support system. It mimics the diagnostic process that teachers using the simulation package INSIGHT give students. The system is written in PROLOG. Unlike SIPDES, the knowledge base contains knowledge concerning the assignments given to students. This should enable it to give more exact advice, whilst being restricted in its application. The authors describe a range of extensions they envisage, along with some words of caution as to the viability of all that may appear desirable!

Elmaghraby and Jagannathan (1985) and Campbell (1986) report on the separate development of an expert system which will help the simulation analyst select a simulation language matched to his/her model and the computer resources.

O'Keefe (1986b) reports on a pilot system that advises on experimentation with transaction flow models. The aim of a consultation with the system is to help indicate which resources, transactions or activities are interesting candidates for possible experiments, and what statistics should be collected given a certain design objective. Lehman *et al.* (1986) have twice published a paper on a general approach to a multistage, hierarchical modelling concept which includes numerical analysis, simulation and hybrid simulation tools for flexible performance analysis of computer systems and communication networks. It is anticipated that this conceptual approach will lead to the development of a dialogue-oriented, knowledge-based system for the selection and construction of models. In the same vein, de Swaan Arons *et al.* (1986) describe an empty shell for building and consulting expert systems which has been used to find an appropriate model of a system to be simulated. It has also been used to recursively validate a simulation model using a knowledge base containing the expert's knowledge on validation.

6.4 Automatic Program Generation

One of the major applications of AI within simulation is automatic program generation. Several such systems exist, and this section starts with a description of one of them developed by CASM. Other AI applications follow in the next subsection.

6.4.1 CASM.AUTOSIM

Barr and Feigenbaum (1982) define automatic programming as the automation of some part of the programming process. Some success has been achieved in this area with systems that help programmers manage large programs, or that produce programs from some specification of what they are to do (beside the code itself). CASM.AUTOSIM is an example of the latter type of application.

CASM.AUTOSIM is an ISPG which accepts a model specification in terms of an ACD representation and produces a simulation program written in Pascal and supported by LIBSIM. It is written in VAX Pascal on a VAX machine and in Turbo Pascal on an IBM microcomputer.

The CASM.AUTOSIM system reflects the general structure of the ISPG in its two distinctive components, namely the interactive input of a model specification and the generation of a Pascal simulation program. Corresponding to these two components CASM.AUTOSIM produces two output files. First there is the interactive data file, which consists of all the input data which is extracted with the help of an ACD through an interactive input session. Second, there is the generated Pascal program file, which contains the Pascal simulation program generated by using as input the interactive data file.

The interactive input session is intended to capture the logic of the proposed simulation model. The description of the ACD and associated data completing the model specification is elicited via an interactive dialogue with the computer. The responses of the user are used to guide the subsequent questioning, to provide a simple analysis of the system described, as well as to assemble a formal specification of the model.

The system requires the specification of the names of each type of object or entity in the model. The life cycle of each entity is then defined by a sequence of alternating active and passive states called activities and queues respectively. Following the entry of the cycles the system permits a review of the specification so far, and gives some simple analysis of the model logic.

The next part of the session allows the definition of particular queuing disciplines for the various queues defined during the description of the life cycles. Where pertinent the relative priority of the activities mentioned in cycle descriptions can be defined. The next series of questions relate to the durations of activities (typically sampled from statistical distributions) and the arithmetic of any entity attributes. The data collection requirement of the simulation model is defined in terms of the production of histograms of attribute values, or of queue lengths or of queue waiting times.

Finally the starting conditions required are specified. The initial disposition of entities within their life cycles is defined. The times of completion of any activities deemed to be in progress at time zero are also requested.

These data defining the model specification are then stored in a named text file for subsequent use. The generation of a simulation program from a previously defined model specification file requires the user merely to select the appropriate option and the relevant data file name. The program can be written in VAX Pascal or Turbo Pascal, and will use the same LIBSIM routines in each case.

CASM.AUTOSIM has been tested on a number of real-life problems and has been used by students at the LSE in simulation project work. As was previously mentioned it is not always possible to specify precisely the desired model within the interactive format provided by CASM.AUTOSIM, and so the program code generated

Automatic Program Generation 159

does not always match exactly the original problem. However, the program, being so well structured, is easily modified (not all students believe this!) to accommodate those features inaccurately represented. Although some handcrafting has proved necessary, the larger part of the coding task is performed by CASM.AUTOSIM.

What has emerged from the development of CASM.AUTOSIM and LIBSIM is a definition of a sound simulation modelling environment. The technical task of turning a formal model description of a problem into a working experimental computer simulation program should be a minor part of the overall problem-solving process. Problem definition and understanding, model verification and model confidence, experimental design in using the computer model and implementation of results are currently difficult expert endeavours. The overall problem-solving process can be made much more efficient if the technical part of the process is executed with minimum effort. Research, teaching and consulting activities suggest that this is best achieved (relative to those methods available) using an effective ISPG and a sound programming structure. The ISPG writes code in a well-supported, widely available high-level programming language, using a programming structure that is readily understood and explicable to customers and other analysts alike. CASM.AUTOSIM and LIBSIM constitute such a desirable working environment. They contribute to an efficient life cycle for a project. Furthermore, this environment encourages and easily permits model updating through its relative simplicity and ease of use. Too often a modelling environment encourages an analyst to 'make do' with the current version of the program because the effort involved in modfying it is too expensive and too slow.

6.4.2 Other interactive simulation support tools

There are many similar systems to CASM.AUTOSIM, for example CAPS, by Clementson (1982). Recently Hollocks (1986) announced the introduction of the WITNESS system. WITNESS sees the world as made up of certain types of components, for example: parts, machines, etc. A real-world system is described as the flow of parts through the other components one by one, stage by stage. As soon as a component is specified it can be run, as though WITNESS operates in interpretive mode. There are no distinct design, construction and running phases as the model is developed.

The new simulation system, VS6, by sysPACK Ltd (1988) incorporates all the benefits of the CASM.AUTOSIM system in a modern colour windowing interface. This provides greater user control and understanding. Graphics through icon definition and movement are also incorporated. A specification for a problem can be tested interactively with a variety of graphics scenes for rapid model prototyping. Program code in Pascal, FORTRAN or C can be generated and amended for complex conditions, or just to provide efficient model processing.

Muetzelfeldt *et al.* (1986) describe an intelligent front end for ecological modelling. The system currently allows an ecologist with little programming or modelling experience to construct a systems dynamics model. It is anticipated that the range of models will be extended. Fjellheim (1986) reports on the development of a knowledge-based support system for creating and modifying so-called flowsheet models for offshore process plants. The user interaction is graphically based. The design activity is supported by a knowledge base. This contains taxonomic knowledge of simulation entities, and rule sets for checking, guiding and automating parts of the model-building task. Luker (1986) describes an interactive dialogue-based computer-assisted modeller of continuous systems. Assistance in conducting model experiments will be provided by expert guidance encapsulated in the system.

Khoshnevis and Chen (1986) describe a rule-based expert system that aids the user with little or no knowledge of simulation model-building to construct simulation models. The system also automatically creates the corresponding computer programs. The system is icon-based, taking the process view of simulation, as depicted by the simulation language SLAM, as the central structure of the visual formulation.

6.5 Other Uses of AI in Simulation

Reilly *et al.* (1985) provide one of many contributions to the incorporation of AI techniques within simulation environments. The future simulation environment is pictured as a distributed processing architecture comprising a model executor (simulation languages), a knowledge engine for record keeping, one or more results analysers (probably on a graphics workstation), and one or more AI builder workstations such as LISP. Groen *et al.* (1986) discuss the integration of simulation and knowledge-based systems with the advent of

Other Uses of AI in Simulation   161

parallel processing in mind. The latter is felt to provide a suitable testing ground for models for which the structure is hard to characterise.

Erickson (1986) discusses the requirements for a successful fusing of AI and simulation in military modelling. The need for such a combination is reinforced by Knapp *et al.* (1987). A submarine interactive attack model is described that represents the tactical situations that can develop between two opposing submarines. The model can handle a wide variety of scenarios, and gives meaningful statistics for expected submarine performance. However, whilst the simulation model allows for substantial flexibility in the choice of tactics, these are input as a predetermined set of plans. Also, the simulation records tactical decisions that are taken during a model run, but provides no explanation for these decisions. The authors anticipate that these limitations could be overcome by incorporating human expertise in a knowledge-based system.

Flitman and Hurrion (1987) have conducted experiments to test the feasibility of linking discrete event simulation models written in a procedural language (FORTRAN) with expert systems written in a declarative language (PROLOG). The two systems have been written on separate micro-computers and linked by a protocol. The combination can be used to develop and test expert systems, and to use an expert system as the control mechanism for a simulation.

Kornell (1985) has reported on the inclusion of expert systems within military simulation models to model the decision processes of individual commanders in combined arms scenarios. A further development is in a wargaming model, where a human player on one side can be replaced by an automated decision module (or even both human players can be replaced). A later paper (Kornell, 1987) discusses experiences by the author in using knowledge-based systems for military simulation. He emphasises the different nature of the task concerning the addition of knowledge-based subsystems to existing simulations, to that of including such systems in the initial specification. Since the author has actually been involved in both activities, it is worth mentioning the stress he puts on the automation of knowledge acquisition. The latter can easily be undervalued by reading the theoretical literature. In practice, knowledge acquisition can easily be the most difficult and time-consuming task, as this author has discovered.

Wahl (1986) reports on the use of declarative simulation programs that allows the inclusion of a rule-based system to augment numeric logic with human judgement. The application area is in aircraft fault isolation and diagnosis, where fault trees have been automated and supplemented by technician judgement. Another area of application of AI within simulation is in the field of process control. Brown *et al.* (1985) describe a system where outputs from a simulation are the facts that describe the state of the system. These facts feed a production expert system that determine the appropriate action (if any) to take. Moreira da Silva and Bastos (1986) describe a special-purpose simulation system based upon a visual interactive event-based package. Within the system an intelligent decision mechanism is designed to enable the testing of different operational rules for batch subdivision, and for transporter scheduling and control.

Balmer and Paul (1986) mentioned the use of an output analyser as an application of artificial intelligence to simulation, as outlined in Section 5.1.3. Haddock (1987) claims to have implemented a simple expert system that controls the running of an automatically generated flexible manufacturing system simulation. The expert system controls the running of the model as either a terminating simulation or as a steady-state simulation. The output statistic employed is the total time in the system for processed units. Popular methods of determining run in periods, run lengths and the number of replications are employed.

Bankes (1986) reports on the development of game-structured simulations of political and military decision-making of various potential combatants. A classic numerical equation-driven simulation is called upon by three knowledge-based subsystems representing the two opponents and a scenario controller. In a recent feature article in *Simulation* (1986), AI to improve nuclear plant availability is reported. A reactor trip simulation environment has been developed as a general rule-based simulation to define the logical connections of components equipments and systems. Maintenance and operations staff can predict whether an action or procedure, about to be taken, would trip the plant; the engineering and design staff can predict if design or procedure changes would reduce the margin to reactor trip.

6.6 Simulation Support for AI Applications

Since there are few real AI applications, this section is disappointingly short. The potential is clear. Simulation could be part of an inference engine, simulating a set of choices under the

Simulation Support for AI Applications 163

control of the AI system from which the latter selects the 'best' with which to continue. Simulation could be an AI model tester, providing 'simulated' inputs prior to using the system in the real world. Alternatively, one could conceive of simulation being used to test the output from an AI system. The following outlines of papers give some of the flavour of this.

Elmaghraby, Jaganathan and Ralston (1985) describe the construction of an expert system designed to control a dynamic chemical process. The actual process considered is a distillation column. The distillation process consumes 30% of the energy consumption in the chemical industry. In order to aid the design, and to test the expert system, a dynamic simulation of the process was interfaced with it. This provided the convenience of experimentation. Elmaghraby, Demeo and Berry (1985) have developed an expert system for flexible manufacturing, with an interactive simulation system used to evaluate it. Both papers hint that the simulation can form the basis of a learning tool, to assist in redefining the expert system rules, and thereby optimising the process being modelled.

The increasing interest in flexible manufacturing systems has led a number of authors to consider an AI system that uses simulation. Ford and Schroer (1987) have developed an expert system with a commercial simulation language for simulating an electronics manufacturing plant. The goals of the system are to develop a simulation capability for the electronics facility, provide a natural language interface so that the decision-maker will not have to learn the simulation language, and embed in the system an expert to assist the decision-maker. The system incorporates a program generator which takes the natural language description as the basis for the specification. Mellichamp and Wahab (1987) have developed an expert system to take the output of a simulation of a flexible manufacturing system design as the basis of a redesign. In this way the expert system can iterate around the designs until some predetermined objectives are met. The limitations of the system are the ability to capture the richness and variety of modifications to designs that human designers display. The authors stress the potential for the system in that, with time, the expert system will slowly improve towards the standard of a human expert.

Moser (1986) sees decision support systems, where artificial intelligence aids the decision-maker in interpreting simulation output, as an area of potential. He has developed a simple system to demonstrate the idea. The problem simulated is that of financial investment decisions, with the expert system interpreting the output from the simulation run for the decision-maker. The system allows the decision-maker to interrogate the results for a variety of possible outcomes.

Lirov *et al.* (1988) propose the AI modelling of control systems. They foresee the AI system designing the model and input definition, and automatically producing the model. A differential games simulator design was chosen to exemplify their ideas. The model generation methodology blends several problem-solving paradigms. Application areas for the example given are claimed to be in the areas of air combat games, and the navigation of mobile robots.

Collins and Feyock (1985) report on aircraft fault diagnosis research. Part of the research involves the use of a simulation model of a physical system to generate the knowledge base for fault diagnosis of that system. Failures are simulated in the model, the symptoms detected from the simulation, and both are stored in a fault dictionary. Hence an expert system is being developed that will aid the pilot. Borden *et al.* (1985) report on the development of an electronic warfare expert system to manage the defences of an aircraft. A computer simulation was written to exercise the expert system.

6.7 Conclusions

This chapter illustrates the effort going into AI research in the simulation community. Oren and Zeigler (1987) and Reddy (1987) indicate promising lines of future research effort. Some of this effort is being rewarded, although the returns so far are low. There is a tendency to make extravagant claims about the benefits of making simulation modelling even more complex by introducing intelligent reasoning. However, simulation as a modelling technique has many unresolved difficulties of its own, for example in the area of validation and verification. As a statistical modelling device, many practical statistical problems concerning experimentation with a model remain very difficult. The addition of intelligent reasoning via structured inference, which in its turn calls on unsubstantiated knowledge, should be treated with caution. Small steps with careful analysis of the process will avoid the fate of pursuing tempting but intangible prizes!

One area of benefit for simulation may be the introduction of

Conclusions

better methodology. For example, Doukidis (1987) points out that explanation facilities in expert systems have potential benefit in simulation modelling as well. Constructing the model so that it can, if required, explain its operation would help validate the model and help understanding of the problem. A simulation model with an explanation facility can be used as a tutor. Simulation currently uses 'canned text' explanation and graphics. Execution traces and rule paraphrasing as used in expert systems could be used to traverse a simulation timing mechanism and paraphrase B and C events respectively.

One criticism of simulation has always been that it models technically hard or numerate problems, but fails on soft or qualitative problems. With caution one can perceive how AI might enable simulation to broaden its horizons into this wider diversity of problem. Gaines (1986) argues for an expert system that formulates requirements, plus an optimiser that gives an optimal solution, combined with a simulation that shows the solution in action to the manager who thereby gains a feel for the sensitivities involved. A second expert system might suggest variations in the simulation that might give improvements. Rajagopalan (1986) has surveyed qualitative modelling and simulation. Two important abilities of human reasoning have been partially automated. Firstly, the ability to apply knowledge of the basic principles of behaviour of proceses and devices in reasoning about novel situations. Secondly, the ability to reason without the benefit of numerical values and without the situation being fully specified. Other authors have looked at the simulation of human thought processes (e.g. Denker *et al.*, 1985) and many authors have looked at a variety of methods of logic modelling (e.g. Futo *et al.*, 1986).

Another aspect of AI that influences simulation modelling is man– machine interfaces, in particular graphics. The conference proceedings edited by Birtwhistle (1985) has several papers on this theme. CASM.AUTOSIM has an automated add-on graphical system that enables a visual representation of the problem to be developed without coding (Knox, 1988). VS6, produced by sysPACK Ltd (1988), is an integrated windowing specification system with full automated graphics and coding facilities. Members of CASM are working on an intelligent graphical specification system that automatically handles code generation from the specification. There is little doubt that the full potential of graphics has yet to be realised, both for the analyst and the customer of such systems.

Researching into intelligent aspects of simulation modelling can lead to spin-off research. The simulation problem formulator described by Paul and Doukidis (1986) led to the development of a skeletal Pascal expert system described by Doukidis and Paul (1987). Doukidis (1986) explains why skeletal expert systems written in a well-structured, well-supported, high-level code are more adaptable and useful than expert shells, or than writing an expert system from scratch. This particular system was used to develop the simulation program debugger expert system described above, and by Doukidis and Paul (1988).

In summary, to quote from Shannon (1986), 'the future of simulation is bound up with AI and the speed with which the advances come. It will be an exciting and challenging time. Profound changes are going to come to the field of simulation as a result of the efforts in AI.'

6.8 References

Balmer, D. W. and Paul, R. J. (1986) CASM — The right environment for simulation. *Journal of the Operational Research Society*, **37**, 443–52.

Bankes, S. C. (1986) Simulating strategic decision making in human organizations. *A.I. Applied to Simulation* (eds E. J. R. Kerckhoffs, G. C. Vansteenkiste and B. P. Zeigler). Simulation Series, Vol. 18, No. 1. Society for Computer Simulation, San Diego, USA.

Barr, A. and Feigenbaum, E. A. (1982) *The Handbook of Artificial Intelligence*, Vol. 2, Pitman, London.

Birtwhistle, G., (ed.) (1985) *AI, Graphics and Simulation*. Society for Computer Simulation, San Diego, USA.

Borden, A. Kao, H., Neyman, W. and Wojciechowski, E. (1985) OPS5 as an electronic warfare design tool. *Artificial Intelligence and Simulation* (ed. W. M. Holmes). Society for Computer Simulation, San Diego, USA.

Brown, T., Alexander, S. M. Jagannathan, V. and Kirchner, R. (1985) Demonstration of an expert system for manufacturing process control. *AI, Graphics and Simulation* (ed. G. Birtwhistle). Society for Computer Simulation, San Diego, USA.

Campbell, R. A. (1986) Development of an expert system for simulation model selection. *Intelligent Simulation Environments* (eds P. A. Luker and H. H. Adelsberger). Simulation Series, Vol. 17, No. 1. Society for Computer Simulation, San Diego, USA.

Clementson, A. T. (1982), *Extended Control and Simulation Language*. Cle.Com Ltd, Birmingham, UK.

References

Collins, W. R. and Feyock, S. (1985) Syntax programming, expert systems, and real-time fault diagnosis. *Artificial Intelligence and Simulation* (ed. W. M. Holmes). Society for Computer Simulation, San Diego, USA.

Crookes, J. G., Balmer, D. W., Chew, S. T. and Paul, R. J. (1986) A three-phase simulation system written in Pascal. *Journal of the Operational Research Society*, **37**, 603–18.

Denker, M. W., Achenbach, K. A. and Keller, D. M. (1985) Computer simulation of Freud's counterwill theory: integrating artificial intelligence and control systems approach. *Artificial Intelligence and Simulation* (ed. W. M. Holmes). Society for Computer Simulation, San Diego, USA.

Doukidis, G. I. (1986) An overview of expert systems. Paper presented at 'Computers: Application in Management and Business', UNESCO International Seminar, University of Patras, Greece.

Doukidis, G. I. (1987) An anthology on the homology of simulation with artificial intelligence. *Journal of the Operational Research Society*, **38**, 701–12.

Doukidis, G. I. and Paul, R. J. (1986) Experiences in automating the formulation of discrete event simulation models. *AI Applied to Simulation* (eds E. J. R. Kerckhoffs, G. C. Vansteenkiste and B. P. Zeigler). Simulation Series, Vol. 18, No. 1. Society for Computer Simulation, San Diego, USA.

Doukidis, G. I. and Paul, R. J. (1987) ASPES — a skeletal Pascal expert system. *Expert Systems and Artificial Intelligence in Decision Support Systems* (eds H. G. Sol, C. A. Th. Takkenberg and P. F. de Vries Robbé). D. Reidel, Dordrecht, Holland.

Doukidis, G. I. and Paul, R. J. (1988) SIPDES: a simulation program debugger using an expert system. CASM Report, Department of Statistics, LSE.

Elmaghraby, A. S., Demeo, R. S. and Berry, J. (1985) Testing an expert system for manufacturing. *Artificial Intelligence and Simulation* (ed. W. M. Holmes). Society for Computer Simulation, San Diego, USA.

Elmaghraby, A. S. and Jagannathan, V. (1985) An expert system for simulationists. *AI, Graphics and Simulation* (ed. G. Birtwhistle). Society for Computer Simulation, San Diego, USA.

Elmaghraby, A. S., Jagannathan, V. and Ralston, P. (1985) An expert system for chemical process control. *Artifical Intelligence and Simulation* (ed. W. M. Holmes). Society for Computer Simulation, San Diego, USA.

Ericksen, S. A. (1986) Fusing AI and simulation in military modeling. *AI Applied to Simulation* (eds E. J. R. Kerckhoffs, G. C. Vansteenkiste and B. P. Zeigler). Simulation Series, Vol. 18, No. 1. Society for Computer Simulation, San Diego, USA.

Fjellheim, R. A. (1986) A knowledge-based interface to process simulation. *AI Applied to Simulation* (eds E. J. R. Kerckhoffs, G. C. Vansteenkiste and B. P. Zeigler). Simulation Series, Vol. 18, No. 1. Society for Computer Simulation, San Diego, USA.

Flitman, A. M. and Hurrion, R. D. (1987) Linking procedural discrete event simulation models with non-procedural expert systems. *Journal of the Operational Research Society*, **38**, 723–33.

Ford, D. R. and Schroer, B. J. (1987) An expert manufacturing simulation system. *Simulation*, **48**, 193–200.

Futo, I., Gergely, T. and Deutsch, T. (1986) Logic modelling. *AI Applied to Simulation* (eds E. J. R. Kerckhoffs, G. C. Vansteenkiste and B. P. Zeigler). Simulation Series, Vol. 18, No. 1. Society for Computer Simulation, San Diego, USA.

Gaines, B. R. (1986) Expert systems and simulation in industrial applications. *Intelligent Simulation Environments*, (eds P. A. Luker and H. H. Adelsberger). Simulation Series, Vol. 17, No. 1. Society for Computer Simulation, San Diego, USA.

Groen, A., van den Herik, H. J., Hofland, A. G., Kerckhoffs, E. J. H., Stoop, J. C. and Varkevisser, P. R. (1986) The integration of simulation with knowledge-based systems. *AI Applied to Simulation* (eds E. J. R. Kerckhoffs, G. C. Vansteenkiste and B. P. Zeigler). Simulation Series, Vol. 18, No. 1. Society for Computer Simulation, San Diego, USA.

Haddock, J. (1987) An expert system framework based on a simulation generator. *Simulation*, **48**, 45–53.

Hill, T. R. and Roberts, S. D. (1987) A prototype knowledge-based simulation support system. *Simulation*, **48**, 152–61.

Hollocks, B. (1986) Another step forward in simulation. *Computer Bulletin*, **2**(4), 16–17.

Khoshnevis, B. and Chen, A. (1986) An expert simulation model builder. *Intelligent Simulation Environments*, (eds P. A. Luker and H. H. Adelsberger). Simulation Series, Vol. 17, No. 1. Society for Computer Simulation, San Diego, USA.

Knapp, B. M., Dudley, A. R. and Ryder, J. S. (1987) Modelling techniques for simulation of submarine engagements. *Journal of the Operational Research Society*, **38**, 891–8.

Knox, P. M. (1988) Automated Graphically-Based Discrete-Event Simulation Systems. Unpublished PhD thesis. University of London.

Kornell, J. (1985) Knowledge-based systems for military simulation: problems, experiences, lessons. *AI, Graphics and Simulation* (ed. G. Birtwhistle). Society for Computer Simulation, San Diego, USA.

Kornell, J. (1987) Reflections on using knowledge based systems for military simulation. *Simulation*, **48**, 144–8.

Lehman, A., Knodler, B., Kwee, E. and Szczerbicka, H. (1986) Dialog-oriented and knowledge-based modeling in a typical PC environment. *AI Applied to Simulation* (eds E. J. R. Kerckhoffs, G. C. Vansteenkiste and B. P. Zeigler). Simulation Series, Vol. 18, No. 1. Society for Computer Simulation, San Diego, USA and *Intelligent Simulation Environments*, (eds P. A. Luker and H. H. Adelsberger). Simulation Series, Vol. 17, No. 1. Society for Computer Simulation, San Diego, USA

References

Lirov, Y., Rodin, E. Y., McElhaney, B. G. and Wilbur, L. W. (1988) Artificial intelligence modelling of control systems. *Simulation*, **50**, 12–24.

Luker, P. A. (1986) Putting expertise into Modeller. *AI Applied to Simulation* (eds E. J. R. Kerckhoffs, G. C. Vansteenkiste and B. P. Zeigler). Simulation Series, Vol. 18, No. 1. Society for Computer Simulation, San Diego, USA.

Mellichamp, J. M. and Wahab, A. F. A. (1987) An expert system for FMS design. *Simulation*, **48**, 201–8.

Moreira da Silva, C. and Bastos, J. M. (1986) The use of decision mechanisms in visual simulation for flexible manufacturing systems modelling. *AI Applied to Simulation* (eds E. J. R. Kerckhoffs, G. C. Vansteenkiste and B. P. Zeigler). Simulation Series, Vol. 18, No. 1. Society for Computer Simulation, San Diego, USA.

Moser, J. G. (1986) Integration of artificial intelligence and simulation in a comprehensive decision-support system. *Simulation*, **47**, 223–9.

Muetzelfeldt, R., Bundy, A., Uschold, M. and Robertson, D. (1986) ECO—An intelligent front end for ecological modelling. *AI Applied to Simulation* (eds E. J. R. Kerckhoffs, G. C. Vansteenkiste and B. P. Zeigler). Simulation Series, Vol. 18, No. 1. Society for Computer Simulation, San Diego, USA.

O'Keefe, R. M. (1986a) Simulation and expert systems—a taxonomy and some examples. *Simulation*, **46**(1), 10–16.

O'Keefe, R. M. (1986b) Advisory systems in simulation. *AI Applied to Simulation* (eds E. J. R. Kerckhoffs, G. C. Vansteenkiste and B. P. Zeigler). Simulation Series, Vol. 18, No. 1. Society for Computer Simulation, San Diego, USA.

Oren, T. I. and Zeigler, B. P. (1987) Artificial intelligence in modelling and simulation: directions to explore. *Simulation*, **48**, 131–4.

Paul, R. J. and Chew, S. T. (1987) Simulation modelling using an interactive simulation program generator. *Journal of the Operational Research Society*, **38**, 735–52.

Paul, R. J. and Doukidis, G. I. (1986) Further developments in the use of artificial intelligence to formulate simulation problems. *Journal of the Operational Research Society*, **37**, 787–810.

Rajagopalan, R. (1986) Qualitative modeling and simulation. *AI Applied to Simulation* (eds E. J. R. Kerckhoffs, G. C. Vansteenkiste and B. P. Zeigler). Simulation Series, Vol. 18, No. 1. Society for Computer Simulation, San Diego, USA.

Reddy, R. (1987) Epistemology of knowledge based simulation. *Simulation*, **48**, 162–6.

Reilly, K. D., Jones, W. T. and Dey, P. (1985) The simulation environment concept artificial intelligence perspectives. *Artificial Intelligence and Simulation* (ed. W. M. Holmes). Society for Computer Simulation, San Diego, USA.

Shannon, R. E. (1986) Intelligent simulation environments. *Intelligent Simulation Environments* (eds P. A. Luker and H. H. Adelsberger). Simulation Series, Vol. 17, No. 1. Society for Computer Simulation, San Diego, USA.

Shannon, R. E., Mayer, R. and Adelsberger, H. H. (1985) Expert systems and simulation. *Simulation*, **44**(6), 275–84.

Simulation (1986) Artificial intelligence to improve nuclear plant availability. *Simulation*, **46**(3), 122–4.

de Swaan Arons, H., Jansen, E. P. and Lucas, P. J. F. (1986) Building and consulting expert systems in simulation with DELFI-2. *AI Applied to Simulation* (eds E. J. R. Kerckhoffs, G. C. Vansteenkiste and B. P. Zeigler). Simulation Series, Vol. 18, No. 1. Society for Computer Simulation, San Diego, USA.

sysPACK Ltd (1988) *VS6 User's Guide*. London.

Wahl, D. (1986) An application of declarative modeling to aircraft fault isolation and diagnosis. *Intelligent Simulation Environments* (eds P. A. Luker and H. H. Adelsberger). Simulation Series, Vol. 17, No. 1. Society for Computer Simulation, San Diego, USA

Computer Modelling for Discrete Simulation
Edited by M. Pidd
©1989 John Wiley & Sons Ltd

7
Simulation in Pascal
M. Pidd

7.1 Developing Simulation Programs

Faced with the task of developing a working simulation, the analyst/programmer has a number of interesting options available. Four overall options are easily identified, and variations are possible within each.

7.1.1 Option one: simulation languages

Firstly, use could be made of simulation programming languages such as ECSL (Clementson, 1982), SIMSCRIPT (Markowitz *et al.*, 1963) or SIMULA (Dahl *et al.*, 1970). Each of these is available in several versions to suit mainframe, mini- or personal computer users. The make-up of such languages is discussed in Pidd (1988) and by Mathewson in Chapter 2. All these languages include a syntax suited to simulation, an executive and a library of useful routines. The vendors of the major languages all claim considerable user bases and offer at least some support to users.

If these languages are well-designed tools for particular purposes, it might be expected that their use is near-universal. Nevertheless, repeated surveys seem to show that only a minority of discrete simulations are written with such simulation languages. Why should this be? To answer this question involves the examination of the other feasible options.

7.1.2 Option two: using FORTRAN

Despite the hopes of the simulation language vendors, many simulations are still written in FORTRAN. As will be made clear later, FORTRAN is far from ideal as a language for discrete simulation. What then is the explanation for its popularity? Perhaps the main reason is conservatism on the part of analysts and their employers. Many management science groups are still committed to FORTRAN as their main language for specialist programs. In addition, a proportion make use of APL and, more recently, C.

What are the reasons for this conservatism? Firstly, most organisations are unwilling to offer long-term support for more than a single scientific programming language. They dread the thought of having to revise programs written in a language known only to employees who left the organisation some years earlier. Given that simulations most certainly can be written in FORTRAN, then innate conservatism means that many will be written in FORTRAN.

A second reason is that libraries of useful routines will probably have been developed over the years. If these are written in FORTRAN, then it is natural to carry on the tradition and write in FORTRAN. Large management science groups may well have developed such FORTRAN libraries for discrete simulation over quite long periods of time. Such an investment is not lightly written off. Thus specialist simulation languages, whatever their inherent virtues or vices, tend only to have a limited market. On a more objective level, a major virtue of FORTRAN is that efficient and bug-free compilers are widely available. These produce well-optimised object code and are fully supported by their vendors. This may not be true of all discrete simulation languages, and it can be difficult to gain proper technical support if the small group supporting the simulation language is in another continent. By contrast, FORTRAN experts seem to be everywhere!

7.1.3 Option three: using data-driven generic models

The second main option open to the analyst/programmer is to make use of pre-programmed generic models. A generic model is one which is well suited to a particular class of system (for some suggestions about the organisation of generic models, see Pidd, 1988). For example, an organisation in the canning industry might develop such a generic model for canning lines. To suit particular lines the generic model might need minor re-programming. Alternatively, the generic model might be general enough to allow the characteristics of the canning lines to be specified purely as data to the model. The latter type of generic model can be purchased from software vendors.

HOCUS (Poole and Szymankiewicz, 1977) is an example of a generic model with a wide range of applications. The plus and minor points of all such generic models are fairly obvious. Their principal attraction is the speed at which particular applications may be developed—often by relatively inexperienced staff. That is, they can be made very easy to use. A well-written generic model might be usable by staff who know little or nothing of its inner workings. In such cases the user may be familiar with the particular system being simulated, but not with the details of computer simulation. The major snag is a consequence of this ease of use. There are bound to be systems to be simulated which fit rather badly onto the structure imposed by the generic model. Hence, particular applications may be better simulated using software other than generic models. As is so often the case, there are horses for courses.

7.1.4 Option four: use some other language

A third option open to the analyst is to write in a general programming language other than FORTRAN. As mentioned above, most surveys report that the majority of simulations are still written in FORTRAN. Such programs need not be written from scratch, but can make use of available libraries of useful routines. This chapter presents the case for Pascal in those circumstances where a general programming language is the best option open to the analyst. In the next chapter, John Crookes argues for C in preference to Pascal—particularly for the development of generic models.

7.2 Discrete Simulation Libraries

When producing discrete simulation programs in general-purpose languages such as FORTRAN, Pascal or C, it is sensible to develop libraries of procedures or subroutines. Depending on the language system in use, these library routines may be separately compiled and linked at run-time. Alternatively, they may be strung together as source code by an editor and then compiled together with the application-specific parts of the program. When a particular simulation needs to be developed, it is often possible to use these library routines as a substantial part of the application. The routines to be provided may be conveniently considered as three groups.

1. Simulation system routines.
2. Useful general-purpose routines.
3. Application-specific routines.

Each will be considered in turn.

7.2.1 Simulation system routines

As pointed out in Pidd (1988), there are four main approaches to simulation modelling. These are the three-phase, activity, event and process interaction approaches. If a simulation language is being used, the analyst need only code the activities, events or processes, the sequencing and scheduling of these being the job of an executive provided in the simulation language. This executive is usually hidden from the user, who is provided with strictly defined ways of communicating with it. Other facilities are also often provided, but hidden from the user. These include routines to allow re-initialisation of the simulation, error traps and tracing facilities.

Given that most simulations are conducted from display screens of different types, it also makes sense to develop routines for standard displays. Depending on the facilities available, these may include monochrome or colour graphics. In Chapter 4, Hurrion gives details of the implementation of useful interactive graphics systems for simulation.

A further possibility is to allow proper interaction in the simulation. Thus there need to be routines which will poll an input device to detect an interrupt. Once stopped, the current state of the simulation needs to be dumped and stored. Interaction may then commence. It makes sense to provide these routines in a planned manner.

The analyst or group faced with developing their own library for simulation must provide similar system routines themselves. Most are not difficult to program, as long as the tasks are properly planned. A couple of three-phase executives in Pascal are provided later in this chapter as illustrations.

Discrete Simulation Libraries   175

7.2.2 Useful general-purpose routines

Most discrete simulations include at least some stochastic behaviour. Therefore, a set of sampling routines must be provided in such a library. Routines which might reasonably be expected as follows.

1. *Random number generation.* A suitable pseudo-random generator must be available. This should generate independently and identically distributed uniform variates on the unit interval. It should have a very long cycle and, by allowing the user to seed the generator, it should allow random number streaming. This control of the streams is an aid to the analysis of the simulation results. For details see Pidd (1988) and Knuth (1981).
2. *Distribution sampling routines.* As these are not particularly difficult to program, at least the following distributions might be provided. Both real and integer variates should be possible.

    uniform
    negative exponential
    normal
    lognormal
    gamma
    Poisson
    Geometric.

    In addition, there should be routines which allow the use of empirical distributions by specifying a histogram or piece-wise approximation.
3. *Sample collection routines.* When testing a simulation program it is often important to examine the sampling distributions for various variables. It is simple to provide routines which automatically produce histograms and moment estimates for these distributions as the samples are generated.

Many discrete simulations are of systems which include queues with a variety of disciplines. It thus make sense to provide standard routines for handling these queues and their disciplines. These routines should maintain queues as linked lists, and should allow new entities to join and leave. Facilities might also be provided to allow the selection of entities from queues according to various criteria.

7.2.3 Application-specific routines

These are routines which are specific to particular applications within the organisation. For example, in an engineering company many simulations may be of systems which include relatively standard robots and guided vehicles. In another case, a food company may need to simulate many conveyor systems. It thus makes sense to develop a library of routines for simulating these. The routines may then be easily incorporated into later simulations.

7.3 Characteristics of Discrete Simulation Programs

One very good reason for not using FORTRAN to write simulation programs is the nature of those programs, and the way in which they tend to be developed. This section points out these characteristic features of discrete simulation programs and their development.

7.3.1 Typical mode of development

It is important to realise that simulation models and programs often develop in an evolutionary fashion. Indeed, it can be argued that this is extremely good practice. It is tempting to attempt to model the whole of a system at once, but this is almost always a mistake. It is much better to proceed step by step in a careful development of the full model. There are three very good reasons for this approach.

Firstly, it makes for easier program testing. It is simpler to test the various components of the model in stages. The fact that each module is valid and verified does not guarantee that the whole program will be correct. However, if the individual modules are incorrect then the whole program is bound to be wrong. Attempting to write and test a finished program in a single pass leads to frustration with confusing error messages and logical mishaps. The finished program must be verified, but after the individual modules are tested; therefore the sensible approach is as follows. Initially develop the skeleton of the program in order to test the overall logic. Once this is OK, set to work on the individual detailed modules. Develop these in turn, with the same approach: i.e. skeleton followed by detail.

The second reason for an evolutionary approach is the organisational context in which simulation projects are conducted.

Characteristics of Discrete Simulation Programs   177

The participants in the study rarely have perfect knowledge at its outset. Usually all the participants are learning as the model and program development proceed. The client may well be learning about the sort of analyses which are most useful from the simulation. The analyst is learning what degree of approximation is acceptable in the model. This learning should be accepted as inevitable and as desirable; hence the development process should be seen as evolutionary. Trying to produce a detailed program specification right at the start is a recipe for later difficulties.

There is a third reason, which may not be so obvious. This is the fact that someone else may need to maintain the model and program at a later date. This is true of those simulations which become part of regular planning process. A correct skeleton which drives individually tested modules makes such patching rather less difficult. However, it is never easy.

Such an evolutionary and modular approach has consequences for the programming language in use. It should be one which encourages a modular approach, possibly with 'top-down' design. In Pascal, programs are tree-structured with functions and procedures as modules. Modularity is an essential feature of the language and thus of Pascal programs. This encourages 'top-down' design and allows the individual development of testable modules. On the other hand, nested tree-structures are not allowed in FORTRAN, only individual functions and subroutines. Modularity in FORTRAN has to be a conscious choice of the programmer rather than a consequence of using the language. Thus Pascal would appear rather better than FORTRAN for modular program development.

7.3.2 Logic not computation

It is important to understand why discrete computer simulations are possible at all. The possibility is based on the use of a computer as a logical engine rather than as a calculating machine. Much management science is based on the ability of computers to carry out rapid, accurate arithmetic. For discrete simulation, speed is certainly important and so is accuracy. But, in addition, another feature is crucial. This is the ability of the computer to undertake logical tasks.

In a typical discrete simulation the state of the model is taken as the aggregate state of all the entities in the simulation. The state of the system changes as these entities themselves change state. So, for example, in a queuing system, service of a particular customer may not begin until a server is ready and the customer is at the head of the queue. These logical interactions between the entities are the basic building blocks of a discrete simulation program. In order to be useful for discrete simulation, a programming language must ease the expression of these logical interactions. There are three ways in which a programming language may do this for the programmer.

(1) Variable names and other names

Firstly, and simplest of all, it ought to be possible to use meaningful names for entities, variables and their states. It is just not sensible to be restricted to names with two, eight or whatever characters in a source file. However, this is a trivial problem to deal with, compared to the others.

(2) Powerful statements

More significant is the ease with which logical statements may be made. The typical form of expression for logical interactions in discrete simulation is as follows:

If ⟨conditions⟩ *then* ⟨actions⟩ *else* ⟨other actions⟩

The inclusion in Pascal of the case statement can make simulation programs easier to read as well as marginally more efficient. It avoids a long list of cascading If . . then . . else statements.

Linked to this is a need for convenient expression of repetitive actions and tests. Though all repetition could be modelled via DO or FOR loops and GOTO's, there are better ways of achieving the same end. Hence most recent programming languages allow the following forms of repetition, and Pascal is no exception.

(a) WHILE
Found in simulation as in the following form:
   While ⟨resources available⟩ Commit resources.

(b) REPEAT . . UNTIL
Found in simulations in the following form:
   Repeat ⟨actions⟩ *Until* ⟨conditions⟩
These statements make for programs which are easy to read and convenient to write.

Characteristics of Discrete Simulation Programs 179

(3) Rich data types

Even FORTRAN enthusiasts will concede that the language is deficient in data types. FORTRAN allows only the following.
REALS: single or double precision.
INTEGERS
BOOLEANS
ARRAYS: of reals, integers or Booleans.
COMPLEX.

There is no convenient way of linking variables of different types. Simulation analysts might reasonably expect rather more variety than this.

Pascal, by contrast, offers a more extensive set of data types. There are built-in (simple) types (reals, integers, Booleans and chars), enumerated types, sub-range types and constructors. Precise definitions of all of these can be found in Jensen and Wirth (1975) or in one of the many books aiming to teach Pascal. Enumeration types, sub-range types and constructors will be considered briefly here from a simulation perspective.

(a) Enumerated types

These allow programmers to declare their own data types as scalars. For example, a simulation of a food plant might include the following.

Type Machine=(Mixer, Cooker, Conveyor, Cooler, Wrapper);
Var Section: machine;

This declares Section to be a variable of type Machine. Thus it may take *only* the values Mixer, Cooker . . Wrapper. The relational operators (=, ⟨ ⟩, >, <, >=, <=) may be applied to these values. In such cases,

Mixer < Cooker < Conveyor < Cooler < Wrapper.

Section may also be used as a Loop control variable. For example

For Section := Mixer to Conveyor do

These types can be great asset to readability and avoid the need for token variables.

(b) Sub-range types

These offer a useful way of avoiding those instances when variables might go out of range, but undetected. The unwary writer of discrete simulations may well fall victim to this problem. For example, if the maximum seating capacity of an aircraft were 350, then the programmer could define the following sub-range type.

Type NoOfSeats = (0 . . 350);
Var Seats : NoOfSeats.

Thus, the variable Sets is declared as being of type NoOfSeats; i.e. an integer in the range 0 to 350. The compiler could then be made to check if Seats ever goes out of range as the program runs.

(c) Constructors

Pascal allows several types of constructor, that is types made of other types. The most familiar to FORTRAN and BASIC buffs is the array. For example.

Type NoOfSeats = (0 . . 350);
    Machine = (Mixer, Cooker, Conveyor, Cooler, Wrapper);
    SeatMat = Array [1 . . 10, 1 . . 7] of NoOfSeats;
    MachineMat = Array [1 . . 5] of Machine;
Var Seatblock : SeatMat;
    MachineBlock : MachineMat;

Thus SeatMat is declared as a two-dimensional array of type NoOfSeats. MachineMat is declared as a vector of type Machine. SeatBlock is declared as a variable of type SeatMat and MachineBlock is a variable of type MachineMat. Variables of these types may then be used in the program. What is particularly convenient is that they may be passed to procedures as parameters. Arrays can be declared as being of any type, whether built-in, enumerated or constructed.

Another constructor type allowed in Pascal and some other languages is the set data type. This can be used to allow very convenient testing of system states. For example.

Type PossStates = (Running, Stopped, Idle, UnderRepair, Clean);
Var State : PossStates;

Characteristics of Discrete Simulation Programs   181

This defines a Set type which includes the values Running . . Clean. State is then declared as a variable of that type. The program might then include the following.

   If State in [Stopped, Idle] then . . .

This makes for convenient and readable programs.

Less familiar to FORTRAN programmers is the idea of a record, as used in Pascal and other languages. This constructor type allows a composite record of several different types to be constructed. For example, suppose a programmer wished to keep linked information about time, availability, state and activities of entities. The programmer could then declare the following.

   Type Machine=(Mixer, Cooker, Conveyor, Cooler, Wrapper);
      Char20=Packed Array [1 . . 20] of char;
      Activity=(Start, Stop, Repair, RepairOver, CleanUp, Cleaned);
      PossStates=(Running, OK, Stopped, Idle, UnderRepair, Clean);
      Entdetails=Record
        Name : Char20;
        Avail : Boolean;
        TimeCell : Integer;
        NextAct, LastAct : Activity;
        State : PossState;
        End;

If the number of entities in the program is small and fixed, then these entity records could be combined into an array. Assuming the above type definitions we could declare the following variable.

   Var Details : Array [Machine] of Entdetails;

This allows very convenient referencing of information for each entity. For example, if we wish to update the information held about the Cooker we could write the following.

   With Details[Cooker] do If State=OK then
      Begin
      TimeCell := 25;
      NextAct := Stop;
      LastAct := Start;
      State := Running;
      Avail := False;
      End;

This makes for readable and efficient programs.

Another type unknown to FORTRAN programmers is the pointer data type. This is used to allow dynamic variables, i.e. ones which are created and destroyed as the program is executed. For simulation applications, this can be an important data type. For example, customer records often need not be kept once the customer has been dealt with. These might be declared as follows.

```
Type Char20=Packed Array[1 .. 20] of char;
     Activity=(Arrive, Serve, Drink, Talk, Leave);
     PossState=(Outside, Waiting, Full, Quiet);
     EntPointer=^EntDetails;
     EntDetails=Record
       Name : Char20;
       Avail : Boolean;
       NextAct, LastAct : Activity;
       State : PossState;
       NextEnt : EntPointer;
       End;
  Var Customer : EntPointer;
```

This example employs a similar record to the previous one, except for the addition of another field. This is called NextEnt, and is of type EntPointer; EntPointer being previously declared as a pointer to EntDetails. Finally, a variable Customer is declared to be of type EntPointer.

The variable Customer is thus a pointer to any specified customer record. Such records may be created and destroyed during the simulation as it proceeds. As customer records are created, they are linked to a previous customer using the field NextEnt — which is itself a point to a customer record. Thus the records could be stored as a forward- or backward-linked list. This avoids the need to specify beforehand what might be the upper limit to the number of customers in the system. Such a limit would be needed for the dimension of an array if it were used as the aggregate record structure. Fairly obviously, similar linked lists can be used to represent queues.

It should be stressed that lists of this type are not as convenient for processing as are arrays. For example, it is possible to go direct to particular array elements, whereas a list must be searched. However, if there are large numbers of temporary entities, then pointer variables can be very useful.

7.4 An Array-based Executive in Pascal

To illustrate the usefulness of the Record type in Pascal, this section describes a simple discrete simulation executive. A three-phase approach is assumed. Many of the features are similar to those shown in the BASIM executive in Pidd (1988). A more refined executive, which makes fuller use of the pointer types of Pascal, is given in Section 7.5 of this chapter. Further examples of Pascal executives and more complete simulation systems can be found in Barnett (1986), Bryant (1981), Crookes *et al.* (1986), Seila (1988) and Jennergren (1984).

As with BASIM, specific information is maintained about each entity. Unlike BASIM, this information is stored in an array of records. The size of this array must be determined beforehand. It would not be sensible to use this array-based approach for more than about thirty entities. Though this seems small, a surprising number of practical simulations require only about this number of entities.

A second array is used during the A phase of the simulation. Again, as with BASIM, this is a simple pushdown stack which contains the identities of any entities due to change state in the B phase. This array, as well as the array of records, must be predetermined in size. The need to search through all entity records is what makes it sensible to restrict this executive to less than about thirty entities. The arrays required are illustrated in Figure 7.1

7.4.1 Essential type definitions

As with all Pascal programs, variable and data types must be defined before use. The executive makes use of the following user-defined data types and variables show in Figure 7.2.

Machine is an enumerated type, which *must* include BotMc as its first value and TopMc as its last value. The remaining values should be meaningful names for the entities of the simulation. BotMc and TopMc are needed because of the difficulty of producing a general sequence from an enumerated type.

BAct and *CAct* are enumerated types which define the possible B and C activities in the simulation. They avoid some of the possible errors in causing the B and C activities to occur.

PossState is another enumerated type, used to define the possible states of the entities making up the system.

The Details Array

	Name (Strng)	Avail (Boolean)	TimeCell (Integer)	NextAct (BAct)	State (PossState)
BotMc					
..					
TopMc					

	Machine
1	
2	
.	
.	
30	

The EntityDue Array

Gives a list of the entities due to change state. The state change is found from the Details array above.

Figure 7.1 Pascal array-based executive: arrays used.

```
{Simple 3 phase executive, using an array for entity records}
Type Machine = (BotMc, ..,..., TopMc);
     BAct = (..);
     CAct = (..);
     PossState = (..);
     Strng = Packed Array [1..10] of char;
     EntDetails = Record
                    Name : Strng;
                    Avail : Boolean;
                    TimeCell : Integer;
                    NextAct : BAct;
                    State : PossState;
                  End;
Var  Details : Array[BotMc..TopMc] of EntDetails;
     NumEntsDue, Clock, RunDuration : Integer;
     EntityDue : Array[1..30] of Machine;
     CurrEnt : Machine;
     EntSet : Set of Machine;
     BSet : Set of BAct;
     CSet : Set of CAct;
```

Figure 7.2 Pascal array-based executive: type and variable declarations.

Strng is used to carry text information for naming the entities for reports. Some Pascals do not need such a data type. *EntDetails* is a record showing the data to be kept about each entity as follows.

An Array-based Executive in Pascal 185

Name: text, giving entity name.
Avail: a Boolean variable used in the A phase.
TimeCell: showing the time of the next state change, if known.
NextAct: showing the next B activity, if known.
State: showing the current state of the entity.

The global variable declaration follow from the type definitions.
Details is a vector of EntDetails. Its size is automatically picked up from the enumerated values of Machine in its type declaration. Three integer variables are then defined as follows:

NumEntsDue: used in the A phase and B phase to indicate how many entities are due to change state.
Clock: the current simulation time.
RunDuration: the time for which the simulation is to run.

EntityDue is a [1..30] vector of type Machine. This is used in the A phase and B phase to indicate which entities are due to change state.
CurrEnt is the Machine which is now due to engage in a particular B activity.
EntSet, Bset and *CSet* are sets of the type shown and are occasionally useful for making sub-range checks.

7.4.2 The A phase

The section of code in Figure 7.3 shows the A phase of this executive using the variables which have been defined above. Its operation is as follows. Firstly, NumEntsDue is set to zero to indicate that no entities have been found as due to change state. Minm is set to MaxInt, the largest integer on the system. Aphase then examines in turn the record of each entity defined to be in EntSet. If the TimeCell is less than Minm, then Minm is set to TimeCell as its new value. NumEntsDue is then set to one. If TimeCell should be equal to Minm then NumEntsDue is incremented. The NumEntsDue cell of EntityDue is set to Entity if TimeCell is less than or equal to Clock.

At the end of Aphase are two error checks, which ought to be needed only rarely but . . . ! The first makes sure that Minm has changed value, and the second that Minm is still non-negative. Finally Clock is reset to its new value.

```
Procedure Aphase;
Var  Entity : Machine;
     Minm : Integer;
Begin
NumEntsDue := 0;
Minm := MaxInt;
For Entity := BotMc to TopMc do If Entity in EntSet then
     With Details[Entity] do If Not Avail then
           Begin
           If Timecell <= Minm then
                Begin
                If TimeCell < Minm then NumEntsDue := 1
                Else NumEntsDue := NumEntsDue + 1;
                Minm   :=   TimeCell;
                EntityDue[NumEntsDue] := Entity;
                End;
           End;
If Minm = MaxInt then Error(3)
Else If Minm < 0 then Error(4);
Clock := Minm;
End;
```

Figure 7.3 Pascal array-based executives: A Phase.

7.4.3 The B and C phases

The main program then moves on to the B and C phases shown in Figure 7.4 Bphase is a simple procedure which goes through the vector EntityDue from 1 to NumEntsDue. From the appropriate entity record the next B activity is identified. The method of causing this B activity to occur is rather clumsy due to a limitation of Pascal. It is necessary to associate a procedure name with each possible enumerated value of BAct. A Case statement is the simplest way to do this.

The Cphase is simply a list of the C activities in the sequence in which they are to be attempted.

7.4.4 Other useful procedures

Three further general procedures are shown in Figure 7.5. Two are essential, one is useful. Error halts execution of the program and prints an error message. It relies on a procedure, shown here as Halt, which will vary in different Pascal implementations. Schedule is used to update the record of a specified entity whenever the programmer wishes to do so. Release is used to set an entity to an available state, which can sometimes be useful.

An Array-based Executive in Pascal

```
Procedure Bphase;
Var Loop : Integer;

Begin
Writeln;
Writeln('Time now .. ', Clock:5);
For Loop := 1 to NumEntsDue do
      Begin
      CurrEnt := EntityDue[Loop];
      With Details[CurrEnt] do
            Begin
            Avail := True;
            Case NextAct of
                 {Add correct procedure names here}
                 End;        {Of Case}
            End;
      End;
End;


Procedure Cphase;
Begin
{Add correct procedure names here in priority order}
End;
```

Figure 7.4 Pascal array-based executives: B and C Phases.

7.4.5 An example

To illustrate the use of this executive, a variation of the harassed booking clerk, described in Pidd (1988), is used. This is a simple system in which a theatre booking clerk has two conflicting tasks to perform. He must serve personal enquirers, that is people who turn up in person at the theatre. Also, he must answer the phone. Personal enquirers have priority should there be two actions open to a clerk. For simplicity, no callers are allowed to ring off before their call is answered. Thus there are queues of unlimited size for both personal enquirers and phone callers. This system can be modelled with five B activities and a single C as follows:

B1: Personal enquirer arrives.
B2: End of personal service.
B3: Phone caller rings in.
B4: End of phone conversation.
B5: Record queue lengths (at regular intervals).
C : Begin work; either personal service or phone conversation.

As the aim is to illustrate the use of the executive, trivial sampling processes are employed. The program assumes that some suitable

```
Procedure Error(Number : Integer);
{Error routine, called as required}
Begin
Case Number of
        1 : Writeln('Attempted  to  schedule  non-existent
            entity');
        2 : Writeln('Attempted  to  schedule  non-existent  B
            activity');
        3 : Writeln('Minm still MaxInt in Aphase');
        4 : Writeln('Minm gone negative in Aphase');
        5 : Writeln('Attempted  to  release  non-existent
            entity');
        End;    {Case}
Halt;           {Procedure which halts execution}
End;


Procedure Schedule(Entity : Machine;
                   NewState : PossState;
                   Activity : BAct;
                   Time : Integer);
{Commits specified entity}
Begin
If Not (Entity in EntSet) then Error(1)
Else if Not (Activity in BSet) then Error(2)
Else With Details[Entity] do
        Begin
        Nextact := Activity;
        If (Time + Clock) < 0 then Timecell := RunDuration + 60
        Else TimeCell := Clock + Time;
        Avail := False;
        State := NewState;
        End;
End;


Procedure Release(Entity : Machine;
                  NewState : PossState);
{Sets specified entity as Avail}
Begin
If Not (Entity in EntSet) then Error(5)
Else With Details[Entity] do
        Begin
        State := NewState;
        Avail := True;
        TimeCell := Clock;
        End;
End;
```

Figure 7.5 Pascal array-based executive: essential procedures.

random number generator is called by the function Random. For details of how to write such a function in implementation of Pascal with limited integer arithmetic, see Jennergren (1985).

The simulation blocks consist of the five B activities and a single C activity. Each activity is a separate, un-nested procedure. The simulation is initialised in Initialisation and a report is generated in Finalisation. A procedure InitEnt is used to simplify the initialisation of entity records. The global type and variable declarations are shown in Figure 7.6. Most of the variables are integers used to keep

An Array-based Executive in Pascal

```
{Simple 3 phase executive, using an array for entity records}

Type Machine  =   (BotMc,   PersEnq,   PhoneEnq,   Clerk1,   Clerk2,
                   Clerk3, Clerk4, Clerk5, Observer, TopMc);
BAct = (Arrive, EndServe, Call, EndTalk, Observe);
CAct = (Work);
PossState = (Busy, Idle);
Strng = Packed Array [1..10] of char;

EntDetails = Record
                Name : Strng;
                Avail : Boolean;
                TimeCell : Integer;
                NextAct : BAct;
                State : PossState;
                End;

Var  Details : Array[BotMc..TopMc] of EntDetails;
NumEntsDue, Clock, RunDuration : Integer;
EntityDue : Array[1..30] of Machine;
CurrEnt : Machine;
EntSet: Set of Machine;
BSet : Set of BAct;
CSet : Set of CAct;

{Now variable definitions for activities..etc..}

NumClerks, NumPhone : Integer;
NumPers, NumServe, NumTalk, NumSeen, NumConv : Integer;
PersQ, PhoneQ : Integer;
ObsPhoneQ, ObsPersQ : Array[1..24] of integer;
Obs : Integer;
```

Figure 7.6 Simple array-based simulation of the harassed booking clerk problem: Declarations.

track of the queue lengths and of the number of services started or completed. The two arrays, ObsPersQ and ObsPhoneQ, are used to record the queue lengths at regular intervals in activity B5. Obs is used to record the number of observations so far.

The variables used in the activities and in the executive need to be initialised. Pascal implementations generally leave it up to the programmer to see to initialisation explicitly. Here, this can be done with a procedure called Initialisation which is shown in Figure 7.7. This makes use of another procedure, InitEnt. This initialisation procedure sets up the number of clerks to be simulated, and also establishes the length of the simulation run. Three sets are established. BSet and CSet are straightforward. EntSet is slightly more complicated, as it depends on the number of clerks in the simulation. The arrival of the first personal enquirer and phone call are also established.

The B and C activities themselves are shown in Figure 7.8; all six are very simple and the comments should make their operation

```
Procedure   InitEnt(Entity  :  Machine;
                   NewState : PossState;
                   Activity : BAct;
                   Time : Integer;
                   Nom : Strng);
{Sets up initial state of specified entity}
Begin
With Details[Entity] do Name := Nom;
Schedule(Entity, NewState, Activity, Time);
End;
```

Figure 7.7a Simple array-based simulation of the harassed booking clerk problem: Initialisation routines.

```
Procedure Initialisation;
Var   Entity : Machine;
      Counter : Integer;
Begin
Clock := 0;           {Set simulation clock to zero}
Writeln;
Writeln('Harassed booking clerk simulation');
Writeln('--------------------------------');
Repeat
     Write('How Many Clerks (1..5)? ');
     Readln(NumClerks);
Until (NumClerks > 0) and (NumClerks < 6);
Repeat
     Write('Simulation duration (20..480 minutes)? ');
     Readln(RunDuration);
Until (RunDuration > 19) and (RunDuration <= 480);
BSet := [Arrive..Observe];
CSet := [Work];
EntSet := [PersEnq, PhoneEnq, Observer];
{Establish base Entity set}
{Set up first arrivals & first observation of queue lengths}
InitEnt(PersEnq, Busy, Arrive, Round(10*Random), 'Personal   ');
InitEnt(PhoneEnq, Busy, Call, Round(15*Random), 'Phone      ');
InitEnt(Observer, Busy, Observe, 20, 'Observer   ');
{Set up all clerks as initially free}
Entity := Clerk1;
For Counter := 1 to NumClerks do
     Begin
     EntSet := EntSet + [Entity];
     Release(Entity, Idle);
     Entity := Succ(Entity);
     End;
{Initialise counters to zero}
NumPers := 0;
NumPhone := 0;
NumServe := 0;
NumTalk := 0;
NumSeen := 0;
NumConv := 0;
PersQ := 0;
PhoneQ := 0;
Obs := 0;
End;
```

Figure 7.7b Simple array-based simulation of the harassed booking clerk problem: Initialisation routines.

An Array-based Executive in Pascal 191

```
Procedure BArrive;          {Arrival of personal enquirer}
Begin
NumPers := NumPers + 1;     {Increment number of arrivals}
PersQ := PersQ + 1;         {Increment queue length}
Writeln('Personal enquirer  ', NumPers, ' arrives, queue now ',
PersQ);
{Schedule next personal arrival}
Schedule(PersEnq, Busy, Arrive, Round(10*Random));
End;

Procedure BEndServe;        {End of personal service}
Begin
{Increment number of completed services}
NumSeen := NumSeen + 1;
Details[CurrEnt].State := Idle;    {Set clerk idle}
Writeln('Clerk finished personal service ',NumSeen);
End;

Procedure BCall;            {Arrival of phone call}
Begin
NumPhone := NumPhone + 1;   {Increment number of calls}
PhoneQ := PhoneQ + 1;       {Increment queue length}
Writeln('Phone  enquirer  ', NumPhone, ' arrives, queue now ',
PhoneQ);
{Schedule next phone call}
Schedule(PhoneEnq, Busy, Call, Round(15*Random));
End;

Procedure BEndTalk;         {End of phone conversation}
Begin
{Increment number of completed conversations}
NumConv := NumConv + 1;
Details[CurrEnt].State := Idle;    {Set clerk idle}
Writeln('Clerk finished phone conversation ',NumConv);
End;

Procedure BObserve;   {Collect time series of queue lengths}
Begin
Obs := Obs + 1;       {Increment number of observations}
ObsPersQ[Obs] := PersQ;
ObsPhoneQ[Obs] := PhoneQ;
{Schedule next observation}
Schedule(Observer, Busy, Observe, 20);
End;
```

Figure 7.8a Simple array-based simulation of the harassed booking clerk problem: B activities.

clear. The finalisation section, B phase, C phase and main program are the final sections of code for this model and are shown in Figure 7.9. In the finalisation, the observed queue lengths are listed, together with the number of customers served and calls answered. The B phase, C phase and main program speak for themselves.

Though this program does nothing which could not be done in either FORTRAN or BASIC, it does illustrate some of the simple, yet convenient, features of Pascal for simulation. The next section shows an executive in which entity records are dynamically created and destroyed in an efficient manner. It also employs a much more

```
Procedure BeginWork;
Var Clerk : Machine;
Time, Counter : Integer;
Begin
Clerk := Clerk1;      {Establish first clerk}
Counter := 0;
Repeat
     With Details[Clerk]do If Avail then  {If clerk available}
         Begin
         If PersQ > 0 then   {If personal queue exists}
              Begin
              {Increment started services}
              NumServe := NumServe + 1;
              PersQ := PersQ - 1;
              {Reduce queue by 1}
              Writeln('Begin service ',NumServe);
              {Schedule end of this service for current clerk}
              Schedule(Clerk,         Busy,         EndServe,
              Round(10*Random));End
         Else If PhoneQ > 0 then  {If phone queue exists}
              Begin
              {Increment started conversations}
              NumTalk := NumTalk + 1;
              PhoneQ := PhoneQ - 1; {Reduce queue by 1}
              Writeln('Begin talk ', NumTalk);
              {Schedule end of this conversation for current
              clerk}
              Schedule(Clerk, Busy, EndTalk, Round(5*Random));
              End;
         End;
         {Set up next clerk}
         Clerk := Succ(Clerk);
         {Count number of clerks tried}
         Counter := Counter + 1;
     Until Counter = NumClerks;
End;
```

Figure 7.8b Simple array-based simulation of the harassed booking clerk problem: C activities.

```
Procedure Finalisation;
Var Counter, Time : Integer;
Begin
Writeln;
Writeln('Simulation with  ',  NumClerks,   ' over after ',
RunDuration);
Writeln('Time     Pers Queue      Phone Queue');
Writeln('----     ----------      -----------');
For Counter := 1 to Obs do
     Begin
     Time := Counter*20;
     Writeln(Time:3,                         ObsPersQ[Counter]:11,
     ObsPhoneQ[Counter]:15);
     End;
Writeln; Writeln('Number of personal arrivals : ', NumPers);
Writeln('Number of phone calls : ', NumPhone);
End;
```

Figure 7.9a Simple array-based simulation of the harassed booking clerk problem: Finalisation routine.

A Simple Pointer-based Executive

```
Procedure Bphase;
Var Loop : Integer;
Begin Writeln;
Writeln('Time now .. ', Clock:5);
For Loop := 1 to NumEntsDue do
    Begin
    CurrEnt := EntityDue[Loop];
    With Details[CurrEnt] do
        Begin
        Avail := True;
        Case NextAct of
            Arrive : BArrive;
            EndServe : BEndServe;
            Call : BCall;
            EndTalk : BEndTalk;
            Observe : Bobserve;
            End;         {Case}
        End;
    End;
End;

Procedure Cphase;
Begin
BeginWork;
End;


Begin         {Main program}
Initialisation;
While Clock <= RunDuration do
    Begin
    Aphase;
    Bphase;
    Cphase;
    End;
Finalisation;
End.
```

Figure 7.9b Simple array-based simulation of the harassed booking clerk problem: B Phase, C Phase and main routine.

efficient method of implementing the time search which is at the heart of the A phase.

7.5 A Simple Pointer-based Executive

As mentioned in Section 4.2, one very useful data type available in Pascal is the pointer. This is especially useful in the creation of dynamic data structures such as stacks, linked lists and trees. For details of the use of such structures see Wirth (1976), Page and Wilson (1985), or similar books which teach the use of Pascal. This section is devoted to another simple executive, this time built around three types of linked list.

7.5.1 Type definitions

Classes

Entities are organised into classes which share common features, new members of any class inheriting these features, and this class information is held in a doubly linked list ClassList. This list has ClassRoot as its first record, its predecessor being Nil. ClassList is terminated by ClassSent, a sentinel which points forward to Nil. Classes are linked forwards and backwards in a list which runs from ClassRoot to ClassSent. Each class record contains the following fields.

RootEnt: a point to the first entity record of this class.
ClassDesc: text information for debugging.
NumEnts: an integer showing how many entities are currently in this class.
MaxEnt: an integer showing how many entities have so far belonged to this class.
PrevClass: a pointer to the previous class in ClassList.
NextClass: a pointer to the next class in the list.

Thus details of any class may be found by scanning the ClassList.

Entities

The entity records themselves are maintained in lists, one list for each class of entities. Locating an entity thus involves locating its class in ClassList and then finding the correct entity. The first record in each EntList is pointed to by a variable RootEnt from ClassList. Each EntList is organised as a doubly linked list, terminated by a Nil record. Each entity record contains the following fields:

TCell: the time cell of the entity.
NextAct: the next activity of the entity, if known.
State: the current state of the entity.
Avail: a Boolean variable indicating whether the entity is currently engaged or is available for scheduling.
EntNumber: the unique number of this entity.
ThisClass: a pointer to the class record of this entity.
Util: an integer variable used to accumulate the total active time of the entity (see the procedure Schedule below).
PrevEnt: the preceding entity record in this EntList.
NextEnt: the following record in this EntList.

A Simple Pointer-based Executive   195

Entity records maybe added to, and deleted from, any of the entity lists as the simulation proceeds. Thus entities can be temporary or permanent, and there is no need to specify any maximum at compilation time.

Times

In the simple array-based executive described in the previous section, it was necessary to check all entity records for the A phase. To avoid this, a third linked list is employed. This list, TimeList, is linked forwards from TimeRoot to TimeSent, these being permanent global variables. Each record merely points (via the Entity field) to an active entity as well as to the succeeding record of TimeList. The records which make up TimeList are ordered chronologically. Thus the A phase is trivial, and involves merely examining the time cell of the first entity noted in TimeList. On the other hand, scheduling an entity is slightly more complicated as it must be inserted at the correct place in TimeList.

Queues

Another pointer-based structure is used to maintain queues of entities if they are required in the simulation. The queues are maintained as circular lists defined as QueueList, each record of which has the following fields:

QSize: the current number of entities in this queue.
QEnd: a pointer of type MembPoint (see below) to the last member of this queue, pointing to Nil if QSize is zero.
QName: a text identifier for the queue which may be useful in debugging.
Class: the class type which can occupy this queue.

The circular list of entities itself is held in dynamic variables of type MembPoint, which provide the sequence of entities in any queue at any time. The fields of MembPoint are defined as follows:

QMember: of type EntPoint and pointing to the entity record which occupies this position in the queue.
NextMember: point to the next member of the circular list.

```
Type TimePoint = ^TimeList; {Single linked list of scheduled entities}
     EntPoint  = ^EntList;  {Doubly linked list used to maintain
                             entity attributes. One list per class}
     ClassPoint = ^ClassList; {Used to keep class information}
     MembPoint = ^Member;    {Member of a queue}
     QueuePoint = ^QueueList; {Queue of entities, circular list}

     BAct = (Arrive, EndServe, Call, EndTalk, Observe); {Valid B activities}
     PossState = (Busy, Idle, Arriving, InQueue, Waiting); {Valid states}
     Char10 = Packed Array [1..10] of Char;

     TimeList = Record Entity : EntPoint;    {Identifies correct entity}
                       NextTime : TimePoint; {Fwd link in time list}
                End;

     EntList = Record TCell : integer;       {Time of next state change}
                      NextAct : BAct;        {Next B activity scheduled}
                      State : PossState;     {Current state of entity}
                      Avail : Boolean;       {Can entity be scheduled?}
                      EntNumber : integer;   {Counter for entities}
                      ThisClass : ClassPoint; {Class membership of entity}
                      Util : Integer;        {Total active time of entity}
                      PrevEnt, NextEnt : EntPoint; {Fwd & Bwd links}
               End;

     ClassList = Record RootEnt : EntPoint;  {Points to Root of list of
                                              entities associated with this class}
                        ClassDesc : Char10;  {Verbal description}
                        NumEnts : Integer;   {Counter of entities currently
                                              associated with this Class}
                        MaxEnt : Integer;    {Total entities created for this
                                              Class during the simulation}
                        PrevClass, NextClass : ClassPoint; {Fwd & Bwd links}
                 End;

     Member = Record QMember : EntPoint;      {Entity in this position}
                     NextMember : MembPoint;  {Next one in the list}
              End;

     QueueList = Record QSize : Integer;      {Current size of queue}
                       QEnd : MembPoint;      {Points into the circular list}
                       QName : Char10;
                       Class : ClassPoint;
                End;

Var TimeRoot, TimeSent : TimePoint;     {Root & sentinel for time list}
    CurrEnt : EntPoint;                 {Entity selected in ABPhase}
    ClassRoot, ClassSent : ClassPoint;  {Root & sentinel for Class list}
    Clock : Integer;                    {Current simulation time}
    RunDuration : Integer;              {Duration of simulation}
    SeeOp : Boolean;                    {Check for runtime output}
```

Figure 7.10 Pointer-based executive: type and global variable definitions.

As the list is circular, it is not terminated by any sort of sentinel. Instead, the following is guaranteed.

1. If QSize is zero, then QEnd points to Nil.
2. If QSize is one, then QEnd points to the single entity in the queue and the NextMember pointer points at the entity itself. That is, the circuit has only one member.

A Simple Pointer-based Executive

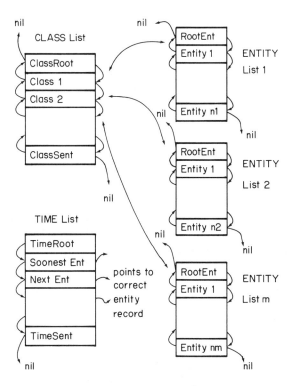

Figure 7.11 Pointer-based executive: linked lists.

3   If QSize equals n, where $(n > 1)$, then QEnd points to the nth entity in the queue (the last one). Then the nth entity points to the first via NextMember, the first to the second, the second to the third and so on until the n-1th points to the nth.

The type declarations needed, together with necessary global variables are shown in Figure 7.10, and Figure 7.11 makes clear the links between the various lists.

7.5.2 The A, B and C phases

Because the A phase is so simple for this executive, it makes sense to use a single procedure, ABphase, to handle both the A and B phases. This is shown in Figure 7.12. Having located the time of the next event, this procedure simply moves down TimeList one record at a time. Each record which indicates an entity with a time cell equal to

```
Procedure ABPhase;
{Carries out the A and B phases of 3 phase discrete event simulation}
Var p1, p2 : TimePoint;
    Time : Integer;
Begin
{Writeln;ShowTimeList;
ShowEntLists;}                              {Use these if having problems debugging}
If TimeRoot^.NextTime <> TimeSent then {Check that time list not empty}
    Begin
    p1 := TimeRoot^.NextTime;               {Find top of time list}
    Time := p1^.Entity^.TCell;              {Note time of the first entity}
    Clock := Time;                          {Move clock to new time}
    If SeeOp then
        Begin
        Writeln;
        Writeln('Time now ',Clock);
        End;
    While p1^.Entity^.TCell = Time do
    {For all entities on list with same TCell}
            Begin
            CurrEnt := p1^.Entity;          {CurrEnt points to the entity}
            CurrEnt^.Avail := True;         {Make entity available}
            p2 := p1;
            p1 := p2^.NextTime;             {Find the next entity}
            TimeRoot^.NextTime := p1;       {Time root linked to next entity}
            Dispose(p2);                    {Destroy CurrEnt pointer from list}
            BList;                          {Do correct B activity for CurrEnt}
            End;
    End
Else Error(9);
End;
```

Figure 7.12 Pointer-based executive: ABPhase.

the new clock time is used to execute a B activity. The record is then deleted from TimeList. This movement down TimeList ceases when an entity with time cell greater then Clock is reached. Cphase follows ABPhase. BList is of the form shown below:

> Procedure BList;
> Begin
> Case CurrEnt^.NextAct of
>   (List of B activities, linked to values defined as type BAct)
> End:

Thus the main program is as follows:

> Begin (Main program)
> InitClassList;
> InitTimeList;
> Initialisation;

A Simple Pointer-based Executive 199

```
While Clock <=RunDuration do
  Begin
  ABphase;
  Cphase;
  End;
Finalisation;
End.
```

InitClassList and InitTimeList are mandatory procedures which establish and initialise the overall ClassList and the TimeList. Failure to call these procedures will result in undefined pointers which may cause havoc in some versions of Pascal. They are shown in Figure 7.13.

```
Procedure InitClassList;
{Establishes new double-linked list of classes at start of simulation.
Creates root and sentinel. Root points forward to sentinel and back to Nil.
Sentinel points back to root and forward to Nil}
Begin
New(ClassRoot);
New(ClassSent);
With ClassRoot^ do
     Begin
     PrevClass := Nil;
     NextClass := ClassSent;
     ClassDesc := 'Root         ';
     End;
With ClassSent  do
     Begin
     PrevClass := ClassRoot;
     NextClass := Nil;
     ClassDesc := 'Sentinel     ';
     End;
End;


Procedure InitTimeList;
{Establish new time list at start of simulation. Creates root & sentinel and
sets Root to point to sentinel and sentinel to point to Nil}
Begin
New(TimeRoot);
New(TimeSent);
TimeRoot^.NextTime := TimeSent;
TimeSent^.NextTime := Nil;
End;
```

Figure 7.13 Pointed based executive: establishing the time and class lists.

7.5.3 Scheduling entities

As mentioned earlier, the task of scheduling an entity to engage in a future B activity is more complicated with this executive than with

```
Procedure Schedule(ThisEnt : EntPoint;
                   NewState : PossState;
                   NextBAct : BAct;
                   Time : Integer);
{Adds an entity pointer to the time list. Time list is sequenced by the
TCell values of the entities}

Procedure InsertTime;
{Finds correct point in timelist and inserts new pointer}
Var Post, Pre, NewTime : TimePoint;
    OK : Boolean;
Begin
Post := TimeRoot;
OK := False;
Repeat                     {Zoom down time list until at the correct spot}
     Pre := Post;
     Post := Pre^.NextTime;
     If Post = TimeSent then OK := True
     Else If Post^.Entity^.TCell > ThisEnt^.TCell then OK := True;
Until OK;
New(NewTime);              {Establish new entry in time list}
NewTime^.Entity := ThisEnt;
NewTime^.NextTime := Post;    {Link new record into time list before Post}
Pre^.NextTime := NewTime;     {Link fwd from Pre to new time NewTime}
End;


Begin
{ShowEntLists;}         {Use this if debugging and program seems lost!}
With ThisEnt^ do
     Begin
     If Avail then
         Begin
         If Time+Clock > MaxInt then TCell := MaxInt
             Else TCell := Time + Clock;  {Update TCell value}
         NextAct := NextBAct;             {Update Next activity of this entity}
         State := NewState;               {Change state of this entity}
         Avail := False;                  {Entity no longer available}
         Util := Util + Time;             {Accumulate entity active time}
         InsertTime;                      {Insert pointer on time list}
         If SeeOp then
             Writeln('Scheduling ', ThisClass^.ClassDesc, EntNumber:5, ' for ',
                          TCell:8);
         End
     Else Error(8);
     End;
End;
```

Figure 7.14 Pointer-based executive: procedures for scheduling entities.

the array-based procedures. Two tasks are involved whenever an entity is to be scheduled. Firstly, its record must be updated; that is, its next activity field (NextAct) and its time cell (TCell) must be updated and it must be shown to be unavailable. Secondly, an entry must be made in the correct place in TimeList. To make this clearer here, the procedure Schedule includes a nested procedure, InsertTime, which updates TimeList. The procedures are shown in Figure 7.14.

A Simple Pointer-based Executive 201

```
Procedure CreateEnt(ClassName : ClassPoint;
                    Num : Integer;
                    FirstState : PossState);
{Adds any number (Num) of entities to a pre-existing class (ClassName)}
Var e1, e2, e3 : EntPoint;
    Counter, Loop : integer;
Begin
With ClassName^ do                 {Update record for this class}
    Begin
    Counter := MaxEnt;
    MaxEnt := MaxEnt + Num;
    NumEnts := NumEnts + Num;
    e1 := RootEnt;
    End;
While e1^.NextEnt <> Nil do e1 := e1^.NextEnt;   {Find end of list}
For Loop := 1 to Num do            {Add each entity record in turn to list}
    Begin
    New(e2);                       {Create new entity}
    e1^.NextEnt := e2;             {Link new entity into list}
    e2^.PrevEnt := e1;
    Counter := Counter + 1;
    With e2^ do                    {Set up entity attributes}
        Begin
        TCell := 0;
        NextEnt := Nil;
        Avail := True;
        Util := 0;
        State := FirstState;
        EntNumber := Counter;
        ThisClass := ·ClassName;
        End;
    e1 := e2;                      {Reset end of entity list}
    End;
End;
```

Figure 7.15a Pointer-based executive: adding entities.

7.5.4 Adding and deleting entities

Given that arrays offer true random access to entity records, then the only reason for using linked lists must be to allow the dynamic creation of entities. Searching linked lists and tree structures can be done efficiently, but it is still quicker to have direct (i.e. random) access to particular records. Without such random access, some means must be provided for locating, adding and deleting entities. Suitable procedures are shown in Figure 7.15.

The procedure CreateEnt allows the additon of Num extra entities of class ClassName, a suitable class having been previously defined. It firstly updates the appropriate class record in ClassList. This involves incrementing the two counters NumEnts and MaxEnt. The new entities, set to some specified state, are then added at the end of the correct EntList for this class. Their Avail field is set to True.

The procedure DestroyEntity is used to completely destroy an entity from the simulation when it is no longer needed. It first checks

```
Procedure DestroyEntity(Var ThisEnt : EntPoint);
{Used to destroy a temporary entity from the simulation, when it is no
loger needed.
The user must ensure that ThisEnt is not sitting in queue somewhere. Entities
in queues must be removed from the queues before deletion.}
Var t1 : TimePoint;
    c1 : ClassPoint;
Begin
t1 := TimeRoot;         {Find start of time list}
Repeat                  {Make sure CurrEnt not on time list! Abort if it is}
    t1 := t1^.NextTime;
    If t1^.Entity = ThisEnt then Error(1);
Until t1 = TimeSent;
With ThisEnt^ do                        {Safe to destroy so go ahead}
    Begin
    c1 := ThisClass;                    {Find correct class on class list}
    c1^.NumEnts := c1^.NumEnts - 1;     {Decrement number of active entities}
    PrevEnt^.NextEnt := NextEnt;        {Remove ThisEnt from the entity list}
    If NextEnt <> Nil then NextEnt^.PrevEnt := PrevEnt;
    If SeeOp then
        Writeln('Deleting ', ThisClass^.ClassDesc, EntNumber:4);
    End;
Dispose(ThisEnt);                       {Destroy the pointer}
End;

Procedure DelEnt(ClassName : ClassPoint;
                 Num : integer);
{Finds and destroys the Numth entity belonging to class ClassName.
As with DestroyEntity, the user must ensure that the entity is not in a queue
somewhere, otherwise expect problems later on.}
Var e1 : EntPoint;
    Found : Boolean;
Begin
Found := False;
With ClassName^ do          {Check that correct number given to entity}
    If Num > MaxEnt then Error(2)
    Else
        Begin
        e1 := RootEnt;
        While (e1 <> Nil) and (Not Found) do
            Begin           {Find correct entity record in list}
            e1 := e1^.NextEnt;
            Found := (e1^.EntNumber = Num);
            End;
        If Found then DestroyEntity(e1) Else Error(3);
        End;
End;
```

Figure 7.15b Pointer-based executive: destroying entities.

that the entity is not currently on the TimeList; were this the case, an error would result. If the entity is available, it is removed from the appropriate EntList and the NumEnts field of the Class record is decremented. All traces of the entity are removed from the Pascal stack by disposing of the pointer. Before using this procedure it is important to ensure that the entity is not in any queue (see above) otherwise the QMember field in the queue will point to some undefined location.

DelEnt is a similar procedure which can be used to destroy an entity by referring to its Class and EntNumber rather than finding the entity itself first. The same caveat about queue membership applies.

A Simple Pointer-based Executive 203

```
Procedure CreateClass(Var ClassName : ClassPoint;
                         Desc : Char10;
                         Num : Integer;
                         FirstState : PossState);
Var c1 : ClassPoint;
{Adds a class (ClassName), initially of Num entities, to the list of classes.
Adds the appropriate list of entities as EntList}
Begin
c1 := ClassSent^.PrevClass;             {Find current end of class list}
New(ClassName);                         {Establish new pointer}
c1^.NextClass := ClassName;             {Link previous last class to this class}
ClassSent^.PrevClass := ClassName;
With ClassName^ do                      {Establish Class record}
    Begin
    NextClass := ClassSent;             {Make this new bottom of class list}
    ClassDesc := Desc;                  {Add verbal description}
    NumEnts := 0;                       {Class initially with no entities}
    MaxEnt := 0;
    New(RootEnt);                       {Establish RootEnt}
    With RootEnt^ do                    {Establish new entity list}
        Begin
        ThisClass := ClassName;         {Point back to Class List}
        NextEnt := Nil;                 {Point forwards to Nil}
        PrevEnt := Nil;                 {Point backwards to Nil};
        End;
    End;
CreateEnt(ClassName, Num, FirstState);           {Add appropriate number of
entities}
End;
```

Figure 7.16 Pointer-based executive: creating classes.

```
Procedure FindFirst(ClassName : ClassPoint;
                     ThisState : PossState;
                     Var ThisEnt : EntPoint;
                     Var Found : Boolean);
{Finds first entity of class ClassName in State ThisState.
Returns the entity as ThisEnt if Found, else returns Found as False}
Begin
Found := False;
ThisEnt := ClassName^.RootEnt;   {Goes to start of correct entity list}
{Find first entity in correct state or end of list}
While (ThisEnt <> Nil) and (Not Found) do
    Begin
    ThisEnt := ThisEnt^.NextEnt;
    Found := (ThisEnt^.State = ThisState);
    End;
End;


Function FindEnt(ClassName : ClassPoint;
                 Num : integer) : EntPoint;
{Locates the Numth created entity of class ClassName}
Var e1 : EntPoint;
Begin
If Num > ClassName^.MaxEnt then Error(4)
    Else
        Begin
        e1 := ClassName^.RootEnt^.NextEnt;
        While (e1^.EntNumber <> Num) and (e1 <> Nil) do e1 := e1^.NextEnt;
        If e1 <> Nil then FindEnt := e1
        Else Error(5);
        End;
End;
```

Figure 7.17 Pointer-based executive: finding entities.

7.5.5 Creating classes

At some stage the classes of entity making up the simulation model must be defined. In this executive each class is a globally defined variable of type ClassPoint. Given such variables, the procedure CreateClass is shown in Figure 7.16. Firstly, a new class record is added to ClassList. The fields of this record are set to initial values. Secondly, a new Entlist is established with RootEnt as its first record pointing to Nil in both directions. By using the procedure CreatEnt, the entity list is initialised with the appropriate number of entities.

7.5.6 Finding entities

Other procedures might be needed to find particular entities, either in general or with specified states. Two such procedures are shown in Figure 7.17. Findfirst returns the first entity which it can find in the state ThisState by searching through the entities in the order in which they appear in the EntList. If no such entity can be located, the Boolean variable Found is returned as False.

```
Procedure CreateQueue(Var Q : QueuePoint;
                    EntityClass : ClassPoint;
                    Name : Char10);
{Establishes a new queue, but of size zero and empty.
 Initially this is an empty list.}
Begin
New(Q);
With Q^ do
     Begin
     QSize := 0;
     QEnd := Nil;
     QName := Name;
     Class := EntityClass;
     End;
End;


Procedure RotateQ(Q : QueuePoint;
                Num : Integer);
{Rotates the circular queue Num places, has the effect of moving each member
Num places relative to the start. Putting Num = 1 puts the second entity at
the head, third at second ..etc.. and the head at the tail}
Var Loop : Integer;
Begin
With Q^ do
     If QSize = 0 then Error(6)
     Else For Loop := 1 to Num do QEnd := QEnd^.NextMember;
End;
```

Figure 7.18 Pointer-based executive: creating and rotating queues.

A Simple Pointer-based Executive 205

```
Procedure FindHead(Var HeadEnt : EntPoint;
                   Q : QueuePoint;
                   Var Found : Boolean);
{Tries to find the head of the queue. Returns this as HeadEnt with
Found = True if successful. Otherwise returns Found = False.
Does nothing to the queue members.}
Begin
If Q^.QSize > 0 then
   Begin
   Found := True;
   HeadEnt := Q^.QEnd^.NextMember^.QMember; {Picks up correct QMember}
   End
Else Found := False;
End;


Procedure FindTail(Var TailEnt : EntPoint;
                   Q : QueuePoint;
                   Var Found : Boolean);
{Tries to find the tail of the queue. Returns this as TailEnt with
Found = True if successful. Otherwise returns Found = False.
Does nothing to the queue members.}
Begin
If Q^.QSize > 0 then
   Begin
   Found := True;
   TailEnt := Q^.QEnd^.QMember; {Picks up correct QMember}
   End
Else Found := False;
End;

Function InQ(ThisEnt : EntPoint;
             Q : QueuePoint) : Boolean;
{Checks whether ThisEnt is in Q. If so, returns InQ as True, otherwise False}
Var Found : Boolean;
    Memb : MembPoint;
    Counter : Integer;
Begin
If Q^.Class = ThisEnt^.ThisClass then
   Begin
   Found := False;                              {Set initial value of Found}
   Memb := Q^.QEnd;                             {Ready to go down the list}
   Counter := 1;                                {Keep count}
   While (Q^.QSize >= Counter) and (Not Found) do    {Find or stop at end}
      If Memb^.QMember = ThisEnt then Found := True  {Found it!}
      Else
         Begin
         Counter := Counter + 1;                {Increment the counter}
         Memb := Memb^.NextMember;              {Try next member}
         End;
   InQ := Found;                                {Return boolean value}
   End
Else Error(10);
End;
```

Figure 7.19 Pointer-based executive: finding entities in queues.

FindEnt returns with entity which has the specified EntNumber in the appropriate ClassList. An Error results if the entity cannot be found.

7.5.7 Creating queues

Once a queue is created, it remains in the simulation until the run is

```
Procedure IntoQueue(Q : QueuePoint;
                    ThisEnt : EntPoint;
                    Var Memb : MembPoint);
{Adds an entity to a queue. Called by AddtoHead() and AddtoTail()}
Begin
New(Memb);                              {Create a new pointer}
Memb^.QMember := ThisEnt;               {Point Memb at ThisEnt}
Q^.QSize := Q^.QSize + 1;               {Increment QSize}
If Q^.QSize = 1 then                    {If this is the only entry .. }
   Begin
   Memb^.NextMember := Memb;            {Link to itself}
   Q^.QEnd := Memb;                     {This entity is last (and first)}
   End
Else
   Begin                                          {Not the only entry ..}
   Memb^.NextMember := Q^.QEnd^.NextMember; {Link from this new entry}
   Q^.QEnd^.NextMember := Memb;         {This entry pointed from last}
   End;
End;


Procedure AddToHead(ThisEnt : EntPoint;
                    Q : QueuePoint);
{Places ThisEnt at the start of a queue}
Var Memb : MembPoint;
Begin
If Q^.Class = ThisEnt^.ThisClass then
   IntoQueue(Q, ThisEnt, Memb)          {Add direct to head of queue}
Else Error(10);
End;


Procedure AddtoTail(ThisEnt : EntPoint;
                    Q : QueuePoint);
{Places ThisEnt at the end of a queue}
Var Memb : MembPoint;
Begin
If Q^.Class = ThisEnt^.ThisClass then
   Begin
   IntoQueue(Q, ThisEnt, Memb);                 {Add direct to head of queue}
   If Q^.QSize > 1 then Q^.QEnd := Memb;        {Now move back one position}
   End
Else Error(10);
End;
```

Figure 7.20 Pointer-based executive: adding entities to queues.

over; thus queues are created as global variables. The procedure CreateQueue, shown in Figure 7.18, may be used to do so. Also shown in Figure 7.18 is the procedure Rotate, which uses the circular list structure of the queues to change the position of the members of a queue. It moves all entities Num places down the queue relative to the start. Rotating with Num equal to 1 puts the old second as the new head, the old third in second position, the old third as fourth and so on.

7.5.8 Finding queue members

A common need is to find entities at the head or tail or a queue. Two

A Simple Pointer-based Executive   207

```
Procedure RemoveFromQueue(Q : QueuePoint;
                          ThisMember : MembPoint);
{General procedure to remove an entity from a queue. The queue links
are reset and the Membership pointer is deleted.
Used by TakeFromHead() and TakeFromTail().}
Begin
With Q^ do
     Begin
     If QSize = 0 then Error(6)             {Q is empty, so fail}
     Else
         Begin
         QSize := QSize - 1;                {Reduce QSize}
         If QSize = 0 then QEnd := Nil      {If Q empty, correct behaviour}
         Else                               {Q not empty .. }
             QEnd^.NextMember := ThisMember^.NextMember;
         Dispose(ThisMember);
         End;
     End;
End;

Procedure TakeFromHead(Var ThisEnt : EntPoint;
                       Q : QueuePoint;
                       Var Found : Boolean);
{Returns with the entity at the head of Q, removes ThisEnt from the head
of Q and returns Found as True if QSize > 0 exists.
Otherwise Found is returned as false and ThisEnt is unspecified.}
Var Head : MembPoint;
Begin
With Q^ do
     Begin
     If QSize = 0 then Found := False       {Queue is empty}
     Else
         Begin                              {Queue is not empty .. }
         Found := True;
         QSize := QSize - 1;                {Decrement QSize}
         If QSize = 0 then
             Begin
             ThisEnt := QEnd^.QMember;      {Find correct entity}
             QEnd := Nil;                   {Protect pointer}
             End
         Else
             Begin
             Head := QEnd^.NextMember;      {Find head of queue}
             ThisEnt := Head^.QMember;      {Find correct entity}
             QEnd^.NextMember := Head^.NextMember;  {Re-establish link}
             Dispose(Head);                 {Remove pointer}
             End;
         End;
     End;
End;
```

Figure 7.21a Pointer-based executive: removing entities from queues.

procedures, FindHead and FindTail, are provided for this purpose and are shown in Figure 7.19, together with a function InQ which checks whether a specified entity may be found in a specified queue. The FindHead and FindTail procedures employ a Boolean variable Found, which is returned with a value of False if the queue is currently empty. If QSize is greater than zero, then the procedures return with entities at the head or tail of the specified queue. They do not alter the position of any entities in the queue.

```
Procedure TakeFromTail(Var ThisEnt : EntPoint;
                      Q : QueuePoint;
                      Var Found : Boolean);
{Returns with the entity at the tail of Q, removes ThisEnt from the tail
of Q and returns Found as True if QSize > 0 exists.
Otherwise Found is returned as false and ThisEnt is unspecified.}
Var Tail, NewHead : MembPoint;
Begin
With Q^ do
    Begin
    If QSize = 0 then Found := False           {Queue is empty}
    Else
        Begin                                  {Queue is not empty .. }
        RotateQ(Q, QSize-1);
        TakeFromHead(ThisEnt, Q, Found);
        End;
    End;
End;
```

Figure 7.21b Pointer-based executive: removing entities from queues.

The functon InQ returns a Boolean value which is True or False depending on whether the entity can be found in the queue. InQ produces an error if the specified entity is not in the Class which may occupy this queue.

7.5.9 Adding entities to queues

Three procedures are shown in Figure 7.20 for this purpose. AddToHead puts the entity at the head of the queue and AddToTail puts it at the tail. Both procedures make use of the procedure IntoQueue to do so, and both return Errors if the entity is of the wrong class for the queue.

7.5.10 Removing entities from queues

It is common to need to remove entities from the head or tail of a queue, and two procedures for that purpose are shown in Figure 7.21. These procedures, TakeFromHead and TakeFromTail, return an entity at the head or tail of the queue if QSize is greater than zero. If QSize is zero then both procedures return with the Boolean variable Found set to False. Note that TakeFromTail uses the procedure Rotate (see Figure 7.18) to make the current tail entity into the head, it then uses TakeFromHead to complete the operation.

7.5.11 Other procedures

Four other procedures are shown in Figure 7.22. One mandatory

An Example: 209

```
Procedure Error(ErrorNum : Integer);
{Stop simulation and show error message if necessary}
Begin
Writeln;Writeln('Stopped at ', Clock);
Case ErrorNum of
     1:Writeln('Tried to kill active CurrEnt');
     2:Writeln('Entity number out of range in DelEnt');
     3:Writeln('No entity found for deletion in DelEnt');
     4:Writeln('Out of range entity in FindEnt');
     5:Writeln('Entity cannot be found in FindEnt');
     6:Writeln('Tried to operate on an empty queue');
     7:Writeln('ClassList empty, cannot print');
     8:Writeln('Tried to schedule unavailable entity');
     9:Writeln('Timelist seems to be empty');
     10:Writeln('Cannot have this entity in this queue, wrong class');
     End;
Halt;                       {Exit from run}
End;


Procedure ShowEntLists;
{Used for debugging, will list current contents of all entity lists on screen}
Var e1 : EntPoint;
    c1 : ClassPoint;
    Loop : Integer;
Begin
If ClassRoot^.NextClass = ClassSent then Error(7)
Else
    Begin
    c1 := ClassRoot^.NextClass;        {Start with first Class}
    While c1 <> ClassSent do
         Begin
         Writeln(c1^.ClassDesc);
         e1 := c1^.RootEnt;            {Point to Root of this EntList}
         For Loop := 1 to c1^.NumEnts do
             Begin
             e1 := e1^.NextEnt;        {Point to next ent record in this EntList}
             With e1^ do
                  Begin
                  Write(EntNumber:5, TCell:5);
                  If Avail then Writeln('    Avail') Else Writeln;
                  End;
             End;
         c1 := c1^.NextClass;          {On to next class in class list}
         End;
    End;
End;
```

Figure 7.22a Pointer-based executive: utility procedures.

procedure is to handle errors, and the other three allow the contents of the various lists to be displayed for debugging purposes.

7.6 An Example:
An Encore for the Harassed Booking Clerk

To illustrate the use of this pointer-based executive, the harassed booking clerk example is programmed below in a different form to

```
Procedure ShowQueue(Q : QueuePoint);
{Lists the contents of the specified queue. Useful for debugging.}
Var M1 : MembPoint;
    Counter : Integer;
Begin
Writeln('Contents of queue ', Q^.QName);
Counter := 1;
If Q^.QSize = 0 then Writeln('Empty')
Else
    Begin
    M1 := Q^.QEnd;
    While Counter <= Q^.QSize do
         Begin
         M1 := M1^.NextMember;
         With M1^.QMember^ do
              Writeln(Counter:5, '    ', ThisClass^.ClassDesc, EntNumber:4);
         Counter:= Counter+ 1;
         End;
    Writeln;
    End;
End;


Procedure ShowTimeList;
Var t1, t2 : TimePoint;
{Used for debugging, will list current contents of time list on screen}
Begin
t1 := TimeRoot^.NextTime;
While t1 <> TimeSent do
     Begin
     With t1^ do With Entity^ do
          Writeln(ThisClass^.ClassDesc, EntNumber:5,    TCell:5);
     t2 := t1;
     t1 := t2^.NextTime;
     End;
End;
```

Figure 7.22b Pointer-based executive: utility procedures.

```
{Now specific variable definitions for activities ..etc..
 Must be edited if the simulation program is modified}

Var PersEnq, PhoneEnq, Observer : ClassPoint;   {Classes to be used}
    PhoneQueue, PersQueue : QueuePoint;         {Queues to be used}


    NumClerks, FreeClerks : Integer;      {Number of clerks available & free}
    NumPers : Integer;                    {Number of personal arrivals}
    NumPhone : Integer;                   {Number of phone calls}
    NumServe : Integer;                   {Number of personal services started}
    NumTalk : Integer;                    {Number of phone conversations started}
    ObsPhoneQ : Array[1..25] of integer;  {Time series of personal queue}
    ObsPersQ : Array[1..25] of integer;   {Time series of phone queue}
    NumSeen : Integer;                    {Number of completed personal services}
    NumConv : integer;                    {Number of completed phone calls}
    Obs : Integer;                        {Number of observations}
```

Figure 7.23 Harassed booking clerk, pointer-based executive: variable declarations.

An Example

```
Procedure BArrive;              {Arrival of personal enquirer}
Var Time : integer;
    NextCust : EntPoint;
Begin
{First handle the latest arrival}
CurrEnt^.State := InQueue;          {Latest customer now InQueue}
NumPers := NumPers + 1;             {Increment number of arrivals}
AddToTail(CurrEnt, PersQueue);      {Add this customer to back of PersQueue}
If SeeOp then
    Writeln('Personal enquirer ', NumPers, ' arrives, queue now ',
                    PersQueue^.QSize);
{Then handle the next personal enquirer}
CreateEnt(PersEnq, 1, Arriving);              {Create next personal arrival}
NextCust := FindEnt(PersEnq, NumPers+1);      {Schedule next personal arrival}
Schedule(NextCust, Arriving, Arrive, Round(10*Random));
End;


Procedure BEndServe;            {End of personal service}
Begin
NumSeen := NumSeen + 1;             {Increment number of completed services}
FreeClerks := FreeClerks + 1;       {Add one to free clerks}
DestroyEntity(CurrEnt);             {Finished with this customer}
If SeeOp then Writeln('Clerk finished personal service ',NumSeen);
End;


Procedure BCall;                {Arrival of phone call}
Var Time : integer;
    NextCaller : EntPoint;
    HeadEnt, TailEnt : EntPoint;
    HeadFound, TailFound : Boolean;
Begin
{First handle the latest phone call}
CurrEnt^.State := Waiting;          {Latest caller now waiting}
NumPhone := NumPhone + 1;           {Increment number of calls}
AddToTail(CurrEnt, PhoneQueue);     {Add this call to the back of PhoneQueue}
If SeeOp then
    Writeln('Phone enquirer ', NumPhone, ' arrives, queue now ',
                    PhoneQueue^.QSize);
{Then handle the next phone call}
CreateEnt(PhoneEnq, 1, Arriving);             {Create next phone call}
NextCaller := FindEnt(PhoneEnq, NumPhone+1);  {Schedule next phone call}
Schedule(NextCaller, Arriving, Call, Round(15*Random));
End;

Procedure BEndTalk;             {End of phone conversation}
Begin
NumConv := NumConv + 1;             {Increment number of completed conversations}
FreeClerks := FreeClerks + 1;       {Add one to free clerks}
DestroyEntity(CurrEnt);             {Finished with this phone call}
If SeeOp then Writeln('Clerk finished phone conversation ',NumConv);
End;
```

Figure 7.24a Harassed booking clerk, pointer-based executive: main B activities.

that of the previous section. Previously, the entities were as follows:

Personal enquirer arrival machine
Phone enquirer arrival machine
Clerks (1 . . NumClerks)
Observer

```
Procedure Bobserve;          {Collect time series of queue lengths}
Begin
Obs := Obs + 1;              {Increment number of observations}
ObsPersQ[Obs] := PersQueue^.QSize;    {Note length of personal queue}
ObsPhoneQ[Obs] := PhoneQueue^.QSize;  {Note length of phone queue}
Schedule(CurrEnt, Idle, Observe, 20);  {Schedule next observation}
End;

{****************************************************************************
                       C Activities start here
*****************************************************************************}

Procedure BeginPersonalService;       {Start to serve a personal enquirer}
Var ThisCust: EntPoint;
    CustomersFound : Boolean;
Begin
CustomersFound := True;
While (FreeClerks > 0) and (CustomersFound) do
      Begin
      TakeFromTail(ThisCust, PersQueue, CustomersFound);
      If CustomersFound then
         Begin
         NumServe := NumServe + 1;      {Increment started services}
         Schedule(ThisCust, Busy, EndServe, Round(10*Random));
         FreeClerks := FreeClerks - 1;  {Decrement free clerks}
         If SeeOp then
             Writeln('Begin service ', NumServe, ' free clerks = ', FreeClerks);

         End;
      End;
End;

Procedure BeginPhoneConversation;
{Start to answer phone call}
Var ThisCaller: EntPoint;
    CallersFound : Boolean;
Begin
CallersFound := True;
While (FreeClerks > 0) and (CallersFound) do
      Begin
      TakeFromHead(ThisCaller, PhoneQueue, CallersFound);
      If CallersFound then
         Begin
         NumTalk := NumTalk + 1;         {Increment started conversations}
         Schedule(ThisCaller, Busy, EndTalk, Round(5*Random));
         FreeClerks := FreeClerks - 1;   {Decrement free clerks}
         If SeeOp then
             Writeln('Begin talk ', NumTalk, ' freeclerks = ', FreeClerks);
         End;
      End;
End;
```

Figure 7.24b Harassed booking clerk, pointer-based executive: C activities plus BObserve.

This time the clerks are modelled by a simple integer variable, FreeClerks, which notes the number of free clerks at any time. On the other hand, both types of enquirer are modelled as individual entities. They are created as their arrival is scheduled, and destroyed as their service is complete. The observer is unchanged. Figure 7.23 shows the global variables which are necessary in addition to those defined in Figure 7.10. The five B and single C activities are shown in

```
Procedure BList;         {Needed because wish to Execute correct B activities}
Begin
Case CurrEnt^.NextAct of
    Arrive : BArrive;
    EndServe : BEndServe;
    Call : BCall;
    EndTalk : BEndTalk;
    Observe : Bobserve;
    End;
End;

Procedure Cphase;        {List of C activities in priority order}
Begin
BeginPersonalService;
BeginPhoneConversation;
End;
```

Figure 7.24c Harassed booking clerk, pointer-based executive: BList and CPhase.

Figure 7.24. There are two arrival-type B activites, BArrive and BCall, in which the arriving entity (returned as CurrEnt) by ABPhase is added to the tail of a queue. Before the next arrival can be scheduled a new entity record must be created and added to the appropriate ClassList. Conversely, when service-type states are complete (i.e. activites BEndServe and BEndTalk), the relevant entities are destroyed.

For clarity, there are two C activities, BeginPersonalService and BeginPhoneConversation, and each works as follows. The start of the service is controlled by a While loop which continues until FreeClerks is zero (all clerks are busy) or CustomersFound is False (none can be found by TakeFromTail in the appropriate queue). Whereas in the previous version the clerks were scheduled to control the end of the state, this time the enquirers themselves are scheduled.

To complete the program, Initialisation and Finalisation procedures are needed. Most of the Initialisation is similar to the previous version, the main differences are that entity classes have to be created and that a variable FreeClerks is introduced. Finalisation is unchanged. Both procedures are shown in Figure 7.25. It is also necessary to ensure that the BList and CPhase procedures are amended to reflect the B and C activities in use.

7.7 Pascal for Discrete Simulation?

It should be clear from this chapter that Pascal can be taken seriously as a candidate language for writing discrete simulations. It has distinct advantages over FORTRAN and BASIC for this type of work because its syntax is expressive, it has useful data

```
Procedure Initialisation;
{Set up initial values of parameters for this model}
Var Counter : Integer;
    Ans : Char;
    x : EntPoint;
    Time : integer;
Begin
Writeln;
Writeln('Harassed booking clerk simulation');
Writeln('--------------------------------');
Repeat
     Write('How Many Clerks (1..5)? ');
     Readln(NumClerks);
Until (NumClerks > 0) and (NumClerks < 6);
Repeat
     Write('Simulation duration (20..480 minutes)? ');
     Readln(RunDuration);
Until (RunDuration > 19) and (RunDuration <= 480);
Repeat
     Write('Run-time O/P to screen (Y/N)? ');
     Readln(Ans);
Until Ans in ['Y', 'y', 'N', 'n'];
If Ans in ['Y', 'y'] then SeeOp := True Else SeeOp := False;
{ **** Create first personal enquirer, first phone caller and observer ***** }
CreateClass(PersEnq, 'Enquirer   ', 1, Arriving);
CreateClass(PhoneEnq, 'Phone Call', 1, Arriving);
CreateClass(Observer, 'Observer   ', 1, Arriving);
{ ******************* Create queues used in the simulation ***************** }

CreateQueue(PersQueue, PersEnq, 'Enq Queue ');
CreateQueue(PhoneQueue, PhoneEnq, 'Call Queue');
{ ************* Set all clerks initially free ********************** }
FreeClerks := NumClerks;
{ ************* Schedule arrival of first personal enquirer ************** }
Time := Round(10*Random);
Schedule(FindEnt(PersEnq, 1), Arriving, Arrive, Time);
{ ************* Schedule arrival of first phone call ********************** }
Time := Round(15*Random);
Schedule(FindEnt(PhoneEnq, 1), Arriving, Call, Time);
{ ************* Schedule first observation ******************************** }
Schedule(FindEnt(Observer, 1), Idle, Observe, 20);
{ ************* Initialise all counters to zero *************************** }
NumPers := 0;
NumPhone := 0;
NumServe := 0;
NumTalk := 0;
NumSeen := 0;
NumConv := 0;
Obs := 0;
End;
```

Figure 7.25a Harassed booking clerk, pointer-based executive: BList and CPhase.

structures and it is block-structured. It is, however, not without its faults. The first being that the ISO Standard Pascal offers no facilities for the development of pre-compiled libraries, though enhancements such as Borland Turbo Pascal v4.0™ have adopted a unitisation system to allow this. The second significant problem is that even libraries of Pascal source code cannot be entirely general, as there is a need to predefine array sizes. For large-scale simulations this latter difficulty may not be a real

```
Procedure Finalisation;         {Final reports on the simulation}
Var Counter, Time : Integer;
Begin
Writeln;
Writeln('Simulation with ', NumClerks, ' clerks over after ', RunDuration);
Writeln;
Writeln('Time     Pers Queue      Phone Queue');
Writeln('----     ----------      -----------');
For Counter := 1 to Obs do
    Begin
    Time := Counter*20;
    Writeln(Time:3, ObsPersQ[Counter]:11, ObsPhoneQ[Counter]:15);
    End;
Writeln;
Writeln('Personal Enquirers, Arrivals : ', NumPers, ', No. Served : ',NumSeen);
Writeln('Phone calls, Arrivals : ', NumPhone, ', No. of Conversations : ',
            NumConv);
End;
```

Figure 7.25b Harassed booking clerk, pointer-based executive: finalisation.

problem though, as pointers are likely to be employed for much of the data representation.

However, it should not be pretended that Pascal, C, FORTRAN, BASIC, APL or the rest are always the best approach to simulation. If the capital cost of software is unimportant then it may be much better to use packages such as SEE-WHY, HOCUS, SIMSCRIPT or SLAM. But this is only true if they are quicker, and if they provide all the facilities needed in particular programs.

7.8 References

Barnett, C. C. (1986) Simulation in Pascal with Micro PASSIM. *Proc. Winter Simulation Conference*, pp. 151–5. Washington DC, 8–10 December 1986. IEEE, Piscataway, New Jersey.

Bryant, R. W. (1981) *SIMPAS User Manual*. Technical Report, Computer Science Department, and Madison Avenue Computing Center, University of Wisconsin-Madison, Madison, Wisconsin.

Clementson, A. T. (1982) *Extended Control and Simulation Language*. Cle.Com Ltd, Birmingham, UK.

Crookes, J. G., Balmer, D. W., Chew, S. T. and Paul, R. J. (1986) A three phase simulation system written in Pascal. *Journal of the Operational Research Society*, **37**(6), 603–18.

Dahl, O.-J., Myhrhaug, B. and Nygaard, K. (1970) *SIMULA 67 Common Base Language*. Publication No. S-22, Norwegian Computer Center, Oslo.

Jennergren, P. (1984) *Discrete Events Simulation in Pascal MT+ on a Microcomputer*. Student-litteratur, Chartwell-Bratt, Lund, Sweden.

Jensen, K. and Wirth, N. (1975) *Pascal User Manual and Report*. Springer-Verlag, New York.

Knuth, D. (1981) *The Art of Computer Programming*, Vol 2: *Semi-numerical Algorithms*, 2nd edn. Addison-Wesley, Reading, Mass.

Markowitz, H. M., Hausner, B. and Carr, H. W. (1963) *SIMSCRIPT: A Simulation Programming Language*. RAND Corporation, RM-3310 pr 1962. Prentice/Hall, Englewood Cliffs, New Jersey.

Page, E. S. and Wilson, L. B. (1985) *Information Representation* and *Manipulation Using Pascal*. Cambridge University Press, Cambridge.

Pidd, M. (1988) *Computer Simulation in Management Science*, 2nd edn. John Wiley & Sons Ltd, Chichester.

Poole, T. G. and Szymankiewicz, J. (1977) *Using Simulation to Solve Problems*. McGraw-Hill, London.

Seila, A. F. (1988) SIMTOOLS: A software tool kit for discrete computer simulation in Pascal. *Simulation*, **50**, 93–9.

Wirth, N. (1976) *Algorithms + Data structures = Programs*. Prentice-Hall, Englewood Cliffs, New Jersey.

Computer Modelling for Discrete Simulation
Edited by M. Pidd
©1989 John Wiley & Sons Ltd

8
Simulation using C

J. G. Crookes

8.1 Introduction— Simulation in General-purpose Languages

An early choice of facing the would-be simulator is between a simulation-specific language or a general-purpose language. When a general-purpose language is selected then it is often enhanced by the use of pre-prepared library routines, either written in-house or obtained from an outside supplier. Given the excellent low-priced compilers now available, coupled with the evident distaste of many computer users at the prospect of learning yet another set of syntactic rules, a decision in favour of such an enhanced general-purpose language is often a wise one. Packages to enhance the common languages are available from various sources, and many companies have their own routines.

I have a strong preference for fast-running simulations, believing those who argue that we should not concern ourselves with such matters (the 'the hardware boys will provide' brigade) probably do not run enough programs. High speed in the final simulation is more readily available if the general-purpose language route is followed. The ease of providing a clean interface between the base language and the library of simulation routines differs markedly between languages, as does the power and ease of use of the resulting system. The variation arises as a result of the attitude of language designers to the provision of libraries, a common assumption being that the user will write a program which will call upon library subroutines for services.

In simulation the executive program, which is prepared independently of any particular model, calls upon the routines specifying the model. So in a sense the executive may be thought of as a 'main' program and the model as a supporting library. As it is desirable for executive programs to be pre-compiled and secure against end-user 'fiddling', this can present problems, the solution of which may be cumbersome, inelegant and possibly slow.

I have written, or made major contributions to, systems of varying degrees of utility, including some supporting visible entities and interactive working, in assembler, ALGOL60, NELIAC, BASIC, Pascal and C. I have also studied the inner workings of other systems. Of these my current preference is for C, with Pascal running second. I anticipate that Pascal will be displaced from this second place in my affections by MODULA2 at some point. Whether C will similarly be displaced is moot. It will not be by ADA if it does occur.

8.2 Why C for Simulation?

8.2.1 C Much better than Pascal

There are a number of sources for my preference for C. I shall discuss them in comparison with Pascal. Most of them are as applicable to general programming as to simulation. Inevitably my preferences are personal, and there are those who see as disadvantages characteristics I regard as advantageous. I assume that the intention is to write substantial simulation models, not pedagogic examples, that these are expected to be of enduring value to the client organisation and thus may need maintenance. A possibility that should be borne in mind whenever producing a model is that it might be better to produce a generic model capable of substantial modification without re-programming.

C is a small language with even fewer reserved words than Pascal, so in one sense it is easy to learn—I certainly found it so. It provides many more operators, and as there are fifteen levels of precedence governing their combination in expressions the generous use of parentheses for clarity of expression is to be recommended. This may be contrasted with Pascal's four levels, which makes Boolean expressions involving relational operators require the use of parentheses to be well formed. The small size, in part, is because some common requirements such as input/output and string handling are not part of the language but are provided as library functions, a mechanism which has proved both popular and efficient, and which is also available to others, such as simulation

Why C for Simulation? 219

developers. Pascal lacks strings too, but, lacking a library mechanism, the defect is normally remedied in implementation-dependent ways.

In stark contrast with standard Pascal, provision is made for a program to be prepared in modules, which may be separately compiled. These modules are then joined together and linked with any required libraries, which may include simulation utility libraries, to produce a run-time program. Some implementations of Pascal allow this as a non-standard extension, but there is little uniformity between implementations.

C is a lineal descendent of BCPL, an early portable language with excellent control constructs but no data typing. It retains excellent control mechanisms and has data typing which may be deliberately and legally violated if required. This is in contrast to the strong typing of Pascal, which can only be evaded with illegal, implementation-dependent, contortions. A separate utility program LINT is available which provides those warnings characteristic of strong typing to users of C. It also provides warnings not always provided by Pascal implementations about use of uninitialised variables and pointers—the source of many seemingly 'impossible' bugs. Some modern compilers now have optional checking comparable with that of Pascal systems. The Pascal programming control statements are broadly similar, though C has the advantage with its 'break' and 'continue' statements which require the dreaded 'goto' in Pascal.

C provides a guaranteed evaluation mechanism for logical expressions in the conditional logical operators || and &&. This allows much clearer expression of loop control conditions without risk of run-time errors that exist in Pascal. The C 'for' statement is unrestricted in contrast with the unit increment enforced in Pascal.

A major difference is in the form a program takes. In Pascal a routine may be either a procedure or a function, and has to be declared textually before use. The definition of a routine takes a similar form to the definition of a program and in particular it may include the declaration and definition of further routines which are then only visible within the enclosing routine environment. In C such nesting of routines (all are called functions) is not permitted, and all functions are at the same level. Modularity is achieved by separation of co-operating routines and data objects into distinct physical files, within which they may share data objects hidden from other routines in other files, and may call upon the services of other, hidden routines (i.e. declared static as distinct from extern—the C term for global). The concept of hidden items is available inside functions where objects may be declared static, and will then retain their value between calls of the function.

Functions in C may be called with a different number of parameters from that specified in their definition. Pascal reserves that right to system procedures such as writeln etc. Though this facility is obviously useful in writing such 'print'-type functions it is not an everyday requirement of general or simulation programming.

Initialisation of variables in Pascal is poor, requiring the use of assignment statements which increases code file sizes with single-use statements. C allows initial values to be specified as required. Re-initialisation would of course require run-time code in C.

C is a permissive language with the design aim of allowing unfettered access to the underlying computer if required, and in simulation programming its ability to permit the storage of routine addresses as data is particularly pleasing. This contrasts with the design aims of Pascal. In Pascal the underlying machine is Pascal and that is that. This results in unwieldy contortions being required to achieve similar ends, causing the simulation programmer to need to set up indirect references to routines and ways of calling them. The impact of this permissiveness on simulation modellers arises out of the differing treatments of pointers in C and Pascal. In C a pointer is the machine address of an item—variables or functions—and may be obtained for all data objects and routines if required.

The ease of use of pointers enables both library routines and generic models to be written that handle objects of sizes determined at run-time. This enables much less restrictive systems to be prepared quite readily, utilising the system library of dynamic memory allocation routines. The built in macro-pre-processor of C enables the programmer to select efficient constructs without producing unreadable programs.

This can be done by the use of parameterised macros. An example taken from the stdio.h header file of the Microsoft C compiler is this macro-definition of the character output function putc(c,f) which outputs the character c to the file f. The action is to decrement the count of buffer space remaining to this file and either add the character to the buffer if space is available for it, incrementing the buffer pointer after that action, or if no space remains to call for the buffer to be flushed along with the character otherwise.

```
#define putc(c,f) >--cnt>=0? 0xff & (*(f)->_ptr++ = (c)): \
__flsbuf((c),(f)))
```

Why C for Simulation? 221

See also the macro-implementation of this or other standard input/output routines in your own compiler's stdio.h file, or the implementation of entity states in the simulation examples given later.

The pre-processor provides other major enhancements to the language beyond the parameterised text substitution referred to above. First is the ability to include other files via the #include statement. This enables programmers to keep control of the communications between modules, by ensuring that identical definitions and declarations actually are identical by being physically the same file. This facility is often provided as an implementation-dependent extension of Pascal. Secondly, it is possible to use the conditional compilation facility to enable one source file to be used to produce different code files depending on compile time parameters. This can be used to produce versions for different machines, or different configurations of one machine. Another common use is to allow extensive debugging code to be optionally included in a test compilation.

C is easily implemented on small machines, and is widely available at bargain prices. If using MS-DOS machines one cannot ignore the excellent Microsoft Compiler which includes a splendid source code debugger called Codeview. My own and my students' experience with this product has been very satisfying, resulting in high work rates.

8.2.2 Disadvantages of C

Needless to say, there are those who do not like C, and their case is well presented in the book (Feuer and Gehani, 1984) which is a compendium of papers discussing the relative merits of ADA, Pascal and C. A major complaint is that the absence of strong typing, coupled with support of the exploitation of side-effects, allows cryptic, write-only, programs which are impenetrable to the author, let alone others, within a relatively short period. This is akin to a complaint that chainsaws can also cut people, as well as wood.

There is no doubt that serious use of C imposes a requirement for a personal programming discipline which Pascal is designed to impose on users. If all the checking options available in good compilers are used, or utilities like LINT, much of this sort of complaint can be set aside, though there is a residue due to the very flexibility of C, in that errors can be made in intention that result in legal C and are only detectable by the run-time behaviour of the program not being as required.

My own most common mistake of this class, when first using C, was confusing the use of the equals sign as assignment with the use of the double equals sign as the relational equality operator. Compilers can sometimes be set to warn of such doubtful usage. The observation that so much successful commercial microcomputer software, including Pascal compilers, is now developed in C, and is successfully ported from machine to machine as new ones appear, indicates that many developers are able to avoid these particular pitfalls.

Arthur Evans Jr, in his conclusion to his contribution to Feuer and Gehani, writes:

> I find C to be a rather curious mixture of things. I get the impression that C's designers were personally charged $1000 for every reserved word in the language and $2000 for each concept, that C programmers are charged $5 for every character in each program they write, and that minimising these costs was a major design goal. It is, in my opinion, very much the wrong metric.

His criterion for comparison was the suitability of the languages for system programming. He eliminated ADA on grounds of size, imposed by the requirements committee. He eliminated Pascal on grounds of capability. He went on to accept that if LINT or equivalent were to be used then many of his complaints against C's design evaporate.

While accepting that there are what for some may be compelling arguments against, for me the balance of advantage is strongly in favour of C for simulation and other use.

8.3 How to Write Simulations In C

8.3.1 Overall design

Our target will be to produce a system capable of expansion to fit it for use in commercially valuable projects. Its design will therefore be modular, exploiting separate compilation and information hiding, while providing efficient functionality thus allowing each new simulation model to be written without excessive demands on the

How to Write Simulations in C   223

modeller. Such a system can be extended by the addition of new modules providing new areas of support, or by the extension of modules to provide additional functions in existing areas.

To meet our target in a sufficiently interesting way we shall create a system with entities having a visual aspect, to provide a visible interface to a model. We shall make provision for the entities to be grouped into ordered sets, i.e. queues. The executive will be without size limitations and will work quickly enough for large simulations. The modules will be glued together by the data structures they share. To enable modules to communicate successfully, details required in more than one module will be kept in a single header file simsys.h.

We shall need one module to contain the executive itself. It will be expedient within the executive to use the concept of linked lists, and as these are also directly useful to simulation modellers to implement queuing systems, a module providing them in a convenient form will be used. Though we shall implement this module using the notion of queues of entities, which is the form most useful to modellers, we shall press it into service in another guise too.

As the discussion of executive design will reveal, we shall use the sorting method known as heapsort as the core of the executive design, so a module implementing this as a general sorting service could provide additional functionality to the modeller. We shall use this style of implementation, without providing the general service. The extension to provide the service adds to running time. If the reader prefers to accept this cost it is easily implemented.

While simulations are often used to model stochastic situations so requiring a sampling module, such a module, which is easily prepared, would mainly add length to this chapter and will not be provided. Nor will a module to support logging of the results of a simulation.

All the above modules can sensibly be provided in a machine-independent way relying on the facilities of the C language and its standard library alone.

If the simulation is to be visual and interactive then further modules implementing these facilities will be wanted, but these would need to call upon a library of machine-dependent functions to move the cursor and to write the screen display with sufficient speed and with the chosen images if bit-mapped graphics were to be used. Ours will be a compromise; we will not use bit-mapped images and so can use standard library calls for writing, accepting whatever they deliver by way of speed, but we will need a machine-dependent module to implement cursor moves at least. The example will be for the IBM PC or clones thereof. We will have five modules and one header file. They are listed as appendices to this chapter:

Appendix 1: simsys.h —the header file
Appendix 2: execmod.c—the executive routines
Appendix 3: heapmod.c—the heapsort system
Appendix 4: queumod.c—the linked list system
Appendix 5: grafmod.c—the display manipulation routines
Appendix 6: machmod.c—the machine-dependent routines.
Appendix 7: phils.c—the hungry philosophers example.

The modules share the common header file simsys.h.

The design of such a system normally has a cyclic aspect as one refines one's ideas of what is desirable with experience. I will try to give an idea of the design process as we proceed, but it will help if a clear idea of the target is kept in mind and if it is always appreciated what tasks must be left to other modules. As it is central we shall design the executive first. Then the design of the other modules will follow, and finally we shall reach the design of a small simulation model using the facilities we have created. At the end of simsys.h is a list of the extern functions created in the modules, and these functions are available to us in the coding of any of our functions.

8.3.2 Executive design

We will base the executive program on the three-phase method. This is simple in itself but it will need at some point to know something of the nature of the entities which will form the subject-matter of the simulation and some strategic decisions will be needed. The function execute(), given in Figure 8.1, will serve us as a starting point. Some variables are needed and are also given. The details are from the file execmod.c. which is given as Appendix 2.

This is nothing more nor less than a direct statement of the three-phase system of executive design. It stops if the variable running is set to FALSE by the user, or if the duration is exceeded, or if nothing more is due to happen as reported by aphase(). Other stopping mechanisms could be used if preferred. Notice that no knowledge of the nature of an entity is required for this function; that level of detail comes later.

We now concern ourselves with the ?phase() functions. The

How to Write Simulations In C 225

```
int running;
/* if set FALSE in a user routine then the simulation will stop    */

long tim;
/* this variable will provide a simulation clock readout for the user */
/* its name is a hangover from the code of the speaking clock service */
/* available by telephone when handsets had letter codes           */

static long trutim;
/* this will hold the system's view of the simulation clock        */
/* it cannot be reached by the user routines and is safe from change */

void execute(duration) long duration; {
    running = TRUE;
    tim = trutim = 0;
    while (running && trutim <= duration && aphase() ) {
        bphase();
        if (running) cphase();
    }
}
```

Figure 8.1 The execute function.

nature of their actions can be specified without further detail. We will do this next. The aphase() function has three tasks: (1) it must discover the time at which the earliest next event takes place and load tim and trutim accordingly; (2) it must prepare a record of all the events due to happen at the selected time, suitable to enable the bphase() function to perform its duties; (3) it must report its success in finding a suitable next event, as if there is not one, the simulation must be terminated.

The bphase() function has one task: for each event due to happen as determined by aphase() it must call the appropriate user B activity, with the appropriate entity as parameter, to handle the user-determined transformations.

The cphase() function has one task: each active user C activity must be called.

This statement of the requirements of the phases points to a need for some decisions: How will aphase() know about future events? How will aphase() communicate with bphase()? How will bphase() know about the correct B activities and parameters for the call? How will cphase() know what a C activity is and whether it is active? The knowledge about future events can only come from the user, so he must be provided with a method of requesting that B activities be carried out, with his choice of entity as parameter, at a future time of his choosing. We can therefore note a requirement to provide a library function with the form: int cause(b__activity,entity,delay) where delay is the time in advance of the current time when the B activity is to be called to act on the entity. Clearly cause() and aphase() must share access to a data structure within which the details of user cause( ) calls are recorded and later extracted in time order by aphase( ).

It is also clear that the functions between them amount to a sorting operation, accepting cause( ) calls in any order and acting on them in order of their chosen simulated time. There are many books and articles in journals and magazines dedicated to discussion of sorting methods, both particular and general. We should note that our requirement is for a method suitable for a dynamic environment where there is a continual stream of new additions to the items to be sorted, and a continual stream of removals as the events are encountered and acted upon. It is relevant that a single call of aphase( ) may find several events due for simultaneous execution, and that the number of outstanding events to be handled may vary substantially. The details that need to be handled by cause( ) and aphase( ) are the triples (entity,b_activity,time) and numerous schemes exist.

A good system, if it is acceptable to place an upper bound on the number of entities in the system before execute( ) is called, is to number the entities from 0 . . MAX and to store the B activity reference and the time in suitable arrays indexed with the entity number, using a null (or other recognisable) B activity reference to indicate an 'uncaused' entity. This was the scheme I used in my BASIM system in BASIC, which worked very well indeed. In such a scheme cause( ) is a very quick operation and most system time is consumed by aphase( ). Even so, if the 'hit rate', that is the number of simultaneous events, is high, then this scheme is competitive for entity numbers into the thousands. It can also be enhanced by using list-processing techniques to directly identify the 'caused' entities. An alternative enhancement is to use a tree structure known as a heap, which can be implemented particularly efficiently within an array and which has substantial advantages in running times if the number of entities is high while the 'hit rate' is not high.

Languages offering dynamic memory allocation facilities, such as C and Pascal, make the acceptance of such schemes with their limitations undesirable, and other structures are preferred. The candidates are linked lists or tree structures. If trees are selected then it is necessary to ensure adequate balance in the trees lest they degenerate into little better than inefficiently processed linked lists. The decision hinges on the number of caused entities likely. I take the view that almost anything works well enough for small models, but when a model is running slowly I would prefer the reason to be the user's code not mine, so I opt for the tree structure referred to

How to Write Simulations In C   227

above, called a heap, which preserves good performance on the largest models with large numbers of entities. This use of the word 'heap' must not be confused with the alternative (later) use to describe the source of dynamically allocated memory in Pascal.

So if we now assume that we can write three functions manipulating or inspecting a heap we can proceed to write both cause() and part of aphase(). If we also agree to use a linked list to communicate between aphase() and bphase() then we can write the whole of aphase(). The heap manipulation functions are in heapmod.c while the linked list functions are in queumod.c.

To write cause() and aphase() necessitates reaching a decision on what is to constitute an entity. This is because we need to arrange that an already 'caused' entity is not available for further causing, and it is convenient to attach this information to the entity itself, so we must decide what it is. We shall use the struct concept and within the struct that holds entity data we shall hold system specified and manipulated attributes, pointers to structs concerned with the visibility of the entity and a pointer to a user-specified struct whose contents are of no interest to any part of the system. Figure 8.2 shows the C code for these entity status descriptors.

We use bits within the status word to quickly determine availability or otherwise of the entities. An entity is either busy (i.e. has been caused but the time not reached or, if the time has been reached, the matching b_activity has not been processed) or available (i.e. not currently the subject of an unsatisfied cause() command). Notice the macro-definitions. Some of the additional bits will find a use later. The time field is to hold the time at which the

```
/* this material is part of simsys.h */

/*         entity status descriptors
*/

#define AVAIL   1
#define BUSY    2

#define avail(e) ((e)->status&AVAIL)
#define busy(e)  ((e)->status&BUSY)

typedef struct entstruct {
        unsigned int status;
        long    time;
        void    (*nextb)();
        pix     *image;
        dpix    *oldimage;
        long    *user;
} *ename, entity;

/* end of part of simsys.h */
```

Figure 8.2 Entity status descriptors.

entity is due for action. The nextb field is a pointer to the function that will carry out the action. It is a user's B activity and will be called with the entity name as parameter when the time is reached. The pix, dpix and user fields will be dealt with later. Cause( ) assumes that insert(ent, &timetree) will store away the ent (which is a pointer to the struct entstruct remember) in something identified by &timetree, such that aphase( ) can get it back on time. We shall see what timetree is and the details of insert( ) when we discuss heapmod.c later.

Notice the XOR operation on status to flip both the BUSY and AVAIL bit. Also notice that in any executive function trutim is used not tim, as tim could be altered by the user in a miguided attempt to turn time backward or some other folly. An attempt to cause( ) earlier than the present or to cause( ) an already busy entity returns a failure indication, and no action takes place. The user should handle the consequences. A zero delay is acceptable and merely indicates an action which logically succeeds the point of the cause( ) call but is less than the chosen time unit in the future.

As it will not surface in the calling routines time beat due to the (necessary) separation of the aphase( ) and the bphase( ) no untoward consequences exist and it is a useful concept. Cause( ) is shown in figure 8.3.

Moving to aphase( ) we can see that it is only to be called from execute( ) and can and should be static. This is also true of bphase( ) and cphase( ). It must recognise an empty heap (nothing in the diary so nothing will happen) and if it finds one then it must report its failure. Otherwise it must determine the next clock time and set tim and trutim accordingly. It must then extract and store the entities to be processed by bphase( ). Finally it must report its success. The features dependent on other modules are the means of recognising an empty heap, the detection of the time of entity next to be delivered by the heap system and the storage of the entity for bphase( ).

The only difficulties for bphase( ) arise from the processing of the queue of entities produced by aphase( ), and this is handled by the qsize( ) and behead( ) commands. The duties are to take each entity

```
int cause(action,ent,dur) void (*action)();   ename ent; long dur; {
        if (busy(ent) ¦¦ dur < 0 ) return FALSE;
        ent->status ^= (BUSY¦AVAIL);
        ent->time = trutim + dur;
        ent->nextb = action;
        insert(ent,&timetree);
        return TRUE;
}
```

Figure 8.3 C code for the Cause routine.

How to Write Simulations in C

from the queue, set its status to be available and not busy, then call the associated b_activity. It may be thought that aphase() and bphase() should not be separate functions, but that as an entity appears at the top of the heap it should be processed by its b_activity. Remember that the user b_activity may call cause() if it chooses, and if the associated delay is zero then the resulting action would not be logically subsequent to the causing time beat, but rather part of it. Figure 8.4 shows the C code for aphase() and bphase().

The problem for cphase() is knowing what is or is not a c_activity. This is handled by using a list of active c_functions, called active_list, and two functions activate() and deactivate() which manipulate two other lists, one for functions to be activated and one for functions to be deactivated. They have to be written in such a manner that no problems arise if a routine has its status changed within a c_activity even within itself. The solution adopted is to change the active list after the processing of the whole time beat, that is changes take effect on the next time beat. The active list is kept in a standard queue by abusing the list processing system using the cast (void (*)()) preceding the head() call and the (ename) casts inside activate() and deactivate().

Any user function at all may be activated, and subsequently deactivated, as long as the function can be sensibly called without a parameter which is all the cphase() function does with them. The order in which the active functions are called is the order in which they are activated. If any 'fancy' activation–deactivation sequences are required then it would be expedient to provide two more functions activate_before() and activate_after() analogous to the

```
static int aphase() {
        if (!timetree) return FALSE;         /* empty heap terminates */
        tim = trutim = toptime(timetree);    /* next time */
        while(timetree && trutim == toptime(timetree) )
                addtofront(exec_queue, top(&timetree));
/*extract all due events and add them to the list for bphase() */
        return TRUE;
}



static void bphase() {
ename current;
        while (qsize(exec_queue)) {
                current = behead(exec_queue);    /* get next entity */
                current->status ^= (AVAIL|BUSY); /* toggle status    */
                (*(current->nextb))(current);    /* call user B activity */
        }
}
```

Figure 8.4 C code for aphase() and bphase().

similar add .... ( ) functions in the queuing module. These functions would take an extra parameter—a function pointer—to indicate a point in the active list.

cphase( ) is shown in Figure 8.5.

The final function in execmod.c is makent( ) which is a utility function creating a 'string' of entities from dynamic memory and delivering a pointer to the first. This is useful for creating classes of similar or related entities. They are initialised and the string is terminated by a 'nul' entity—one with a nul status. This is recognisable as a sentinel and enables a macro implementation of loops scanning each entity of the string, or pairs of entities of matching strings. The definitions are from simsys.h. Figure 8.6 shows the definitions and the function itself.

The code of makent( ) is straightforward and the only item of note is the error-handling which returns responsibility for failure to the caller.

8.3.3 The heap module

The executive uses two functions and one function style macro originating from the heap module. These are insert( ), top( ) and toptime( ). The macro is toptime( ). The data structure manipulated by the system is the heap__node defined in simsys.h and shown in Figure 8.7.

The heap__node contains two pointers, one to the left and one to the right son of the heap__node, one pointer (the ename) to the entity

```
static void cphase() {
int cnum;
void (*cact)();
        for (cnum = qsize(active_list) ; cnum ; cnum -- ) {
                cact = (void (*)()) head(active_list);
                frotate(active_list,1);
                (*cact)();
        }
        while (qsize(enact_list)) addtoback(active_list,behead(enact_list));
        while (qsize(deact_list)) qremove(behead(deact_list),active_list);
}
void activate(cact) void (* cact)(); {
        addtoback(enact_list,(ename)cact);
}

int deactivate(cact) void (* cact)(); {
        if (find((ename)cact,active_list) || find((ename)cact,enact_list) ) {
                addtoback(deact_list,(ename)cact);
                return TRUE;
        }
        return FALSE;
}
```

Figure 8.5 C code for cphase().

How to Write Simulations In C

```
/*
        entity class access macros - function style
        only works if terminated by a null status entity
*/

#define foreach(e,c) for(e=c;*(int*)e;(ename)e++)
#define                                              forpairs(e1,e2,c1,c2)
for(e1=c1,e2=c2;*(int*)e1&&*(int*)e2;(ename)e1++,(ename)e2++)

ename makent(n) unsigned int n; {
unsigned int i;
ename b,e;
        if (!n || (!(e =  (ename)  calloc(  n+1,  sizeof(entity)  )))  ) return
(ename) 0;
        for (b = e, i = 0; i<n ; ++i, ++e ) {
                e->status = AVAIL;
                e->time = MAXLONG;
        }
        e->status = 0;
        return b;
}
```

Figure 8.6 Definitions and C code for the MakeEnt() function.

referenced by the link and a field called sons which counts the total descendents of a node and is used to keep the trees tending towards balance on insertion. The heap property is that at any node of the heap the entity referenced by the node is always earlier (in that its time field is less) than those referenced by its sons, if they exist. Notice that no relationship is implied between the times of the two sons of a node, this lack of relationship allows the use of the sons field to determine the insertion policy when a choice exists between descending either to the left or to the right when seeking a home for an insertion. True balance is not always preserved, but each insertion is used to improve it. Whatever happens on extraction is accepted, i.e. no re-balancing ever takes place and the maximum depth of the tree will, in the worst case, be that which arose when the maximum size was attained.

Tree processing is easily understood as a recursive process. The two main routines, insert( ) for inserting a new node in a tree and fix( ) for tidying up a tree spoiled by having its top element removed, could have been written recursively. As they are both tail recursions

```
typedef struct heap_struct {
        struct heap_struct *rson;
        struct heap_struct *lson;
        ename ent;
        int sons;
} *heap_tree, heap_node;
```

Figure 8.7 Definitions of the heap.

```
void insert(new_ent,tp) ename new_ent; heap_tree *tp; {
ename spare;
heap_tree tree;
        while (TRUE) {            /* continue till finished */
                tree = *tp;       /* remember tp is a pointer to a pointer */
                                  /* tree points to the current node */
                if (!tree) {      /* if it is null make a node */
                        tree = new_heap_node();
                                  /* initialise it */
                        tree->sons = 0;
                        tree->lson = tree->rson = (heap_tree)0;
                        tree->ent = new_ent;
                                  /* point the (null) parent at it */
                        *tp = tree;
                        return; /* all done */
                }
                                  /* remember it is getting an extra descendant */
                ++(tree->sons);
                if (!earlier(tree->ent,new_ent)) {
                                  /* if the new_ent is earlier than the existing */
                                  /* one then swap them over */
                        spare = tree->ent;
                        tree->ent = new_ent;
                        new_ent = spare;
                }
                                  /* descend and repeat loop again */
                if (left_choice(tree)) tp = &(tree->lson);
                else tp = &(tree->rson);
        }
}
```

Figure 8.8 C code for Insert().

the recursive processing is unnecessary. As these two routines are central to the time processing of the simulation system it is worth seeking efficiency above clarity at this point. To aid clarity there are two macro-definitions, earlier( ) to compare the time of two entities and left__choice( ) to decide whether to descend to the left son of a node or not when inserting. Insert( ) is shown in Figure 8.8

The action of insert( ) is to compare the time of a candidate entity with the time of the entity at a node of the tree (initially the top one). If it is earlier than the node's entity they are swapped. Then a child node is selected based on the number of sons of the two child nodes, the one with the smallest number being selected. The process is repeated with the new candidate (either the original or the swapped one) and the new node. The process terminates when no node is found. At that point a new node is created and attached holding the current candidate. The main work is done by fix( ) which follows top( ) in Figure 8.9. The extraction operation top() obtains the entity at the top of the tree and then calls the static function fix() to repair the tree. This it does by promoting the earlier of the two sons and repeating the same action on the resulting damaged tree at the son's position. This process terminates when a son is null. A normal promotion is achieved by copying the ent field. The final promotion prior to termination is a write to the parent pointer as there may be a

How to Write Simulations In C

```
ename top(tp) heap_tree *tp; {
ename e;
                /* remember that tp is a pointer to a pointer */
        if (!(*tp)) error("top");       /* no top to a null tree */
        e = (*tp)->ent;                 /* get the ent */
        fix(tp);                        /* fix the heap */
        return e;                       /* return the entity */
}
static void fix(tp) heap_tree *tp; {
                /* fix gets a tree with a discarded entity field */
                /* remember that tp is a pointer to a pointer */
heap_tree tree;
        while (TRUE) {          /* continue till finished */
                tree = *tp;     /* tree points to entity-less node */
                                /* which will lose a descendant */
                --(tree->sons);
                if (!(tree->rson)) {
                        /* no right son so promote the whole left tree */
                        /* then quit the loop */
                        *tp = tree->lson;
                        break;
                }
                else if (!(tree->lson)) {
                        /* no left son so promote the whole right tree */
                        /* then quit the loop */
                        *tp = tree->rson;
                        break;
                }
                else if    (earlier(tree->rson->ent,tree->lson->ent))   tp =
&(tree->rson);
                else tp = &(tree->lson);
                /* otherwise promote  the earlier of the sons entity */
                /* and descend to repeat the loop again */
                tree->ent = (*tp)->ent;
        }
        /* now discard the unused node */
        old_heap_node(tree);
}
```
Figure 8.9 C code for Top( ).

substantial tree below an only son. It is also possible that both sons are null, in which case the parent pointer becomes null. One heap_node becomes unused and this is disposed of via the static function old_heap_node( ) which either keeps it for later re-use or gives it back to the storage allocator via free( ) depending on whether or not the extern int holdmem is set to TRUE. This same variable holdmem controls the dynamic storage of the queuing system too. Generally if memory is not a problem then it is faster to keep the dynamic links and re-use them. If memory is a problem then holdmem is set FALSE. A compromise would be possible whereby a certain number of links is administered by the simulation system and the rest returned to the allocator.

8.3.4 The queue module

This module is primarily a utility module for the benefit of the user of the system, though it is used also by the executive.

The important thing to understand, in order to easily understand all its functions, is the storage method chosen for the queues. Each queue has an administrative structure, a pointer to which is called a queue. This struct contains a count of the members of the queue and a pointer to the first and last elements of the queue. These elements are themselves structs containing a pointer to an entity and two pointers to elements. The elements pointed to are the element's predecessor, and successor elements in the queue. The elements are

```
typedef struct qdummy {
        struct qdummy *pred;
        struct qdummy *succ;
        ename ent;
} *link,element;

typedef struct qstruct {
        int count;
        link first;
        link last;
} *queue,queueimp;

queue makeq(n) int n;{
queue q;
        if (!(q = (queue)calloc(n,sizeof(queueimp))))  error("no  memory  in makeq");
        return q;
}

void addtofront(q,e) queue q; ename e; {
link l;
        l = newlink(e);
        if (!(q->count)++) q->first = q->last = l;
        else {
                inbefor(l ,q->first);
                q->first = l;
        }
}

static link newlink(e) ename e;{
link l;
        if (qbase) {
                l = qbase;
                qbase = l->pred;
        }
        else if (!(l = (link) malloc(sizeof(element))))
                        error("no memory for queue system");
        l->ent = e;
        return (l->succ = l->pred = l);
}

void inbefor(l,s)
link s,l;
{
        s->pred->succ = l;
        l->pred = s->pred;
        s->pred = l;
        l->succ = s;
}
```

Figure 8.10 Definitions for queues and C code for Makeq( ), AddToFront( ), NewLink and InBefor( ).

How to Write Simulations In C

thus kept in a circle with forward and backward pointers, and the circle is referenced by the first and last fields of the administrative struct, the queuimp. The definitions are shown in Figure 8.10.

A sample of the functions will be described, but as they mainly provide simple manipulations of the above structure the code file should be consulted for full details. As many of the actions on the structs are common to many of the public library functions a hidden static group of functions does much of the work and the public functions use these. The inner functions have no checking, relying on the interfacing functions to make correct calls or not care. The first function to consider is makeq( ) which returns a pointer to an array of queueimp of size determined by the parameter. The array is from calloc( ) and so is of zeroed memory. Makeq( ) is also shown in Figure 8.10.

To put entities into queues the add????( ) functions are used. Addtofront( ) adds the entity given as second parameter to the queue given as first. It uses the static function newlink( ) to get memory for its operation, the static inbefor( ) for its operation, unless the queue is empty and attends to the administrative struct details. This is almost a general pattern, the public function attending to entity and administrative structure details and letting the circular system be modified by the static functions. Note that nothing is done to the entity other than remember it in the link, and so any pointer of similar size can in fact be added to queues by suitable casting, as is the case in the executive.

The entity is remembered by newlink( ) which obtains memory for the new link, stores the entity, points the link's predecessor and successor links at itself, thus making a degenerate circle, and returns the link.

The inbefor( ) function inserts the link which is the first parameter into the circle of the second parameter link. It assumes that the first parameter predecessor and successor fields may be changed without harm. As with all linked list operations the correct sequencing of the actions is important.

The size of a queue is obtained either by inspecting the count field directly, or possibly more conveniently using a macro qsize( ) to do the access and defined in simsys.h #define qsize(q) q->count. Probably the commonest operation is to inspect the head of the queue, and if satisfactory perform some operation using that entity. The functions head( ) and behead( ) are helpful here; both are straightforward with head( ) inspecting the queue while behead( ) changes it. They both return the entity. There are similar functions

```
ename head(q) queue q; {
        if (q->count) return q->first->ent;
        return (ename)0;
}

ename behead(q) queue q; {
link l;
ename e;
        if ((q->count)--) {
                l = q->first;
                if (q->count) q->first = l->succ;
                else q->last = q->first = (link)0;
                e = l->ent;
                extrax(l);
                oldlink(l);
                return e;
        }
        error("behead");
}

static link qfind(e1,q) ename e1; queue q; {
link l;
int i;
        for (i = q->count, l = q->first ; i-- ; l = l->succ) {
                if (e1 == l->ent) return l;
        }
        return (link)0;
}

/* forward rotate a queue
*/void frotate(q,n) queue q; int n ;{
link l;
        for ( l = q->first ; n-- ; l = l->succ ) ;
        q->first = l;
        q->last  = l->pred;
}
```

Figure 8.11 C code for Head ( ), Behead ( ), QFind ( ) and FRotate ( ).

for the tail of the queue and analogous ones for specific entities within a queue. These latter involve a search of the queue to find the link of the entity involved, and this is handled by the static function qfind( ).

The final type of function is that which rotates a queue. Here is the one that does forward rotations, frotate( ) which works by creating a spare link l and using it to track the appropriate numbers of links of the circle.

8.3.5 The grafmod module

This module provides for the drawing, erasing and moving of entities on the screen. With some extension it can be easily modified to work with colour, a larger pseudo-screen with the actual glass being a window onto the larger one. If required it can be replaced by

How to Write Simulations In C 237

alternatives using plotting-style commands on a bit-mapped screen without much change to the simulations. This is because the fundamental notion is the simple one of an entity having an appearance and being located at a place. The appearance can be anything that can be made to appear on the glass, and the place can be anywhere either on a pseudo screen or on the glass if the two coincide.

The changes required to simulations are not in the resulting drawing style commands, but in the initialisation of entities with appearances and their later modification. As this can mainly be achieved by pointer assignments, writing a new approach to the graphics is a matter of rewriting this module and providing functions to create, edit and transfer appearances.

The images handled by this version of grafmod are the simplest available, to illustrate the concepts needed to incorporate them into a simulation model, as our topic is simulation, not graphics programming. They are monochrome, mobile text strings. A complication imposed by the requirement of displaying a simulation's progress correctly is that, to represent the simultaneity embodied in the model, all drawing associated with a time beat should take place simultaneously, otherwise a watcher would become conscious of the within-time beat processing sequence and might draw unwarranted conclusions based upon what is, and should be (in the b__phase) an arbitrary processing order.

```
void redraw(e) ename e; {
        if (e->status&DIRTY) return;   /* already done this so return */
        addtoback(screenset,e);         /* remember this entity */
        e->status |= DIRTY;             /* mark it */
}

void move(e) ename e; {
pix *p;
dpix *o;
        if (e->status & MOVED) return;  /* if original image stored */
        /* immobile entities never get an oldimage - no wasted space */
        if (!(e->oldimage))
                if (!(e->oldimage = (dpix *) malloc(sizeof(dpix))))
                        error("no space for oldimage ");
        /* store the old image size and location */
        p = e->image;
        o = e->oldimage;
        o->row = p->row;
        o->col = p->col;
        if (p->text) o->slen = strlen(p->text);
        else o->slen = 0;
        /* it may already have been redrawn() */
        if (!(e->status&DIRTY)) addtoback(screenset,e);
        /* mark it */
        e->status |= (DIRTY|MOVED);
}
```

Figure 8.12 C code for ReDraw() and Move().

```
void draw(e) ename e; {
register pix *p;
        p = e->image;             /* using p should be quicker */
        cursor(p->col,p->row);    /* move the cursor */
        cputs(p->text);           /* write to the console */
}

void erase(e) ename e; {
register pix *p;
int l;
        p = e->image;             /* using p should be quicker */
        cursor(p->col,p->row);    /* move the cursor */
        l = strlen(p->text);      /* determine image size */
        blank_string[l] = 0;      /* prepare suitable length blank string */
        cputs(blank_string);      /* erase the image */
        blank_string[l] = ' ';    /* restore the blank string */
}
```

Figure 8.13 C code for Draw( ) and Erase( ).

The screen after the first screen changing b__activity would be incorrect until after the last screen changing c__activity. If this in general were a high proportion of the total time, as it should be if the a__phase is efficient, then most of the time the screen would be simply wrong. To handle this the status field of the entity is used with two bits being assigned the task of determining whether an entity appearance has changed, in which case it is DIRTY, or whether it has moved, in which case it is (DIRTYMOVED). The redraw( ) and move( ) functions then become simple, merely changing the entity status, storing the entity in a list for later physical drawing and in the case of move( ) noting the details of the image to be erased if this has not already been done. The field oldimage is used for this latter purpose. Redraw( ) and move( ) are shown in Figure 8.12.

```
void update_screen() {
ename e;
register dpix *o;
register pix *p;
int i;
        /* first all moving entities are erased in their current place */
        for (i = qsize(screenset);i--;) {
                /* we do not change the screenset membership details */
                e = head(screenset);
                frotate(screenset,1);
                if (e->status & MOVED ) erase(e);
        }
        /* now we empty the screenset as we draw its members */
        while (qsize(screenset)) {
                e = behead(screenset);
                draw(e);
                /* mark them unmoved and clean */
                e->status &= (~(DIRTY|MOVED));
        }
}
```

Figure 8.14 C code for Update__Screen( ).

How to Write Simulations In C

If the user wishes he should be able to draw and erase his entities so draw( ) and erase( ), which act without delay, are provided. Notice the erasure method used of having a prepared string of blanks of sufficient length to cope with any image. This has its length changed by slotting in a terminating null to match it to the length of the image string to be erased. The writing is done with cputs( ), which is a console writing function provided by compiler vendors. Faster routines writing directly to screen memory could be provided on systems with memory-mapped screens, but of course this requires machine-specific code. Draw( ) and erase( ) are shown in Figure 8.13.

The routine of drawing a simulation screen is carried out by update__screen( ) shown in Figure 8.14: This first of all erases any entities which have moved—if this was not done first then late erasures could interfere with the results of earlier drawing. Then the entities are drawn and their status changed to record the new state. The set holding them is emptied. In this presentation of this function the drawing and erasure is done by calling draw( ) and erase( ) for clarity, but in the file grafmod.c it is done by inline code as these are small routines.

8.3.6 The machine-dependent module

This module supplies routines to support cursor movement and other useful facilities, such as inhibiting the effects of CTRLC, coloured text, etc., on IBM PCs or clones. They mainly use compiler vendor-supplied library functions to achieve their effects, and are not of direct concern from a simulation writer's viewpoint—merely necessary. Again for improved speed the cursor handling can be obtained by directly programming the chip that handles the screen, but this is not the place for such code.

8.3.7 The hungry philosophers example

This is a well-known example problem (due to Dijkstra) in which some philosophers sit in a circle surrounding their food supply. Their lives consist of an endless cycle of thinking, being seized with hunger and then, if possible, eating. The qualification placed upon their eating is that they may only eat if the two forks adjacent to them are both free. As the forks are placed between adjacent philosophers, it is possible for them to be in use if a neighbour is eating. In this case they wait till both forks are available then eat.

The code for a simulation of this situation is very straightforward. It is given in appendix 7. The entities selected are 6 philosophers and 6 forks. It is sometimes argued that the forks are redundant, as the rules can be suitably expressed in terms of the states of a philosopher's neighbour, which is true. My experience is that in real problems the specifications change (the philosophers can eat ice-cream or sandwiches without forks, or only using one fork—sometimes) in which case I find it easier to cope if the main features of a situation are explicitly present in the model, rather than implicitly so. My two entity types are handled by two b-activities for the philosophers and one trivial one for the forks. There is one c-activity to arrange eating. This is where any priority rules would be implemented. Initialisation is carried out in the initialise() routine and a final report() routine concludes the simulation.

The three phase system lends itself to control uses as well as to simulation, so there are additional c-activities to implement the screen display and user interaction, in this case control of single stepping. The screen is drawn by the activation of the routine update__screen(), the clocktime is reported by the activation of the timeshow() routine and the control is handled by the pair of routines sinstep() and free__run() only one of which is ever active at a given time. The order of activation is important, as it is normally required to see the situation after any model c-activities before a user interaction is permitted, so update__screen() should follow the model c-activities and precede interaction activities.

8.4 References

Feuer, A. and Gehan, N. (1984) *Comparing and Assessing Programming Languages*. Prentice-Hall, Englewood Cliffs, New Jersey.

Computer Modelling for Discrete Simulation
Edited by M. Pidd
©1989 John Wiley & Sons Ltd

Appendices

Appendix 1 :- simsys.h - the header file

```
/*      this is file SIMSYS.H    */
char    *malloc(int);
char    *calloc(int,int);

#define bool int
#define TRUE 1
#define FALSE 0
#define MAXLONG 0x7fffffff
#define DZERO (double)0.0
#define NULLPTR (void *) 0

/*      entity status descriptors
*/

#define AVAIL   1
#define BUSY    2
#define DIRTY   64          /* needing a redraw */
#define MOVED   128         /* needs erase prior to redraw */

typedef struct pixstruct {
        unsigned int    row;
        unsigned int    col;
        char *text;
        int colfont;
} pix;

typedef struct dpixstruct {
        unsigned int    row;
        unsigned int    col;
                int     slen;
} dpix;

#define avail(e) ((e)->status&AVAIL)
#define busy(e)  ((e)->status&BUSY)
#define appearance(e) (e)->image->text

/*
        entity class access macros - function style
        only works if terminated by a null status entity
*/

#define foreach(e,c) for(e=c;*(int*)e;(ename)e++)
#define                                                  forpairs(e1,e2,c1,c2)
for(e1=c1,e2=c2;*(int*)e1&&*(int*)e2;(ename)e1++,(ename)e2++)

#define qsize(q) q->count
```

241

```
typedef struct entstruct {
        unsigned int status;
        long    time;
        void    (*nextb)();
        pix     *image;
        dpix    *oldimage;
        long    *user;
} *ename,entity;


typedef struct heap_struct {
        struct heap_struct *rson;
        struct heap_struct *lson;
        ename ent;
        int sons;
} *heap_tree,heap_node;


typedef struct qdummy {
        struct qdummy *pred;
        struct qdummy *succ;
        ename ent;
} *link,element;

typedef struct qstruct {
        int count;
        link first;
        link last;
} *queue,queueimp;



#ifndef EXECMOD
extern int running;
extern int holdmem;
extern long tim;
#endif
```

Appendices 243

```c
typedef struct histruct{
    char    freqcnt;   /* FALSE if a state record type is wanted  */
    int     histsize;  /* total number of cells not including  two overflow cells */
    double  *cell;     /* points to an array of cells size [2 + histsize] */
    double  count,     /* holds number of data items logged */
            lcount,    /* copy of count at last statistics update */
            width,     /* cell width */
            base,      /* values logged less than this go into overflow */
            mean,      /* average of logged data - when histogram is up-to-date */
            variance,  /* variance of logged data - when  histogram is up-to-date */
            sd,        /* standard deviation of logged data - when histogram is up-to-date */
            total,     /* total of logged data  */
            sosq;      /* sum of sqares of logged data */
} *histogram,hdata;

#define EPSILON 0.0001


typedef struct seedstruct {
        unsigned int ur,ur1;
} *seed,seedat;

typedef struct distruct {
        double *dx; /* monotonic increasing - allowable minus  to plus infinity */
        double *dy; /* start at 0.0 and end at 1.0 */
} *distribution,distdat;

/* definitions for MACHMOD.C */

#ifdef TURBOC
#define signal(x,y) ssignal(x,y)
#endif

/* word registers */

struct WORDREGS {
        unsigned int ax;
        unsigned int bx;
        unsigned int cx;
        unsigned int dx;
        unsigned int si;
        unsigned int di;
        unsigned int cflag;
        };
```

```
/* byte registers */

struct BYTEREGS {
        unsigned char al, ah;
        unsigned char bl, bh;
        unsigned char cl, ch;
        unsigned char dl, dh;
        };

/* general purpose registers union - overlays the corresponding word and
 * byte registers.
 */

union REGS {
        struct WORDREGS x;
        struct BYTEREGS h;
        };

/* segment registers */

struct SREGS {
        unsigned int es;
        unsigned int cs;
        unsigned int ss;
        unsigned int ds;
        };

#define SIGINT   2          /* interrupt - corresponds to DOS int 23H */

        /* FUNCTION PROTOTYPES*/

/* The functions provided by each module are now given as formal    */
/* prototype definitions, a form which enables some compilers to    */
/* check the parameter lists of function calls for correct          */
/* parameter types.                                                 */

/* formal global function prototypes from execmod.c                 */

int cause(void (*)(),struct entstruct *,long );

/* cause() communicates a request from a user model to the system */
/* for a B_activity (the first parameter) to be carried out on a  */
/* named entity (the second parameter) after a delay supplied as  */
/* the third parameter.                                           */

void activate(void (*)());

/* activate() tells the system that the function supplied as the  */
/* parameter is a C_activity.                                     */

int deactivate(void (*)());

/* deactivate() tells the system that the function supplied as the*/
/* parameter is no longer a C_activity.                           */
```

Appendices _____245

```
void execute(long );

/* execute() tells the system to run the model from time zero to   */
/* the first time beat beyond the duration specified as parameter. */

struct entstruct *makent(unsigned int);

/* makent() supplies a pointer to a 'string' of properly           */
/* initialised entities of length specified by the parameter. The  */
/* string is terminated by a 'nul' entity. Entities may also be    */
/* created by any of the space reserving methods allowed by the    */
/* language of course.                                             */

/* formal global function prototypes from heapmod.c                */

void insert(struct entstruct *,struct heap_struct * *);

/* insert() puts the entity supplied as the first parameter into   */
/* the heapstructure supplied as the second parameter.             */

struct entstruct *top(struct heap_struct * *);

/* top() removes the top of the heapstructure supplied as          */
/* parameter and returns a pointer to the entity removed.          */

/* formal global function prototypes from machmod.c                */

void printcrt(void );

/* printcrt() prints the display - it is equivalent to pressing    */
/* the shift/PrtSc key                                             */

void breakoff(void );

/* breakoff() inhibits Ctrl-C processing and thus lets the         */
/* programmer control the termination arrangements.                */

void set_video_mode(int );

/* set_video_mode() does just that.                                */

void cursor(int ,int );

/* cursor() moves the cursor to the x,y point supplied as          */
/* parameters.                                                     */

void get_cursor(int *,int *);

/* get_cursor() finds the current position and loads the pointer   */
/* parameter targets accordingly.                                  */
```

```c
void write_char_attr(int ,char ,char );

/* write_char_attr() writes a number (first parameter) of copies    */
/* of a character (second parameter) in the style or attribute      */
/* specified by the third parameter.                                */

void clrscr(void);

/* clrscr() clears the screen.                                      */

/* formal global function prototypes from queumod.c                 */

struct qstruct *makeq(int );

/* makeq() returns a pointer to an array of initialised queues.     */
/* The array size is specified by the parameter.                    */

void addtofront(struct qstruct *,struct entstruct *);
void addtoback(struct qstruct *,struct entstruct *);
void addafter(struct entstruct *,struct qstruct *,struct entstruct *);
void addbefor(struct entstruct *,struct qstruct *,struct entstruct *);

/* All the add.....() functions add an entity to a queue in         */
/* position specified by the name and extra parameter, if any.      */

struct entstruct *head(struct qstruct *);

/* head() returns the entity at the head of a queue without         */
/* changing the queue.                                              */

struct entstruct *tail(struct qstruct *);

/* tail() returns the entity at the tail of a queue without         */
/* changing the queue.                                              */

struct entstruct *behead(struct qstruct *);

/* behead() returns the entity at the head of a queue and           */
/* removes it from the queue.                                       */

struct entstruct *betail(struct qstruct *);

/* betail() returns the entity at the tail of a queue and           */
/* removes it from the queue.                                       */

int qremove(struct entstruct *,struct qstruct *);

/* qremove() removes the named entity from the named queue if it    */
/* finds it in the queue. It returns 0 if it fails or 1 if it       */
/* succeeds.                                                        */
```

```c
struct entstruct *find(struct entstruct *,struct qstruct *);

/* find() returns 0 if the named entity is not in the named queue */
/* and 1 if it is. The queue is unchanged.                        */

void rrotate(struct qstruct *,int );
void frotate(struct qstruct *,int );

/* ?rotate() rotates the named queue by the second parameter      */
/* places. The rotation is forwards or rearwards depending on     */
/* the function name.                                             */

/* formal global function prototypes from grafmod.c               */

void redraw(struct entstruct *);

/* redraw() is an instruction to redraw an entity without it      */
/* moving position. This is delayed drawing operation.            */

void move(struct entstruct *);

/* move() is an instruction to redraw an entity in a new location */
/* - implying that it must be erased from its original location.  */
/* This is a delayed drawing operation.                           */

void draw(struct entstruct *);

/* draw() does a physical draw of an entity.                      */

void erase(struct entstruct *);

/* erase() is a physical erase of an entity;                      */

void update_screen(void );

/* update_screen() carries out all outstanding delayed drawing    */
/* operations.                                                    */

/* formal definition of functions to be provided by user          */

void error(char *);

/* error() is called by the system functions if fatal errors      */
/* occur. The user writes it so that any preservation of          */
/* information required may be undertaken. The char pointer       */
/* points to an explanatory string for use as a screen display.   */


/*      this is end of file SIMSYS.H    */
```

Appendix 2 :- execmod.c - the executive routines

```c
/*        this is file EXECMOD.C  */
#define EXECMOD           /* required for conditional compilation in simsys.h */
#include "stdio.h"
#include "simsys.h"

static int  aphase(void );
static void bphase(void );
static void cphase(void );

#define toptime(x)      x->ent->time

int holdmem = TRUE;     /* inhibit use of free() for system temporary items */

static heap_tree timetree;  /* used by heap system to store future events */

int running;
/* if set FALSE in a user routine then the simulation will stop */

long tim;
/* this variable will provide a simulation clock readout for the user */

static long trutim;
/* this will hold the system's view of the simulation clock */
/* it cannot be reached by the user routines and is safe from change */

static queueimp exec_queueimp = {0,0,0};
static queue exec_queue = &exec_queueimp;

static void bphase() {
ename current;
        while (qsize(exec_queue)) {
                current = behead(exec_queue);   /* get next entity */
                current->status ^= (AVAIL|BUSY);/* toggle status   */
                (*(current->nextb))(current);   /* call user B activity */
        }
}


static int aphase() {
        if (!timetree) return FALSE;            /* empty heap terminates */
        tim = trutim = toptime(timetree);                 /* next time */
        while(timetree && trutim == toptime(timetree) )
                addtofront(exec_queue,top(&timetree));
/*extract all due events and add them to the list for bphase() */
        return TRUE;
}
```

Appendices 249

```
int cause(action,ent,dur) void (*action)();   ename ent;  long dur; {
        if (busy(ent) || dur < 0 ) return FALSE;
        ent->status ^= (BUSY|AVAIL);
        ent->time = trutim + dur;
        ent->nextb = action;
        insert(ent,&timetree);
        return TRUE;
}

static   queueimp   active_listimp   =    {0,0,0}  ,enact_listimp  =  {0,0,0} ,
deact_listimp = {0,0,0} ;
static   queue    active_list    =    &active_listimp,enact_list   =   &enact_listimp,
deact_list = &deact_listimp;

static void cphase() {
int cnum;
void (*cact)();
        for (cnum = qsize(active_list) ; cnum ; cnum -- ) {
                cact = (void (*)()) head(active_list);
                frotate(active_list,1);
                (*cact)();
        }
        while (qsize(enact_list)) addtoback(active_list,behead(enact_list));
        while (qsize(deact_list)) qremove(behead(deact_list),active_list);
}

void activate(cact) void (* cact)(); {
        addtoback(enact_list,(ename)cact);
}

int deactivate(cact) void (* cact)(); {
        if (find((ename)cact,active_list) || find((ename)cact,enact_list) ) {
                addtoback(deact_list,(ename)cact);
                return TRUE;
        }
        return FALSE;
}

void execute(duration) long duration; {
     running = TRUE;
     tim = trutim = 0;
     while (running && trutim <= duration && aphase() ) {
                bphase();
                if (running) cphase();
     }
}

ename makent(n) register unsigned int n; {
register unsigned int i;
register ename b,e;
        if (!n || (!(e = (ename) calloc( n+1, sizeof(entity) ))) ) return
(ename) 0;
        for (b = e, i = 0; i<n ; ++i, ++e ) {
                e->status = AVAIL;
                e->time = MAXLONG;
        }
        e->status = 0;
        return b;
}
/*      this is the end of file EXECMOD.C        */
```

Appendix 3 :- heapmod.c - the heapsort system

```c
/* this is file HEAPMOD.C        */

#define HEAPMOD

#include "simsys.h"
static  void fix(struct heap_struct * * );
static  struct heap_struct *new_heap_node(void);
static  void old_heap_node(struct heap_struct *);

/*      defines for the heap system     */

#define  left_choice(t)   ((t->lson  &&  t->rson)  ?  (t->lson->sons  <=
t->rson->sons): !(t->lson))
#define earlier(x,y) ((x)->time <= (y)->time)

void insert(new_ent,tp) ename new_ent; heap_tree *tp; {
ename spare;
heap_tree tree;
        while (TRUE) {          /* continue till finished */
                tree = *tp;     /* remember tp is a pointer to a pointer */
                                /* tree points to the current node */
                if (!tree) {    /* if it is null make a node */
                        tree = new_heap_node();
                                /* initialise it */
                        tree->sons = 0;
                        tree->lson = tree->rson = (heap_tree)0;
                        tree->ent = new_ent;
                                /* point the (null) parent at it */
                        *tp = tree;
                        return; /* all done */
                }
                        /* remember it is getting an extra descendant */
                ++(tree->sons);
                if (!earlier(tree->ent,new_ent)) {
                        /* if the new_ent is earlier than the existing */
                        /* one then swap them over */
                        spare = tree->ent;
                        tree->ent = new_ent;
                        new_ent = spare;
                }
                        /* descend and repeat loop again */
                if (left_choice(tree)) tp = &(tree->lson);
                else tp = &(tree->rson);
        }
}

static void fix(tp) heap_tree *tp; {
                /* fix gets a tree with a discarded entity field */
                /* remember that tp is a pointer to a pointer */
```

```
heap_tree tree;
        while (TRUE) {              /* continue till finished */
                tree = *tp;         /* tree points to entity-less node */
                                    /* which will lose a descendant */
                --(tree->sons);
                if (!(tree->rson)) {
                        /* no right son so promote the whole left tree */
                        /* then quit the loop */
                        *tp = tree->lson;
                        break;
                }
                else if (!(tree->lson)) {
                        /* no left son so promote the whole right tree */
                        /* then quit the loop */
                        *tp = tree->rson;
                        break;
                }
                else    if    (earlier(tree->rson->ent,tree->lson->ent))    tp   =
&(tree->rson);
                else tp = &(tree->lson);
                /* otherwise promote  the earlier of the sons entity */
                /* and descend to repeat the loop again */
                tree->ent = (*tp)->ent;
        }
        /* now discard the unused node */
        old_heap_node(tree);
}

ename top(tp) heap_tree *tp; {
ename e;
                /* remember that tp is a pointer to a pointer */
        if (!(*tp)) error("top");       /* no top to a null tree */
        e = (*tp)->ent;                 /* get the ent */
        fix(tp);                        /* fix the heap */
        return e;                       /* return the entity */
}

static heap_tree tbase = 0;

static heap_tree new_heap_node() {
heap_tree l;
        if (tbase) {
                l = tbase;
                tbase = l->lson;
        }
        else if (!(l =(heap_tree) malloc(sizeof(heap_node))))
                        error("no memory for system call");
        return l;
}




                static void old_heap_node(l) heap_tree l; {
                        if (holdmem) {
                                l->lson = tbase;
                                tbase = l;
                        }
                        else free((char *)l);
                }

                /* this is end of file HEAPMOD.C            */
```

Appendix 4 :- queumod.c - the linked list system

```c
/* this is file QUEUMOD.C      */

#define QUEUMOD

#include "stdio.h"
#include "simsys.h"

static void    extrax(struct qdummy *);
static void    inafter(struct qdummy *,struct qdummy *);
static void    inbefor(struct qdummy *,struct qdummy *);
static  struct qdummy *newlink(struct entstruct *);
static  struct qdummy *qfind(struct entstruct *,struct qstruct *);
static void oldlink(struct qdummy *);

queue makeq(n) int n;{
queue q;
        if  (!(q  =  (queue)calloc(n,sizeof(queueimp))))  error("no  memory  in makeq");
        return q;
}

/* a disconnected link always points at itself both ways */
/* and a chain is circular both ways */
/* no checking is done by the basic procedures - inserting & extracting */

/* removes a link from its current chain */
static void extrax(s)
link s;
{
        s->pred->succ = s->succ;
        s->succ->pred = s->pred;
}

/* inserts a link l before s in s's chain */
static void inbefor(l,s)
link s,l;
{
        s->pred->succ = l;
        l->pred = s->pred;
        s->pred = l;
        l->succ = s;
}
/* inserts a link l after s in s's chain */
static void inafter(s,l)
link s,l;
{
        s->succ->pred = l;
        l->succ = s->succ;
        s->succ = l;
        l->pred = s;
}
```

Appendices 253

```
static link qbase = 0;

static link newlink(e) ename e;{
link l;
        if (qbase) {
                l = qbase;
                qbase = l->pred;
        }
        else if (!(l = (link) malloc(sizeof(element))))
                        error("no memory for queue system");
        l->ent = e;
        return (l->succ = l->pred = l);
}

static void oldlink(l) link l; {
        if (holdmem) {
                l->pred = qbase;
                qbase = l;
        }
        else free(l);
}

static link qfind(e1,q) ename e1; queue q; {
link l;
int i;
        for (i = q->count, l = q->first ; i-- ; l = l->succ) {
                if (e1 == l->ent) return l;
        }
        return (link)0;
}

void addtofront(q,e) queue q; ename e; {
link l;
        l = newlink(e);
        if (!(q->count)++) q->first = q->last = l;
        else {
                inbefor(l ,q->first);
                q->first = l;
        }
}
void addtoback(q,e) queue q; ename e; {
link l;
        l = newlink(e);
        if (!(q->count)++) q->first = q->last = l;
        else {
                inafter(q->last,l );
                q->last = l;
        }
}
```

```
void addafter(e1,q,e) queue q; ename e1,e; {
link l,m;
        l = newlink(e);
        if (!(q->count)++) q->first = q->last = l;
        if ((m = qfind(e1,q)) != q->last) inafter(m,l);
        else {
                inafter(q->last,l );
                q->last = l;
        }
}
void addbefor(e1,q,e) queue q; ename e1,e; {
link l,m;
        l = newlink(e);
        if (!(q->count)++) q->first = q->last = l;
        if ((m = qfind(e1,q)) != q->first) inbefor(l,m);
        else {
                inbefor(l ,q->first);
                q->first = l;
        }
}
ename head(q) queue q; {
        if (q->count) return q->first->ent;
        return (ename)0;
}
ename tail(q) queue q; {
        if (q->count) return q->last->ent;
        return (ename)0;
}
ename behead(q) queue q; {
link l;
ename e;
        if ((q->count)--) {
                l = q->first;
                if (q->count) q->first = l->succ;
                else q->last = q->first = (link)0;
                e = l->ent;
                extrax(l);
                oldlink(l);
                return e;
        }
        error("behead");
}
```

Appendices 255

```c
ename betail(q) queue q; {
link l;
ename e;
        if ((q->count)--) {
                l = q->last;
                if (q->count) q->last = l->pred;
                else q->last = q->first = (link)0;
                e = l->ent;
                extrax(l);
                oldlink(l);
                return e;
        }
        error("betail");
}
bool qremove(e1,q) queue q; ename e1; {
link l;
        if (l = qfind(e1,q)) {
                if (--(q->count)) {
                        if ( q->first == l) q->first = l->succ;
                        if ( q->last == l) q->last = l->pred;
                }
                else q->last = q->first = (link)0;
                extrax(l);
                oldlink(l);
                return TRUE;
        }
        return FALSE;
}

ename find(e1,q) queue q; ename e1; {
        if (qfind(e1,q)) return e1;
        return (ename)0;
}
/* reverse rotate a queue      */
void rrotate(q,n) queue q; int n ;{
link l;
        for ( l = q->first ; n-- ; l = l->pred );
        q->first = l;
        q->last  = l->pred;
}
/* forward rotate a queue
*/void frotate(q,n) queue q; int n ;{
link l;
        for ( l = q->first ; n-- ; l = l->succ ) ;
        q->first = l;
        q->last  = l->pred;
}

/* this is end of file QUEUMOD.C          */
```

Appendix 5 :- grafmod.c - the display manipulation routines

```c
/* this is file GRAFMOD.C         */

#define GRAFMOD

#include "stdio.h"
#include "simsys.h"


static queueimp screendat;
static queue screenset = &screendat;

char blank_string[] = "                                                                    ";


void redraw(e) ename e; {
        if (e->status&DIRTY) return;    /* already done this so return */
        addtoback(screenset,e);         /* remember this entity */
        e->status |= DIRTY;             /* mark it */
}

void move(e) ename e; {
pix *p;
dpix *o;
        if (e->status & MOVED) return;  /* if original image stored */
        /* immobile entities never get an oldimage - no wasted space */
        if (!(e->oldimage))
                if (!(e->oldimage = (dpix *) malloc(sizeof(dpix))))
                        error("no space for oldimage ");
        /* store the old image size and location */
        p = e->image;
        o = e->oldimage;
        o->row = p->row;
        o->col = p->col;
        if (p->text) o->slen = strlen(p->text);
        else o->slen = 0;
        /* it may already have been redrawn */
        if (!(e->status&DIRTY)) addtoback(screenset,e);
        /* mark it */
        e->status |= (DIRTY|MOVED);
}

void draw(e) ename e; {
register pix *p;
        p = e->image;                   /* using p should be quicker */
        cursor(p->col,p->row);          /* move the cursor */
        cputs(p->text);                 /* write to the console */
}
```

Appendices 257

```c
void erase(e) ename e; {
register pix *p;
int l;
        p = e->image;              /* using p should be quicker */
        cursor(p->col,p->row);     /* move the cursor */
        l = strlen(p->text);       /* determine image size */
        blank_string[l] = 0;       /* prepare suitable length blank string */
        cputs(blank_string);       /* erase the image */
        blank_string[l] = ' ';     /* restore the blank string */
}

void update_screen() {
ename e;
register dpix *o;
register pix *p;
int i;
        /* first all moving entities are erased in their current place */
        for (i = qsize(screenset);i--;) {
                /* we do not change the screenset membership details */
                e = head(screenset);
                frotate(screenset,1);
                if (e->status & MOVED ) {
                        /* do the erasures */
                        o = e->oldimage;
                        cursor(o->col,o->row);
                        blank_string[o->slen] = 0;
                        cputs(blank_string);
                        blank_string[o->slen] = ' ';
                }
        }
        /* now we empty the screenset as we draw its members */
        while (qsize(screenset)) {
                e = behead(screenset);
                p = e->image;
                cursor(p->col,p->row);
                cputs(p->text);
                /* mark them unmoved and clean */
                e->status &= (~(DIRTY|MOVED));
        }
}

/* this is end of file GRAFMOD.C          */
```

Appendix 6 :- machmod.c - the machine dependent routines

```
/* this is file MACHMOD>C        */
#define MACHMOD
#include "simsys.h"

static  void newbreak(void);


void printcrt() {
union REGS xall;
        int86(5,&xall,&xall);
        /* interrupt 5 is the shift/prtscr equivalent */
}
static void newbreak() {
        signal(SIGINT,newbreak);
}
void breakoff() {
        signal(SIGINT,newbreak);
}

/* Video Handling */

static char refpage = 0;

void set_video_mode(m) int m; {
union REGS xin,xout;
struct SREGS segs;
        segread(&segs);
/*      xin.h.ah = 0;   */      /* set video mode function */
/*      xin.h.al = m & 0x7; */
        xin.x.ax = m & 0x7;     /* same as above in effect */
        int86x(0x10,&xin,&xout,&segs);
}

int get_video_mode(m) {
union REGS xin,xout;
struct SREGS segs;
        segread(&segs);
        xin.h.ah = 0xf;  /* get video mode function */
        int86x(0x10,&xin,&xout,&segs);
        return xout.h.al;
}

void cursor(col,row) int col,row; {
union REGS xin,xout;
struct SREGS segs;
        segread(&segs);
        xin.h.ah = 2;   /* sets cursor position */
        xin.h.dh = row;
        xin.h.dl = col;
        xin.h.bh = refpage;
        int86x(0x10,&xin,&xout,&segs);
}
```

Appendices

```c
void get_cursor(pcol,prow) int *pcol,*prow; {
union REGS xin,xout;
struct SREGS segs;
        segread(&segs);
        xin.h.ah = 3;     /* gets cursor position */
        xin.h.bh = refpage;
        int86x(0x10,&xin,&xout,&segs);
        *prow = xout.h.dh;
        *pcol = xout.h.dl;
}

void write_char_attr(count,c,a) int count; char c,a; {
union REGS xin,xout;
struct SREGS segs;
        segread(&segs);
        xin.h.ah = 9;     /* write char + attr    */
        xin.h.bh = refpage;
        xin.h.al = c;
        xin.h.bl = a;
        xin.x.cx = count;
        int86x(0x10,&xin,&xout,&segs);
}

void clrscr() {
int m;
        m = get_video_mode();
        set_video_mode(m);
}

/* this is end of file MACHMOD.C        */
```

Appendix 7 -: phils.c - The hungry philosophers example.

```
/* all files should have a name symbol defined so that
conditional compilation can be used, primarily in header files.
See SIMSYS.H  for example        */

#define USER
#include <stdio.h>
#include <conio.h>
#include <stdlib.h>
#include <simsys.h>

void initialise(void);
void timeshow(void);
void report(char *);
void eat(void) ;
void forkisfree(struct entstruct *);
void main(void);
void sinstep(void);
void stopeating(struct entstruct *);
void stopthinking(struct entstruct *);


/* The simulation will run faster if the utilities that use
dynamic memory do not return it via free() but hang on to it
for their own re-use. If this is done and memory is tight
though, the simulation may fail while part of the program is
holding currently unused memory. The decision is controlled in
the queue module and the exec module by an external int
holdmem. The option is offered or not by defining or not the
symbol MEMOPT in this program     */

#define MEMOPT

#define PHILNUM 6

typedef struct {
        ename lfork,rfork;
} philsdata;

philsdata philsforks[PHILNUM];

ename phils,forks;

/* for this simulation an image consistes of a location and a string.
*/

char
        hunger[]    =   "HUNGRY  ",
        eating[]    =   "EATING  ",
        thinking[]  =   "THINKING",
        in_use[]    =   "IN USE  ",
        not_in_use[] ="FORK FREE";
```

Appendices 261

```c
/* it is easy to initialise the entity images in C     */
pix philsplace[PHILNUM] = { {12,12,thinking},
                            { 6,24,thinking},
                            { 6,48,thinking},
                            {12,60,thinking},
                            {18,48,thinking},
                            {18,24,thinking}
                                             },
    forksplace[PHILNUM] = { { 9,18,not_in_use},
                            { 4,36,not_in_use},
                            { 9,54,not_in_use},
                            {15,54,not_in_use},
                            {20,36,not_in_use},
                            {15,18,not_in_use}
                                             };
long eatime ,thinktime,duration;

void main() {

        initialise();
        execute(duration);
        report("Normal termination");
}


/* The B activities are all nearly trivial     */

void stopthinking(aphil) register ename aphil; {
        move(aphil);
        appearance(aphil) = hunger;
}

void stopeating(aphil) register ename aphil;{
        move(aphil);
        appearance(aphil) = thinking;
        if (!cause(stopthinking,aphil,thinktime)) error("stopeating cause");
}

void forkisfree(afork) register ename afork;{
        move(afork);
        appearance(afork) = not_in_use;

}
```

```c
/* The main C activity is where the decisions are made in this
   model   */

void eat() {
ename temphil,left,rite;
philsdata *tempuser;
        foreach (temphil , phils) {
                if ( busy(temphil)) continue;
                tempuser = (philsdata *)(temphil->user);
                left = tempuser->lfork;
                if ( busy(left) ) continue;
                rite = tempuser->rfork;
                if ( busy(rite) ) continue;
                move(temphil);
                move(left);
                move(rite);
                if (!cause(stopeating,temphil,eatime)) error("1st. eat cause");
                if (!cause(forkisfree,left,    eatime)) error("2nd. eat cause");
                if (!cause(forkisfree,rite,    eatime)) error("3rd. eat cause");
                appearance(left) = in_use;
                appearance(rite) = in_use;
                appearance(temphil) = eating;
        }
}

/* The C activity mechanism lends itself to control uses as
   well as the simulation, aided by the activate() -
   deactivate() pair. So we have free_run(), sinstep() and
   timeshow() as below. We start by defining the name free_run
   so that it may be referenced in sinstep(). Notice the mask
   with 0x5f in the switch statement in sinstep incidentally. I
   find it the easiest way of reacting to both upper and lower
   case ascii.
*/

void free_run();

void sinstep() {
static int screen_off = FALSE;
        timeshow();
        switch(getch() & 0x5f ) {
                case 'Q':
                        if (deactivate(sinstep)) {
                                activate(free_run);
                                break;
                        }
                        error("can not turn off single stepping");
                case 'A':
                        report("aborted");
                        exit(1);
                case 'N':
                        if (deactivate(update_screen) ) {
                                screen_off = TRUE;
                                break;
                        }
                case 'S':
                        if ( screen_off ) {
                                deactivate(sinstep);
                                activate(update_screen);
                                activate(sinstep);
                                screen_off = FALSE;
                        }
                        else {
                                deactivate(sinstep);
                                deactivate(update_screen);
                                activate(free_run);
                                screen_off = TRUE;
                        }
                        break;
                case 'T':
                        running = FALSE;
                        break;
                default:;
        }
}
```

Appendices 263

```
void free_run() {
        if (kbhit() ) {
                if ( deactivate(free_run)) activate(sinstep) ;
                else error("can not turn on single stepping");
                sinstep();       /* sinstep will read and interpret the character
 */
        }
        else timeshow();
}

void timeshow() {
        cursor(60,22);
        fprintf(stderr,"Time now %ld",tim);
}

void report(message) char *message; {
        cursor(0,23);
        fprintf(stderr,message);
        fprintf(stderr," after %ld time units\n",tim);
}
```

```
void initialise() {
long i;
ename temphil,temfork;
philsdata *tempuser;
        clrscr();

#ifdef MEMOPT
        fprintf(stderr,"holdmem is ");
        if (holdmem) fprintf(stderr,"TRUE");
        else fprintf(stderr,"FALSE");
        fprintf(stderr,"\nwill you use free (y/n) .. ");
        holdmem = ((getchar() & 0x5f) != 'Y');
        clrscr();
#endif
                                if (0 == (phils = makent(PHILNUM))) error("no sp
ace for phils");
                                if (0 == (forks = makent(PHILNUM))) error("no sp
ace for forks");
        cursor(0,12);
        fprintf(stderr,"Please give the eating time .. ");
        scanf("%ld",&eatime);
        fprintf(stderr,"Please give the thinking time .. ");
        scanf("%ld",&thinktime);
        fprintf(stderr,"Please give the run duration .. ");
        scanf("%ld",&duration);
        fprintf(stderr,"Confirming eat %ld    think %ld    duration %ld   press
<ret>",eatime,thinktime,duration);
        i = getchar();
        i = getchar();
        clrscr();
        i = 0;
        forpairs (temphil,temfork , phils ,forks ) {
                temphil->image = philsplace + i;
                temfork->image = forksplace + i;
                tempuser =      &philsforks[i] ;
                (temphil->user) = (long *) tempuser;
                tempuser->lfork       = forks + i;
                if (i) tempuser->rfork = forks + (i - 1);
                else   tempuser->rfork = forks + (PHILNUM - 1);
                move(temfork);
                move(temphil);
                if (!cause(stopthinking,temphil,i++ + thinktime)) error("initial
ise cause");
        }
        activate(eat);
                                activate(update_screen);
        activate(sinstep);
}

/* It is a user obligation to provide an error handler. This
   simple one suffices, but more complex ones are possible for
   none fatal errors
*/
void error(s) char *s; {
        fprintf(stderr,"\n** Error termination **\n%s\nat time %ld\n",s,tim);
                                exit(1);
}
```

Author Index

Abed S. Y. 61, 98
Achenbach K. A. 165, 167
Adelsberger H. H. 115, 118, 122, 142, 144, 145, 147, 154, 166, 168, 170,
Aikins J. 131, 147
Alexander S. M. 162, 166
Alsop J. W. 104, 117
Anderen L. 108, 110, 117
Ariav G. 85, 90

Balci O. 24, 25, 54
Balmer D. W. 123, 124, 137, 144, 145, 154, 162, 166, 167, 183, 215
Balzer R. 131, 147
Bankes S. C. 162, 166
Banks J. 65, 98
Barnett C. C. 52, 55, 183, 215
Barr A. 121, 128, 132, 134, 144, 157, 166
Barta, T. A. 98
Barton A. 143, 144
Basden A. 131, 144
Bastos J. M. 162, 169
Bauman R. 142, 144
Bazjanac V. 104, 117
Becker L. 53, 56
Bell P. C. 104, 109, 110, 117
Bell T. E. 18, 22, 104, 117
Belogus D. 100
Benoit J. 131, 147
Berry J. 163, 167
Bezivin J. 53, 54, 55
Birnbaum L. 131, 147
Birtwistle G. M. 26, 50, 51, 55, 81, 91, 93, 98, 122, 142, 144, 145, 146, 147, 165, 166, 167, 168
Black J. T. 99
Bobrow D. G. 131, 144
Bolshoi A. 100
Bonnet A. 125, 144
Boothroyd H. 108, 117

Borden A. 164, 166
Bramer M. A. 131, 135, 144
Bright J. G. 104, 109, 117
Brown J. C. 104, 106, 117
Brown T. 162, 166
Bryant R. W. 52, 55,183, 215
Bundy A. 160, 169
Burns A. 99
Buxton J. N. 16, 22

Cammarata 53, 55
Campbell J. A. 121, 145
Campbell R. A. 156, 166
Cannon R. L. 73, 100
Carr H. W. 16, 22, 171, 215
Carson J. S. 65, 98, 114, 118
Cellier F. E. 47, 56
Chaharbagi K. 29, 55
Chan A. W. 108, 109, 117, 118, 119
Chen A. 160, 168
Chew S. T. 123, 124, 137, 145, 146, 150, 154, 167, 169, 183, 215
Chi U. H. 104, 108, 118
Cleary J. 141, 145
Clementson A. T. 18, 22, 47, 55, 73, 98, 123, 145, 159, 166, 171, 215
Cobbin P. 63, 98
Collins W. R. 164, 166
Comfort J. C. 37, 55
Conway R. 71, 72, 98
Cox S. 61, 98
Crookes J. G. 47, 55, 124, 137, 140, 145, 147, 154, 167, 183, 215
Curnow R. 12, 22
Curran S. 22, 22

Da Silva C. M. 111, 117
Dahl O-J. 55, 171, 215
Davies B. L. 29, 55
de Carvahlo R. S. 47, 55
de Swaan Arons H. 157, 170

de Vries Robbé P. F. 167
de Wael L. 90, 144, 147
Demeo R. S. 163, 167
Denker M. W. 165, 167
Deutsch T. 141, 165, 168
Dey P. 160, 169
Donovan J. J. 104, 117
Doukidis G. I. 27, 56, 125, 137, 138, 144, 145, 146, 149, 154, 156, 164, 166, 167, 169
DuBois D. F. 32, 55
Dudley A. R. 161, 168

Elmaghraby A. S. 156, 163, 167
Engi D. 62, 98
Ericksen S. A. 161, 167

Feigenbaum E. A. 121, 128, 132, 134, 144, 157, 166
Feyock S. 164, 166
Fiddy E. 104, 105, 106, 109, 117
Fisher M. J. W. 104, 110, 111, 117
Fjellheim R. A. 160, 167
Flitman A. M. 114, 115, 117, 142, 145, 161, 167
Ford D. R. 163, 168
Fox M. S. 143, 144, 146, 147
Futo I. 141, 145, 165, 168

Gaines B. R. 144, 145, 165, 168
Gates B. 55
Gergely T. 141, 145, 165, 168
Ginzberg M. J. 85, 98
Glicksman J. 144, 145
Goh K. 141, 145
Goldestein I. P. 130, 145
Goodhead T. C. 108, 110, 117
Gordon G. 60, 98
Graefe P. W. U. 108, 109, 118, 119
Greenberg S. 16, 22
Groen A. 160, 168
Groundwater E. H. 142, 145

Haddock J. 162, 168
Hastings N. A. J. 7, 22
Hausner B. 16, 22, 171, 215
Haverty J. P. 104, 118

Hayes-Roth F. 131, 140, 146, 147
Heginbotham W. B. 105, 118
Heidorn G. E. 27, 55
Hill T. R. 156, 168
Hills P. R. 43, 50, 55
Hofland A. G. 160, 168
Hollocks B. W. 110, 118, 159, 168
Holmes W. M. 122, 146, 166, 167, 169
Hooper J. W. 44, 55
Hurrion R. D. 102, 104, 110, 114, 115, 117, 118, 119, 142, 145, 161, 167
Husain N. 143, 144, 146, 147

Jagannathan V. 156, 162, 163, 166, 167
Jansen E. P. 157, 170
Jefferson D. R. 54, 55
Jennergren P. 183, 188, 215
Jensen K. 179, 215
Johnson N. 103, 118
Jones M. M. 104, 117
Jones W. T. 160, 169

Kao H. 164, 166
Kaplan R. M. 131, 144
Kay M. 131, 144
Katske J. 104, 118
Keller D. M. 165, 167
Kendall J. 142, 144
Kerckhoffs E. J. H. 122, 145, 146, 147, 160, 166, 167, 168, 169, 170
Khoshnevis B. 160, 168
Kirchner R. 162, 166
Kiviat P. J. 27, 35, 47, 55, 56
Klahr P. 143, 146
Knapp B. M. 161, 168
Knodler B. 157, 168
Knox P. M. 165, 168
Knuth D. 175, 215
Kornell J. 161, 168
Krasnow H. S. 66, 99
Kreutzer W. 56
Kurose, J. F. 86, 99
Kwee E. 157, 168

Laski J. G. 16, 22
Laughery K. R. 63, 99

Author Index

Law A. M. 55, 94, 99, 114, 118
Lehman A. 157, 168
Lembersky M. R. 104, 108, 118
Lenat D. B. 140, 146
Lenz J. E. 69, 70
Lirov Y. 164, 168
Looney M. W. 108, 118
Lucas P. J. F. 157, 170
Luker P. A. 73, 81, 99, 122, 144, 145, 147, 160, 166, 168, 169, 170

MacNair E. A. 99
Mahoney T. M. 108, 110, 117
Malloy 52
Markowitz H. M. 16, 22, 46, 55, 171, 215
Marsh C. A. 142, 146
Mathewson S. C. 18, 22, 49, 55, 73, 74, 76, 99, 123, 146
Maxwell W. 72, 98
Mayer R. 113, 142, 144, 147, 154, 169
McArthur D. 91, 99
McElhaney B. G. 164, 168
McRoberts M. 143, 146
McRoberts, K. L. 98
Mellichamp J. M. 163, 169
Merikallio R. A. 66, 99
Micheletti G. F. 103, 118
Michie D. 134, 145, 146
Middleton S. 142, 146
Mitrani I. 36, 55
Moose Jnr, R. I. 55
Moreira da Silva C. 162, 169
Moser J. G. 162, 169
Muetzelfeldt R. 160, 169
Myhrhaug B. J. 55, 171, 215

Nance R. E. 26, 55, 91, 97
Nenonen L. K. 108, 109, 118
Neyman W. 164, 166
Norman D. A. 131, 144
Norman T. A. 108, 118
Nygaard K. 55, 171, 215

O'Donovan T. M. 61, 99
O'Keefe R. M. 52, 56, 104, 109, 110, 117, 137, 142, 144, 146, 154, 156, 169
Oren T. I. 164, 169

Page E. S. 193, 216
Palme J. 118
Papp I. 141, 145

Parnas D. L. 122, 146
Paul R. J. 27, 56, 91, 123, 124, 125, 137, 144, 145, 146, 149, 150, 154, 156, 162, 166, 167, 169, 183, 215
Pazirandeh M. 53, 56
Peacock J. B. P. 7, 22
Pegden C. D. 63
Pidd M. 3, 4, 6, 8, 18, 22, 26, 27, 33, 56, 77, 99, 102, 118, 124, 140, 146, 171, 174, 175, 183, 187, 215
Pooch U. W. 144
Poole T. G. 16, 22, 27, 56, 123, 146, 173, 216
Pope D. N. 104, 118
Pritsker A. A. B. 27, 47, 56, 62, 99

Rajagopalan R. 165, 169
Ralston P. 163, 167
Reddy Y. V. 144, 147, 164, 169
Reilly K. D. 160, 169
Rimvall M. 47, 56
Roach J. W. 142, 146
Roberts R. B. 130, 145
Roberts S. D. 73, 99, 156, 157, 168
Robertson D. 160, 169
Robertson P. 144, 147
Rodin E. Y. 164, 168
Rogers M. A. M. 109, 118
Rooda J. E. 52
Rothenberg J. 55
Rozenblit J. W. 90, 99
Ruiz-Mier S. 143, 147
Ryder J. S. 161, 168

Saceroti E. 131, 147
Sampson J. R. 104, 118
Schriber T. 61, 99
Schroer B. J. 65, 99, 163, 168
Secker R. J. R. 102, 118
Seila A. F. 52, 56, 183, 216
Shannon R. E. 115, 118, 142, 144, 147, 154, 166, 169
Shaw M. L. G. 144, 145
Simulation 162, 169
Sohnle R. C. 104, 118
Sol H. G. 167
Sowizral H. 54, 55, 91, 99
Spinelli de Carvalho 140, 147
Stairmand M. C. 53, 56
Standridge C. R. 83, 100
Stefic M. 131, 147

Stoop J. C. 160, 168
Subrahmanian E. 73, 100
Sulonen R. K. 104, 118
sysPACK Ltd 123, 147, 159, 165, 170
Szczerbicka H. 157, 168
Szymankiewicz J. 16, 22, 27, 123, 146, 173, 216

Takkenberg C. A. Th. 167
Talavage J. 143, 147
Tartar J. 104, 118
Taylor R. P. 114, 116, 119
Thomasma T. 53, 56
Thompson H. 131, 144
Tocher K. D. 12, 14, 22
Turano T. A. 142, 144

Udo P. W. 108, 119
Ulgen O. 53, 56
Unger B. 91, 100, 141, 145
Uschold M. 160, 169

van den Herik H. J. 160, 168
Vansteenkiste G. C. 122, 145, 146, 147, 166, 167, 168, 169, 170
Varkevisser P. R. 160, 168
Vaucher J. G. 137, 141, 147

Villanueva R. 55
von Neuman J. 12, 22

Wahab A. F. A. 163, 166
Wahl D. 161, 170
Warby A. H. 108, 118
Waterman D. A. 140, 146
Welch P. D. 99
Wilbur L. W. 164, 168
Wilkinson D. G. 143, 147
Williams G. N. 144
Wilson J. R. 109, 119
Wilson L. B. 193, 216
Winograd T. 128, 131, 144, 147
Wirth N. 179, 193, 216
Wojciechowski E. 164, 166
Woods W. A. 130, 147
Worona S. 98
Wortman D. B. 62, 100, 109, 119

Yazdani M. 145

Zanconato R. 142, 146
Zeigler B. P. 26, 64, 89, 90, 92, 100, 122, 144, 145, 146, 147, 164, 166, 167, 168, 169, 170
Zhang S. X. 99

Subject Index

A phase   137-141, 183, 185, 197
action sentences   150
active c activity list   228, 230
activities   3, 8, 174
activity cycle diagrams   4, 7, 123, 150, 151, 157, 158
ada   221, 222
adding entities   201
adding queue members   208
advice-giving simulation expert system   154
Algol   15, 16
Algol 60   218
animation   101
animation, AUTOCAD   67
animation, CINEMA   65
animation, management access   95
animation, PCModel/GAF   67
animation, TESS   84
aphase( )   224, 225, 228, 230
APL   172, 215
Apple Macintosh   19
application specific routines   176
applications, chemical   109
applications, manufacturing   104
arrays   183
artificial intelligence   22, 121-170
artificial intelligence comparison   137-141
ASPES   156
assembler   218
autocorrelation   11
AUTOSIM   123, 124, 157-159, 165

B activities   184, 225, 228, 230
B events   137-140, 165
B phase   186, 197, 225, 228, 230
backward chaining   136-137, 155
BASIC   193, 213, 218, 216
BASIM   183, 226

batch computing   16
batch simulation   101
BCPL   219
bi-directional chaining   136-137
bit mapped screen   236
BLOBS   143
boolean expressions   218
bounded executive design   226
built-in types   179
business graphics   101

C   21, 173, 215
C activities   184, 225
C events   137-140, 165
C phase   186, 197, 225, 228, 230
CAPS   81, 123, 159
case statement   178
CASM   123-125, 137, 141, 149-160, 153-156, 165
cellular   140
circular lists   234
classes of entities   194
classes, creating   204
classical experimentation   10
COBOL   15
Codeview   221
colour graphics, terminals   102
combining with artificial intelligence   149-170
combining with simulation   149-170
commercial projects   222
compiler vendors   239
computer graphics   101
computers, first generation   13
computing, batch   16
computing, interactive   17
concurrent PROLOG   141
conservatism   172
constructor types   179, 180
contingent logic   3

continuous systems 160
control structure 132
conveyor systems 176
creating classes 204
creating queues 205
criticism 122
CSL 16, 18
cyclic design 224

data structure 223, 225
data types 179, 219
database 5, 9, 21
database languages 85
debugging 4, 17, 221
DEC PDP8 17
decision simulator 104
decision support 30
decision support systems 163
definition 121, 131-132
deleting entities 201
demons 137, 139-140
dialogs, ANDES 82
dictionary 129-130
display methods, logical 110
display methods, schematic 109
distribution sampling 175
do loop 178
domains 129-130
double linked lists 234
DRAFT 74, 123
dynamic effects 11
dynamic memory allocation 220, 227
dynamic store administration 233
dynamic variables 182

ECSL 18, 171
entities 139, 152-153, 194
entities, adding 201
entities, deleting 201, 239
entities, finding 204
entity classes 194
entity cycle diagram 33
entity status 238
enumerated types 179
error traps 174
ESSO 16
evaluation of logical operators 219
events 3, 8, 174
evolutionary development 176
examples 142-143, 156, 161-165

execution speed 14
executive program 14, 174, 217, 218, 224
executive, three phase 185
experimental design, PROLOG advisor 115
experimental frame 64, 89
experimentation 2, 5, 7, 10
expert simulation system 154
expert systems 126, 131-137, 154-156
explanation facility 134

Ferranti Mk I 13
financial modelling 18
finding entities 204
finding queue members 206
first generation computers 13
flexible manufacturing systems 109
flow diagram systems 16, 27
FMS modelling 29
for loop 178
FORTRAN 13-21, 172-177, 182, 193-230
forward chaining 136-137, 140, 155
frame systems 132-133
function pointer 230

gaming 10
gamma distribution 175
GASP 16, 21
general purpose language 217
generic models 20, 66, 172, 218
generic models 220
geometric distribution 175
glass screen 237
goto's 178
GPSS 16, 18, 142
GPSS derivatives 60
grafmod module 236
graphics 53, 223
graphics, bit mapped 103
graphics, character 103
graphics, interactive 110
graphics, passive 110
graphics, playback 102

Subject Index

guided vehicles 176
GUS 131

harassed booking clerk 187, 209
hardware, parallel processing 53
header file simsys.h 223
heap 226, 227, 228, 230
heapsort 223
hit rate 226
HOCUS 16, 18, 20, 173, 215
hybrid models 95
hybrid models, discrete continuous 85

IBM 4
IBM 360 14, 18
IBM 370 18
IBM-compatibles 19
IBM PC 224
iconic graphics 9
if-then rules 136-138
image understanding 126
implementation dependent methods 219
inference 135-137
inference engine 135-137, 139-140
initialisation 188
initialisation of variables 220
inline code 239
inline functions 220, 221
input-output model 7
INSIGHT 156
integrated circuits 15
integrated environments 91, 97
integrated environments, CASM 91
integrated environments, JADE 91
integrated environments, TESS 83
integration 12
Intel 19
intelligent front end 159
interaction 10
interaction, 'bullet-proofing' 111
interaction, entity 110
interaction, general 102
interaction, intelligent 113
interaction, menu 111
interaction, tree 111
interactions, logical 6
interactive computing 17
interactive graphics 174
interactive model building 104

interactive program generators 18
interactive search for solutions 108
interactive support tools 159-160
interfacing functions 235
ISO Pascal 214
ISPG 123-125, 135-155, 157-159

KBS 143-144
keyboards 10, 20
knowledge acquisition 161
knowledge base 132, 134-135, 139-149
knowledge based systems 161
knowledge representation 132-135

language structure, CLASS 50
language structure, object oriented 52
language structure, process 49
languages 141-144
languages, ALGOL 36
languages, APLOMB 85
languages, DEMOS 51
languages, DSSL 29
languages, ECSL 47
languages, FORTRAN 36
languages, GASP 47
languages, GCMS 69
languages, GPSS 58
languages, INSIGHT 73
languages, MAP/1 83
languages, MAST 68
languages, MICRO PASSIM 52
languages, MODELMASTER 72
languages, Pascal 36, 52
languages, PCModel 66
languages, POSE 53
languages, PROLOG 52
languages, Q-GERT 62
languages, QNET4 86
languages, RESQ 85
languages, ROSS 53
languages, SAINT 62
languages, SAME 70
languages, SDL 85
languages, SEE-WHY 49
languages, SIMAN 63
languages, SIMCAL 52
languages, SIMFACTORY 68
languages, SIMON 49
languages, SIMON75 50
languages, SIMPAL 52

languages, SIMPLE_1 73
languages, SIMSCRIPT 27, 34, 46
languages, SIMTOOLS 52
languages, SIMULA 34, 36, 40, 49
languages, SLAM 27, 34, 62
languages, SMALLTALK 52
languages, SOLE 52
languages, summary 58
languages, WITNESS 70
languages, XCELL 71
large simulations 8
learning systems 130, 150
learning techniques 126
learning via PROLOG 115
LEO 13
library approach 8, 217
library functions 218
library routines 220
LIBSIM 124, 157-159
life cycle 152, 158
light pen 10
linked lists 175, 182, 193, 223, 226, 227
lint 221, 222
LISP 141-144, 160
list processing 36, 226, 230
logging module 223
logic modelling 165
logic, contingent 3
logical engines 177
logical interactions 3, 6
lognormal distribution 175
LOOPS 143
LUNAR 130

machine address 220
machine dependence 223
macro definitions 227, 232
macro pre-processor 220
man-machine interfaces 165
man-model interface 106
management perception 106
management science 12
mathematical models 2
menus 9, 18
micro-computer simulation 101
micro-computers 19
military example 161
mini-computers 17

MINITAB 21
model building 92
model development 28, 176
model life cycle 25
model specification, bottom up 92
model specification, via database 92
model structure 7
modelling macros 88
modelling macros, component types 90
modelling of control systems 164
models 122
models, mathematical 2
Modula 2 218
modular design 222
modular development 219
modular structure 4
modularity 6, 7, 14
monitoring using PROLOG 114
Monte Carlo method 12
Motorola 19
mouse 10, 20
MSDOS 19, 20
multi-programming 17

natural language 27
natural language understanding 126-131, 149-153
negative exponential distribution 175
Neliac 218
networks, queueing 61
Normal distribution 175
NUDGE 131

object-oriented programming 121
operating systems 20
operational research 12
OPS5 142
OS/2 19, 20
output analysis 125

parallel processing 160
parallel processing, TimeLock 54
parallel processing, TimeWarp 54
parameters 6, 9
Pascal 21, 171, 218, 221, 222, 227
Personal computer 66

Subject Index   273

personal workstations 18
Petri nets 142
philosophy 123
physical drawing 237
plot commands 236
pointer 220
pointer based executive 197
pointer type 182, 183
pointers, undefined 199
Poisson distribution 175
policy comparison 5
POPLOG 143
portable language 219
porting of software 15
pre-processor 221
precedence levels 218
printers 20
probability distributions 4
problem definition 26, 125, 149-153, 165
procedural representation 133-4
process interaction 8
process of simulation 2
processes 3, 174
production rules 133-137, 140
production systems 135-140, 142
program debugging 93, 153-156, 166
program generation 123, 150, 153-155, 157-160, 163
program generators, CAPS 49
program generators, CAPS/ECSL 73
program generators, DRAFT 49
program generators, DRAFT/DRAW 73
program generators, TESS 73
program maintenance 218
program specification 177
program structure 8
program structure, machine based 44
program structure, material based 44
programming languages 8
project management 94
PROLOG 141-142, 156, 161
pseudo screen 236
punched cards 16
pushdown stack 183

qualitative modelling 165
queue 230
queue members, adding 208
queue members, finding 206
queue members, removing 208

queue module 233
queues 139, 175, 182, 194, 223
queues, creating 205
queuing system 178

random number generation 175, 188
random sampling 12
range checking 180
re-usable code 8
record data type 181
recursive process 231
removing queue members 208
repeat .. until 178
report generators 9
reserved words 218
RESQME 86
robots 176
root 194
ROSS 143
rule based example 160
rule based systems 22
rules of system 6, 7

sample collection 175
sampling 5
sampling experiments 12
sampling module 223
SAS 21
scheduling rules (simulation of) 106
SEE-WHY 21, 215
semantic analysis 127-130, 150-151
semantic filtering 129
semantic grammars 129
semantic nets 133
sentinel 194, 230
separate compilation 222
set data type 180
shell 157
side effects 221
silent film 102
SIMFACTORY 21
SIMON 16
SIMSCRIPT 16, 18, 20, 171, 215
SIMULA 171
SIMULA availability 51
simulation comparison 137-141
simulation languages 171
simulation process 2
simulation project, phases of 112
simulation specific language 217
simulation support environments 22

Subject Index

simulation system routines 174
simultaneity 237
SIPDES 154-156
skeleton program 176
SLAM 20, 160, 215
small models 226
software libraries 8, 172, 173
software vendors 4
sorting 226
source code 173
speech recognition 127
speed of execution 14
spreadsheet 9, 21, 71
SPSS 21
stacks 193
standard library 223
standardisation 14
state of system 3, 177
static 228
static routines 219
statistical modelling 5
statistical packages 9
statistics, inadequacy of tools 94
statistics, rv generation 45
statistics, variance reduction 45
status descriptors 227
status field of entity 238
stdio.h 221
stochastic behaviour 4, 11, 175, 223
string handling 218
strong typing 219
structs 227
sub-range types 179, 180
support environments 22
support for artificial intelligence 162-164
syntactic analysis 127-129, 150-151
system rules 6, 3
system state 3, 177
system theory 89
systems dynamics 160

tail recursion 231
TC-PROLOG 141
text output 9
thermionic valves 13
three phase approach 123, 137-140, 142, 153
three phase executive 185
three phase executive design 224
three phase method 174, 183
time beat 227, 228, 230
time processing 232

time series analysis 9
time structure 37, 43
time structure, event based 38, 46
time structure, process 40
time structure, three-phase 39, 47
time-sharing 17
times 194
timetable 5
token variables 179
top-down design 177
tracing 174
tracker ball 20
transaction flow 58
transaction flow models 156
tree balance 226, 231
tree processing 232
tree structure 226
tree-structuring 177
trees 193
trutim 228
TS-PROLOG 141
Turbo Pascal 214
types, built-in 179
types, constructor 179, 180
types, enumerated 179
types, pointer 182
types, record 181
types, set 180
types, sub-range 179, 180

undefined pointers 199
uniform distribution 175
UNIVAC 13
Unix 20
unlimited executive 223

validation 4-7, 102, 151-152
variable names 178
VAX 19
visual interactive models 223
visual interactive simulation 102, 105
VS6 123-124, 159, 165

while statement 178
Winchester disks 19
WITNESS 21, 159
workstations 18
worst case tree depth 231

Xenix 19
xor 228

zero delay 228